No Surrender! No Retreat!

No Surrender! No Retreat!

African American Pioneer Performers of Twentieth-Century American Theater

Glenda E. Gill

Palgrave Macmillan

NO SURRENDER! NO RETREAT!
Copyright © 2000 Glenda E. Gill. All rights reserved.
Softcover reprint of the hardcover 1st edition 2000 978-0-312-21757-0
No part of this book may be used or reproduced in any
manner whatsoever without written permission except in the case of brief
quotations embodied in critical articles or reviews. For information, address St.
Martin's Press, Scholarly and Reference Division, 175 Fifth Avenue, New York,
N.Y. 10010.

ISBN 978-1-349-62002-9   ISBN 978-1-137-05361-9 (eBook)
DOI 10.1007/978-1-137-05361-9

Library of Congress Cataloging-in-Publication Data to be found at the Library
of Congress.

Design by Letra Libre, Inc.

First edition: April 2000
10 9 8 7 6 5 4 3 2 1

*To the memory of my mother and father,
Olivia Dunlop Gill
and Melvin Leo Gill Sr.
and to the memory of my maternal grandparents,
Sanford Lee and Lucy Tandy Dunlop*

*Until the lions have their own historian,
the tale of the hunt will always glorify the hunter.*

—Kenyan proverb

Table of Contents

Preface and Personal Memoir — xi
Foreword by Daniel Larner — xv
Acknowledgements — xix

Chapter I	What Shall the Negro Dance About?	1
Chapter II	Crucible and Community: The Vision of Rose McClendon	21
Chapter III	The Silencing of Paul Robeson	35
Chapter IV	Measure Her Right: The Tragedy of Ethel Waters	59
Chapter V	Marian Anderson: A Serene Spirit	75
Chapter VI	Five Interpreters of *Porgy and Bess*	91
Chapter VII	Swifter than a Weaver's Shuttle: The Days of Canada Lee	107
Chapter VIII	Pearl Bailey: The Black Dolly Gallagher Levi	137
Chapter IX	Ossie and Ruby are One!	151
Chapter X	James Earl Jones: "My Soul Looks Back and Wonders How I Got Over"	173
Chapter XI	Morgan Freeman's Resistance and Non-Traditional Roles	193
Chapter XII	Has Anything Changed?	205

Index — 219

Preface and Personal Memoir

On 15 April 1999, distinguished African American actor Charles S. Dutton exclaimed on national television, "Theatre advances civilization!" I have written this book with that credo as a motivating factor. My passion for the theatre began when I was five years old, and I was growing up on "The Hill" at Alabama A. and M. College, at Normal, where my mother, Olivia Dunlop Gill, was a professor in the Department of Business, and my father, Melvin Leo Gill, Sr., a postmaster.

We had a host of top-drawer artists and first-rate speakers who came to campus from the time I was five until I left at age 30, for good. It was the greatest artistic feast from which I have partaken in my life—Marian Anderson, Talley Beatty, Carol Brice, Dorothy Maynor, Langston Hughes, The Shakespearean Players of Catholic University, Pearl Primus, Adam Clayton Powell, Jr.—an amazing array. Except for the summer of 1961 and one year (1962–63), during which I attended Wisconsin-Madison, I spent 25 years of my life at Alabama A. and M., and went from the first grade through my senior year in college there. I also taught for two years at Councill Training High School, the laboratory school for A. and M., and in 1963 began my teaching career at A. and M.

At the age of five, I played Little Emily in Thornton Wilder's *Our Town*; Eunice (Warren) Moore was the grown-up Emily. I return from the dead to celebrate my twelfth birthday. While at the time I most looked forward to eating the bacon Lillie Webb, a college student, prepared for my stage breakfast, in more mature years, I realize the importance of valuing "clocks ticking" and "warm baths" while I live. Acting in plays and teaching drama have taught me many lessons.

I have written this book not just because I have been fascinated with theatre all of my life, but because I am equally interested in justice and positive social change. While not every person in this series of mini biographies is an activist, many are. Paul Robeson, according to Charles S. Dutton, "made more money than the President of the United States," yet he sacrificed his career, his family, and his health for the sake of dignity and respect. Most African Americans, regardless of profession, have something in common with those whose lives appear in this collection. In many ways, I write about the universal human condition—the sheer tenacity, good will, and courage that it takes to live.

I also write for the 18-year-old brilliant white male student currently enrolled in my HU352 18th Century and Restoration class who came into my office yesterday and asked, as he saw *Black Women in America,* edited by Darlene Hine (Brooklyn: Carlson Publishing, Inc., 1993) on top of my file cabinet, "Do you write only about black people?" And I think of those Caucasian children, aged eight to ten, in Mobile, Alabama, this morning, interviewed on ABC's *Good Morning America* who said, "Black people murder more." I also write for those students in and out of my classes who understand the worth, already, of all in the human race, and that all races have both good and some very flawed people, as well as achievements and struggles.

I write this book also because, in my own acting experiences with the Alabama A. and M. Thespians, I came to understand the power of theatre. The late and extraordinary J. Preston Cochran cast me, starting when I was 12 years old, in adult roles. I was Reba, the maid, in Kaufman and Hart's *You Can't Take It with You;* Tolton Rosser played Grandpa Vanderhof. I was also Mazie, a maid, in George Kelly's *Craig's Wife,* with Dora Scruggs in the title role.

Sometimes some black directors can perceive black women as maids as much as some white directors. After protesting my maid status to a black director at an all-black college, I got better roles. I have always had a low tolerance for accepting less than I felt I deserved, even though I was there by J. P's graces, to begin with. I was not yet a college student. Cochran was generous to cast me at all.

At the age of 14, I played Mrs. Bradman in Noel Coward's *Blithe Spirit,* also directed by J. Preston Cochran. It was the first time I had seen a seance conducted; it was also the last. I was Stella Carlisle, a rather meaty role of a has-been actress in a summer production Cochran mounted of *Rehearsal for Death.* For that, I wore a flaming red dress. I graduated from high school at age 16 and moved up "The Hill" to college. I auditioned my freshman year for the Thespians.

I hoped that lessons were learned and that there was an aesthetic appreciation for drama when an audience saw me play the evil housekeeper, Mrs. Danvers, in Daphne du Maurier's *Rebecca* directed by Fannie Ella Frazier Hicklin. Mrs. Danvers sets the house on fire rather than serve the second wife of Maxim de Winter, played in our 1956 production by Emily Veale. Edward Harris was de Winter. Rebecca, the first wife, has died. Mrs. Danvers had an obsession with Rebecca. I fully realized how good a part I had been given when I saw Judith Anderson play the role in a 1940 pro-

Preface and Personal Memoir   xiii

duction after I moved to Houghton, Michigan, in the 1990s. I was also the Princess of San Luca in Alberto Casello's *Death Takes a Holiday,* also directed by Dr. Hicklin.

I understood the archetype of the Cannibal Mother who devours her son when I was the wealthy Mrs. Phelps in Sidney Howard's *The Silver Cord,* directed by Fannie Ella Frazier Hicklin in 1957 at Alabama A. and M. As my younger son, Robert, played by Charles Ray, knelt at my feet as a swift final curtain closed, I hoped that those like Mrs. Phelps in the audience might change. I had, clad in my mother's silver fox furs, played a very self-absorbed woman, bent on smothering two sons, but managing, successfully, to break the engagement of one.

I came to understand how vastly different the white world was as I left an all-black college campus in 1962, on Alabama Out of State Aid for Negroes, to attend one heavily white, the University of Wisconsin-Madison. My second summer at Madison, without hesitation, I auditioned for a part. Initially, I played a maid role, Cleota, in Thurber's *The Male Animal,* directed by Lowell Manfull, and then several bit parts in Brecht's *Galileo,* directed by the late Ronald Mitchell.

The resources at Madison were vastly different from those at Alabama A. and M. We had a paid head usher at Madison who happened to be African American. Madison's Union Theatre, perched on splendid Lake Mendota, and built in 1939, was listed at the 1940 San Francisco World's Fair as "one of the twenty-five most distinguished buildings in the world." It seated 1300 and remains an architectural wonder.

At Alabama A. and M. we had performed on the stage of Bibb Graves Auditorium, in a classroom and office building. Our dressing room, unlike the ones at Madison, was Rev. Bradford's adjacent office, which we hoped we would not upset. Rev. Bradford recalled in an early May 1999 telephone conversation that he made unusually adaptable artists, such as Alexandra Danilova, comfortable, by bringing in ironing boards and lights for make-up mirrors, all of which were imported from his home. He wanted privacy for the ladies and, so, put up large sheets of brown paper with masking tape over the rather ample windows that looked out on the main paved street of the college.

Wisconsin-Madison had paid costumers, paid lighting designers and technicians (one a woman), paid publicists, and a photographic studio downtown that did our professional photography. It was as if I had been transported to another planet. At Alabama A. and M., the art teachers made the posters and the electricians handled the technical matters. The printing shop did the programs and students made the costumes or provided their own clothes. On rare occasion, we rented costumes. Madison had a profusion of luxury.

I became a college professor at Alabama A. and M. in 1963, the year I left Madison. Since then, I have taught drama and attended plays as well as meetings of professional theatre societies. I have published since 1974. I believe in the power of theatre to advance civilization, whether or not it is Ruby Dee in Emily Mann's *Having Our Say* or Charles S. Dutton in August Wilson's *The Piano Lesson*, or with the students who study Congreve, Shakespeare, Hansberry, or O'Neill in my classroom. In the formal lectures I have given at home and abroad, I hope that I have touched a life. In the pages of this book, I hope that students and others will be inspired and informed to become better than we are.

One word more. This book is by no means exhaustive. I have not tried to write a history of all African Americans in the theatre and I have not tried to write about African American theatre, *per se*. I define African American theatre as that which is *by, for, about,* and *near* us. This is a book of portraits that are, of necessity, selective. I leave it to others to continue to fill in the gaps.

Glenda E. Gill
Houghton, Michigan
14 June 1999

Foreword

Glenda Gill writes with a particular passion, and a particular perspective, which grow out of her background and her dispositions. The passion is to bring to us, her readers, the information and the context we need to appreciate the achievements of African Americans in the American theatre of the twentieth century. She tells a very challenging story about irrepressible talent, aspiration, and determination, and the overcoming of difficult, painful, and persistent obstacles. Gill's assertion is clear: the actors we read about here are both pioneers and heroes. They have broken new ground, fought the terrors of racist institutions and prejudiced individuals, of stereotyped expectations, and their own weaknesses and flaws, and somehow nourished and developed their huge talents to become landmarks in the history of the American theatre.

Gill's perspective is more complex. She grew up in a university environment in the Deep South, as she reveals here. As she makes clear, this was a "traditionally black" university, Alabama A. and M. College. The operative words here, "black" and "traditional," are both important. From an early age, she developed a love of the culture she was introduced to by her parents and their colleagues. This included a certain graciousness, delicacy and manners, a pride in the culture of her family and people, and an equal pride in the ability of African Americans to appreciate and participate in the culture of the world around them—what would much later come to be known as the "dominant culture." It also included a healthy respect for the particular contributions African Americans were making to the society. That society was not seen as white or black, but as a dynamic, whole fabric. It is hardly that oppression and prejudice were absent from this environment, or awareness of them suppressed, but those who taught Gill refused to be stifled, to be cheated of their love for history, for the arts, and especially in Gill's case, for the theatre.

The history of theatre at Alabama A. and M. College was crucial to the development of Gill's sensibilities. Her family and her teachers had large vision. The history and experience of theatre in America, to say nothing of wider frameworks, was not to be denied them, nor was it denied her. This book shines with the conviction that the contributions African Americans have made to the American theatre—again seen as a dynamic, whole fabric—are important, sometimes crucial, always vital and unique. Their heroism is that they made it against odds. Their eternal success is that they made the justice they were denied by the social structures that restricted them. They changed minds and hearts.

How do we best hear the voices that Gill brings to us in this book? One issue that emerges persistently in the history of American performances of Shakespeare's *Othello*, which arises with frequency in the professional lives of nearly all the actors treated in this book and is still very much alive in all our theatres, is the question of cross-casting, particularly casting across racial lines. Can blacks play white roles, or whites black roles? In Shakespeare's time white men routinely played all roles, white or black, human or divine, male or female. Should blacks and whites now devote their energies to separate theatres? And play only their own roles? Gill discusses the recent argument between August Wilson and Robert Brustein, and the rift of sensibilities it represents. Since this book implicitly takes a stand by defending the participation of the actors discussed here in the larger context of the American theatre and film world, and makes the case for the greatness of these actors, the underpinnings of that stand are worth examining.

The world of the theatre has traditionally involved a set of crucial assumptions about its own workings and the worlds it depicts. While in the postmodern view a play (or any work of art) is essentially a collage of the prevailing views and social influences from the surrounding society, and has no existence independent from those "texts," the traditional ("modern") assumption has been that a play is a whole organism, with its own meanings and understandings derived, as Aristotle first pointed out, from the action it depicts. It is an intentional vehicle for meaning, with all its elements (plot, character, setting, and more) there for the purpose of expressing those meanings. The actor's job, under these circumstances, is to work as an integral part of this human meaning factory, serving the whole, illuminating the action. The assumption is, integrally, that an actor *must* portray the character in the script, which, whoever that character might be, is surely different from the "character" of the actor himself or herself. That is, the actor is always using her tools to "other" herself, to be someone different from herself in a context that, at least in some respects, is other than the one she occupies in her own life, as actor, as person. This extends to other "identities." That is, in some respect, every role will also be "other," at least to some extent, with respect to group identity, nationality, sexuality, cultural or educational background, and more.

To put it another way: what acting means is to play someone other than yourself. When it is yourself, you are not acting. As much as it may be fashionable to draw parallels between acting and the "performance" of gender or culture or "race," or other identity, these parallels are weak forms of what it means to "act," a deeply difficult, probing, and practiced form of "othering."

Given this point of view, it becomes possible in theory for anyone to enact any character, across any line of identity, including performance of self, gender, culture, or "race." The same theory that sees the actor as deliberately creating an "other" for the delectation of the audience, sees that audience as an active perceiver and appreciator of those "others," using the imagination to fill in the inevitable organic gaps in the portrayal. "Eke out our imperfections with your thoughts," invites Shakespeare, and we do that, in the same way that as children we learn to see persons in the animals of stories and cartoons.

What follows from this is that cross-casting, across any line, may be a commercial consideration, it may be a social or aesthetic consideration in a particular context, but as a matter of principle, it is not only possible and permissible but highly desirable. The more imaginative the production, the more imaginative the audience is challenged to be, and the deeper and more profound the possibilities of meaning become. Like everything else in the complex and multi-disciplined art of theatre, it can be mishandled. Cross-casting, like any other consideration of design, can muddy the waters or clarify them, or simply not be of much importance. And members of any given audience will be likely to disagree about the correctness of any cross-casting decision in these rapidly changing times. The essence of the decision must lie in how the details of the decisions made fit into the vision of the world that the show as a whole is trying to evoke. What is that large vision? What is the action that will purvey it? And what are the details of design—of casting, character, and setting—that will best express it? Cross-casting should, ideally, follow the answers to these questions, not precede them.

In this book, Gill shows us those who fought for the causes they thought were just, the crises of their times: Paul Robeson, Canada Lee, Ossie Davis, and Ruby Dee; and those who let their art speak for them, eschewing activism: Marian Anderson, James Earl Jones, Morgan Freeman. Then there are others who fall neatly in neither category. She makes it plain that each of them, regardless of their personal problems and convictions, knew they had a legacy to claim, one that they shared with every other human being, not the least with their white colleagues, whether supporters or oppressors. It is the size of this knowledge that fuels the hugeness of their determination to succeed, to win against odds, to affirm the humanity, which, if we could all live up to, would mean a world so much more rich, both in art and in justice, than the one we currently know.

Daniel Larner
Bellingham, Washington
27 June 1999

Acknowledgements

There have been so many people who have positively touched my life and this book that it is impossible for me to give all of them credit. First and always, I give glory and thanks to God for all that He has made possible in opening doors, giving me strength and focus.

Secondly, I thank my mother, the late Olivia Dunlop Gill, and my maternal grandfather, Sanford Lee Dunlop. It was my mother who set me on my course of love for the theatre by moving me from Clarksville, Tennessee, the home of my maternal grandparents, when I was five, to Alabama A. and M. College, where I witnessed so many in the performing arts and had an opportunity to perform in good amateur theatre. My grandfather, one of the most loving and strongest men I have ever known, cried for joy and in pride, I hope, when I played "Silent Night" for him on "Miss" Lillian's piano, when I was ten years old. Louise Foston Gachette and Malcolm Gachette of Clarksville, whom I knew as friends of over 50 years, supported me and my work as a theatre historian.

Clearly one of the most talented directors I have ever met, the late J. Preston Cochran of the Alabama A. and M. Thespians allowed me to perform in six of his plays when I was an adolescent growing up on the campus. Thank you, "J.P.!" Fannie Ella Frazier Hicklin, who is perhaps the strongest and most organized woman I have ever met, deserves thanks for giving me my very best leading role, and a strong supporting one, as a college student at Alabama A. and M. Eunice Warren Moore, Katherine Inez Hewitt Lee, and the Henry Bradfords, all connected for many years with Alabama A. and M. College, have been lifelong sources of inspiration. I am grateful to Anne Quick Drake, who died at 104, for her interview regarding Ethel Waters, Marian Anderson, and Josephine Baker. I thank Dean Robert A. Carter and Rev. Henry Bradford for their hard work on the Lyceum Committee. I am also grateful to Rev. Bradford for his interview which is interwoven in the chapter on Marian Anderson.

At Wisconsin-Madison, where I earned my M.A., I am indebted to the late Ronald Mitchell and Lowell Manfull, who cast me in Brecht's *Galileo* and Thurber's *The Male Animal*, respectively, in 1962, bold and generous acts for white men at that time in this country. It was at Wisconsin-Madison that I also met Daniel M. Larner, who played Tommy Turner, the lead in *The Male Animal*. I am very grateful to him for the Foreword, and for helping me envisage how I could best complete this book, by my writing abstracts for the unfinished chapters as the book progressed. He also did a thorough reading of the manuscript near its final stages and made extremely helpful suggestions for revision. Maxine Fleckner Ducey of the Film and Theatre Archive of Madison's State Historical Society has been helpful since 1979.

I thank the Lyceum Committee of the University of Texas-El Paso for the 1975 presentation of Ossie Davis and Ruby Dee. It was while I was serving on that committee that I first met the artists. I also am appreciative of the late Bart Lanier Stafford, III, whom I met in El Paso, for his letters, his encouragement, and his gifts of a Paul Robeson and a Marian Anderson record long before this book was conceived. Bart saw further than I.

The research for this book began in 1976 when I wrote a paper on Paul Robeson at the University of Iowa. The staffs of the main and the law libraries deserve thanks. At Iowa, I also met Donald G. Marshall, now of the University of Illinois at Chicago, who became my Ph.D. adviser. He has remained a constant source of inspiration and information since 1976. I appreciate his suggestions of identity, resistance, and representation for this book given me at the 1998 San Francisco Modern Language Association convention.

Tom Pawley, who spent most of his life at Lincoln University at Jefferson City, Missouri, taught me Black Man in American Drama at the University of Iowa in 1976, an experience that was a motherlode of material and excitement. Tom was a guest professor at Iowa that spring semester. Through Tom Pawley, I met Winona Fletcher, now retired from Indiana University-Bloomington. She has given vital information for this book and other research projects.

I also owe thanks to Yale University's Beinicke and Sterling Libraries, Wayne Shirley of the Performing Arts Division of the Library of Congress, Amy Henderson, Wendy Reaves, and Carolyn Carr of the National Portrait Gallery of the Smithsonian Institution, Annette Fern of the Harvard Theatre Collection, Joann Elbashir at Howard University's Moorland-Spingarn Collection, Howard University's Pollock Theatre Collection, the Kennedy Center Performing Arts Library, Duke University Libraries, the libraries of the University of North Carolina at Chapel Hill, Debra Elliott of the Oregon Shakespeare Festival, Bob Taylor of the Billy Rose Theatre Collection of the New York Public Library and Jim Huffman of the Schomburg Center for Research in Black Culture.

Acknowledgements

I am grateful to Donald Hugh Smith, Professor Emeritus of Speech at Bernard Baruch College of the City University of New York, another person I met at Wisconsin-Madison in 1962, and Charles Smith for the generous Rockefeller grant I received in 1976 and 1977 as a doctoral student at the University of Iowa. It allowed me to travel to New York City in May of 1977 for my first research trip as a theatre historian. I also went to Fairfax, Virginia, to the Research Center for the Federal Theatre Project where Lorraine Brown of George Mason was a jewel.

I am grateful to Frances Lee who financed my trip to New York to see the Canada Lee Papers in June of 1980 when I was a graduate student at the University of Iowa. I stayed in her home and enjoyed her hospitality for ten days. Five large file boxes of Canada Lee's papers had lain dormant for 28 years until we unearthed them in Tommy Anderson's garage in Englewood, New Jersey. They contained his glass eye, vast Carl Van Vechten photographs, a letter from his son, and other rare memorabilia, including plans to mount an *Othello* in Italy.

I am especially thankful to Dave Lepse, Pauline Moore, Amanda Binoniemi, Janet Locatelli, Kathy Geier, Stephanie Pepin, Barbara Wilder, Dave Krym, and Dave Bezotte of the Van Pelt Library of the Michigan Technological University. Sandy Slater, Joe Pyykkonen, Cathy Greer, and Bill Tembruell of Photo Services have been most helpful.

Bob Slater and Chris Webb, both, then, of Photo Services, as well, were invaluable in accompanying me to Morgan Freeman's ranch in February of 1997. Myrna Colley-Lee, Morgan Freeman's wife, and Carolyn Tyler, his secretary at his Charleston, Mississippi home, deserve thanks for arranging the personal interview with Mr. Freeman and for sending me newspaper clippings, which Myrna had collected through the years. I am very grateful to Mical Whitaker of Metter, Georgia, for giving me Morgan Freeman's unlisted home phone number.

Robert Hansen, Supervisor of Instructional Resources at Michigan Tech, without charging me a cent, brought a tape recorder to my home on a Saturday when I suddenly learned that I could talk to James Earl Jones on a Sunday night in September of 1998. It was that Sunday evening when Mr. Jones and I set up a time for the 15 September 1998 interview which occurred at 8:00 A.M. on a Tuesday morning. Mr. Jones deserves special thanks for rising at that hour, which he set; he wished to be in the Toronto stores at 9:30 A.M. to do his Christmas shopping.

I also thank Dean Sung Lee and the Faculty Development Committee of Michigan Tech for three generous grants. Dean Maximilian Seel of Sciences and Arts was very supportive. I thank Mike Abbott of the Accounting Office of Michigan Tech, as well as Carol Johnson, Departmental Coordinator in the Department of Humanities. Words are not adequate to thank Sylvia Matthews, Assistant Director, and Nancy Grimm, Director of the Writing Center at Michigan Technological University who served, ably and tirelessly, as my readers.

Karla Kitalong, a genius at computer problems, should be canonized for sainthood. Eunice Carlson, Professor of Biology at Michigan Tech, carted me at midnight from the airport on several research trips and voluntarily parted with two rare Paul Robeson treasures—two records made in the 1960s. Thank you, Eunice and Karla. Gloria Melton of Student Affairs voluntarily mailed me a Paul Robeson and a Marian Anderson tape of their music. Sue Niemi and Jeanne Fricke fielded faxes, phone calls, and Xerox problems. Marjorie Lindley provided services for the final computer disks. Matt Buss assisted with the computer, and Karen Snyder of Fine Arts was a jewel in several ways, including sharing her photocopier when ours in Humanities was swamped.

Sally Hruska, one of my best friends in Houghton, entertained James Guines, formerly of the Alabama A. and M. Thespians, at her fabulous Lake Superior retreat, gave me a video of Paul Robeson, and managed other extraordinary gestures that supported my research. Karen Pearson of Milwaukee's Urban League volunteered to transcribe the tapes of the interviews with Morgan Freeman and James Earl Jones. The Office of Dee and Davis was most helpful, as well, in facilitating the interview with Miss Dee and in providing photographs.

I especially thank Robert Earl Jones, the late Rosamond Gilder, Woodie King Jr., Lloyd Richards, Ruby Dee, Morgan Freeman, the late Dick Campbell, Maya Angelou, William Warfield, Leonard de Paur, the late Tommy Anderson, and the many other theatre practitioners who gave me interviews or wrote me letters.

I am grateful to members of their families. Carl Lee, Canada Lee's son, comes to mind; he met me at a New York City restaurant two hours before my friend Joan Carter and I, in 1982, went to see James Earl Jones in *Othello*. I still see myself eating T-bone steak in Abe and Ruth Hill's Harlem apartment as they talked about the American Negro Theatre and Addie Anderson's exquisite fried chicken. Some of these people became close friends. I recall sitting in Fred O'Neal's Time Square office and his incredibly warm manner.

I thank again all those at Tuskegee University who assisted in hosting Federal Theatre actors for the 1982 artistic luncheon. I fondly remember Claudine Penson's exquisite breakfast soufflé. I thank Jo Taylor, again, for hosting that wonderful luncheon of 14 November 1982, where Leonard de Paur, Abe Hill, and Tommy Anderson talked and performed.

Nena Couch, Curator of the Lawrence and Lee Theatre Research Center at The Ohio State University, has been wonderful in assisting me with

Porgy and Bess, and it was through Alan Woods of that center that I ever had the need to write on the opera; I spoke on it, first at Michigan Technological University on April 23, 1991, with soprano Gabrielyn Watson and pianist Mary Rodeck. Then, in May of 1991, I spoke on *Porgy and Bess* at the Frank W. Hale Jr. Black Cultural Center at Ohio State.

I thank all the people in Hanover, New Hampshire, who, although we were total strangers, picked many of us up free from various spots at the 1998 Dartmouth Drama Conference. I thank my sister, Bonita, for coming to that conference and for introducing me, earlier, to the work of Bill T. Jones.

The Acting Company staff deserves thanks for its unusual generosity in sending me photographs and for other material. It was John Houseman, who co-founded the group, who endorsed my first book for the cover. Valerie Pegg, Director of Cultural Affairs at Michigan Technological University, put me in touch with the main office of the group. Thanks, Valerie.

I am indeed grateful to the many people who voluntarily mailed me clippings from newspapers and magazines, Cecelia Jeffries, in particular, who also indulged my talking about the manuscript on Saturdays. Debra S. Van Tassel of Colorado did an extensive bibliography of James Earl Jones while she was still a Reference Librarian in Boulder.

I am deeply indebted to Ruth Mannes, Production Editor, Donna Cherry, Amanda Johnson, Karin Cholak, and Michael Flamini, Editorial Director of St. Martin's Press. Mr. Flamini invited me first to lunch in Chicago on 8 August 1997, at the Palmer House, where we first looked at an in-depth plan prior to my signing a contract. I am most grateful for his unusual assistance in bringing this to completion! To Bob Johnson, I owe thanks for his unusual faith in and respect for me. I thank Sandi Schroeder, my caring indexer. Finally, to Michael Moore, who sat on my living room couch and read the manuscript, voluntarily, for three hours on a September Sunday morning, I thank you for nourishing my spirit during the final tedious months of preparation. For any omissions, I ask indulgence.

Glenda E. Gill
Houghton, Michigan
8 February 2000

Josephine Baker, 1906–1975, *Dancer,* G. Rader, Chromo-lithographic poster, National Portrait Gallery, Smithsonian Institution.

Chapter I

What Shall the Negro Dance About?

> Tap. Tap. Tap.
> Whirl! Whirl!
> Sammy Davis, Jr.
> Bill "Bojangles" Robinson
> Janet Collins, prima ballerina
>
> First on the heel
> and then on the toe.
> Every time I jump about,
> I jump Jim Crow.

"What shall the Negro dance about?" asked Hemsley Winfield after a dance performance at the Harlem YMCA in October 1933. The question is a metaphor for all African American performing artists who faced, throughout the twentieth century, overwhelming discrimination, but triumph on the stage. Those performers who have been most fulfilled and respected were those who had a strong sense of identity as African Americans and who, at some point in their careers, either danced, sang, wrote about, or performed dramatic roles that showed this strong sense of identity. They resisted racism in their daily lives and in the theatre. They demanded that African Americans be represented authentically on the stage.

Pearl Primus, a dancer/choreographer best known in the 1940s for her "Strange Fruit," a dance about lynching, firmly declared:

> Dance has been my vehicle. Dance has been my language, my strength. . . . Dance has been my freedom and my world. It has enabled me to go around, bore through, batter down or ignore visible social and economic walls.

> Dance is my medicine. It is the scream which eases for awhile the terrible frustration common to all human beings who, because of race, creed or color, are invisible. Dance is the fist with which I fight the sickening ignorance of prejudice. It is the veiled contempt I feel for those who patronize with false smiles, handouts, empty promises, insincere compliments. . . . I am able to dance out my anger and my tears—I dance not to entertain, but to help people better understand each other (Estrada, n.p.).

Dance was a soothing balm for artists of color.

This book is about 15 theatre practitioners, mainly dramatic actors, who personify an era in African American theatrical productions of the twentieth century: Rose McClendon, Paul Robeson, Ethel Waters, Marian Anderson, Todd Duncan, Anne Wiggins Brown, Leontyne Price, William Warfield, Maya Angelou, Canada Lee, Pearl Bailey, Ossie Davis, Ruby Dee, James Earl Jones, and Morgan Freeman. Each actor was a courageous pioneer who took a stand, some more quietly than others, and one, with emotional and physical violence. The word "performers" is used to include those who sang, but not to include the broader field of popular entertainment.

To describe the challenge of being black and a performer is difficult. One might think of the Harlem Renaissance poet, Countee Cullen, who questioned why God would "make a poet black and bid him sing." In the area of public accommodations, the African American has made significant gains in the course of the twentieth century. There have also been some economic benefits, and more diverse employment opportunities. Educational opportunities have opened and home ownership has increased. But housing remains rigidly segregated. Interracial marriages, while on the rise, are still not abundant between white and black. The eleven o'clock hour on Sunday remains the most segregated in the nation's churches.

All 15 performers in this study experienced some formal segregation. Public accommodations were closed to African Americans for most of the first six decades of the twentieth century. Performers had to stay in rooming houses or houses of prostitution if they were on the road. Demeaning signs, saying "White" or "Colored" loomed darkly over water fountains, in theatres, on public bathroom doors at filling stations and in bus and train stations, a profound inconvenience for performers on the road. Most college graduates who were black attended and graduated from virtually all-black colleges. Throughout the twentieth century, the median black income has not kept pace with white.

> Every time I jump about,
> I jump Jim Crow.

What Shall the Negro Dance About?

As the twentieth century closed, Ellis Cose wrote on 7 June 1999, in *Newsweek:*

> In fact, when blacks compare themselves with whites in virtually any arena, the picture is unsettling.
>
> Black income, for instance, is at its highest level ever, and unemployment is lower than it has been in a quarter of a century. Yet black unemployment (at 8.9 percent) remains more than twice the rate for whites (3.9 percent).
>
> ... And though black median income (for a family of four) reached a record high of $34,644 in 1997, that was still $21,378 less than the average for whites.
>
> It is not, however, just the difference in numbers that makes so many blacks loath to believe American society is serious about racial equality (40).

Then, Cose cites police brutality, the vast number of black men in prison, the drug culture, black children having children, the welfare myth, the popular culture of television, which is racially segmented, and the general distancing that many whites generate toward African Americans in the social fabric of their lives. Cose concludes: "And despite the lip service we pay to the concept of equality, we look with equanimity, even pride, upon a statistical profile of black Americans that, were it whites, would be a source of horror and consternation" (40).

"What shall the Negro dance about?" is a question still being answered on the American stage. How does the African American create? In 1926, Harlem Renaissance writer Langston Hughes also answered in his "The Negro Artist and the Racial Mountain,"

> We younger Negro artists who create now intend to express our individual dark-skinned selves without fear or shame. If white people are pleased we are glad. If they are not, it doesn't matter. We know we are beautiful. And ugly too. The tom-tom cries and the tom-tom laughs. If colored people are pleased we are glad. If they are not, their displeasure doesn't matter either. We build temples for tomorrow, strong as we know how, and we stand on top of the mountain, free within ourselves [quoted by Richard Long in the American Dance Festival pamphlet, *The Black Tradition in American Modern Dance* 18].

The Negro danced in celebration, in mourning, and in alienation. He or she danced to Negro spirituals and tapped to African drums. "Chuck" Davis and his African drummers and dancers are premier examples, as is the Alvin Ailey troupe. The artist of color never gave up. Through the art of song, dance, dramatic performance, instrumental music, and pantomime, the Negro artist found the spirit to overcome. Dance was a medicine, a refuge, a healing art.

> "Do the split!"
> The Nicholas Brothers
> Tap! Tap! Tap! Tap! Tap!

The Negro danced about racism, which was as pervasive in the theatre as it was in the broader America throughout the first six to seven decades of the twentieth century. There was a separate booking agency for black performers, the Theatre Owners Booking Agency, sometimes referred to as "Tough on Black Actors," in the early part of the twentieth century. Unionization was unheard of for most blacks during the first three decades. Stereotypes pervaded. Salaries for all but a few were meager. How did the artist resist? David Krasner posited:

> Theatrical resistance to racism during the late nineteenth and first decades of the twentieth century was, in general, neither an overt act of confrontation nor an admixture of revolutionary dogma, but rather a gradual movement, a phenomenon of advances and retreats. Resistance was often combined with an appearance of accommodation (5).

The African-American performing artist came to understand that art was, for many, also a weapon.

Not all artists used performance as a militant statement. Marian Anderson stated that she was ill-equipped for hand-to-hand combat, yet no other Negro performer of the twentieth century did more to bring about positive opportunities and respect for underrepresented groups than she, in her quiet and dignified manner. She simply made people cry with her song and self-possession under stress. Ossie Davis and Ruby Dee, while playing some non-traditional roles, have been and are activists and artists who write about and perform material that profoundly represents the African American. The Negro also danced to tell his or her history.

> *Jelly's Last Jam*
> *Bring in Da Noise. Bring in Da Funk.*
> Savion Glover
> Gregory Hines
> Tap. Tap. Tap.

The Negro also "danced" to demand inclusion. One such effort that paid off was the black theatre practitioner's inclusion in the Federal Theatre, a major moment in America. It is the only time in the history of the United States that the government has acted as a producer. Out of the needs of the Great Depression, Franklin Delano Roosevelt created the

Federal Theatre Project, with a grant of $46 million. Rose McClendon, an actor of quiet power, and best known for her role of Cora in Langston Hughes's 1935 *Mulatto* on Broadway, was also instrumental in persuading John Houseman to include actors of color in the Federal Theatre of 1935–39.

As a result, 851 actors of color were included in the famous government project, which had 13,000 people total. Harry Hopkins, Relief Administrator for President Roosevelt, appointed Hallie Flanagan as National Director, and there were regional administrators. Actors of all colors earned $23.86 a week, regardless of the size of the role. The Negro Units performed in either 16 or 22 separate groups, depending on the sources one reads, in 75 different dramas, including vaudeville, classical theatre, Negro drama, children's theatre, and a dance unit. Chicago, Birmingham, Raleigh/Durham, San Francisco, Peoria, Hartford, and New York City were a few of the venues. One dance unit was headed by Katherine Dunham.

> L'Ag Ya. Groove!
> *Ballet Fedre!* Jump!
> Tap. Tap. Tap. Tap.

Many African American dramatic groups arose during the early part of the twentieth century, which would permit "not an isolated Robeson" but many more actors of color to practice their craft in authentic representations. Socialist forces of government emerged in America in the 1930s. Times were bleak, and they were especially difficult for all but a few African American actors who were eager for better opportunities. The Negro People's Theatre put on plays by white playwrights such as Clifford Odets's *Waiting for Lefty*, about striking taxi workers of the Great Depression, because the black artists in The Rose McClendon Players were supported by the Communists and they were too poor to refuse.

James Earl Jones has almost always been apolitical in his statements to the press, but his resistance in roles such as that of Jack Johnson in Howard Sackler's *The Great White Hope* speaks volumes. Morgan Freeman, who has not created any controversy, makes a powerful statement of resistance in the films *The Shawshank Redemption* and *Glory*. Pearl Bailey, who was generally perceived as anything other than political, had the courage to say, when she selected an all-black cast for the 1967 *Hello Dolly!* amidst protests from black and white, that a lot of talented people showed up and they happened to be black. Protest comes in many forms. Slavery taught the African American that.

> Hello, Dolly, well hello Dolly!
> It's so nice to have you back where you belong.

The Negro actor, for much of the twentieth century, was the stepchild of the American theatre. The 1999 *Rollin' on the TOBA* reflects much of the hardships performers of color, especially in vaudeville, had to face. Acting, as a career, has always been a profession of high risk for anyone. It was profoundly frightening for anyone black because regular work, even in boon times, was even less available to him or her. Managers reneged on contracts. Black actors were often stranded and left on the road to get home the best way they could. Pearl Bailey earned $15 a week in Pennsylvania mining towns during the Great Depression. A New York group of black actors rehearsed for one year in 1927, and when the show closed, they got no money.

The Negro "danced" to demand union protection, which he/she ultimately obtained, especially after the venerable Frederick O'Neal became the only black President of Actors Equity from 1964 to 1973.

Sheila Rule observed of O'Neal:

> A soft-spoken, big-boned six-footer, his gentleness sometimes irritated the more militant younger black members of Equity. When meetings got tense, he had a knack for breaking the strain, either by a quip or by calling for a coffee break. He told lively jokes that often surprised those who expected staider comments from him (B8).

I interviewed Fred O'Neal at his Times Square Office on 24 June 1980. He had the following to say about the union:

> In 1913 Actors Equity came about. Black actors could join, but a paternalistic attitude prevailed. Equity took the position that there was so little work for black actors that it did not pay them to pay the initiation fee, which at that time was approximately $75. Actors Equity negotiates a "standard agreement" of a minimum salary. On that base salary, the actor may negotiate a higher salary.
>
> There are minimum conditions. There are hours of rehearsal after which there must be meal time. The employer pays for social security, pension, and welfare. Hospitalization and disability payments are required. . . . Everyone has a two-week bond—has two weeks' salary already in hand if a show fails. If they are on the road, Equity will bring them home (Personal interview with author).

Before O'Neal, Ethel Waters dressed under a set of stairs and so did Canada Lee. O'Neal, himself, ate fish and potatoes as a struggling actor who eventually performed in over 50 productions on stage and screen. The Negro actor resisted abuse.

> And every time I jump about,
> I jump Jim Crow.

Minstrelsy put great emphasis on dance, beginning with the "Jim Crow" dance initiated by Caucasian performer Thomas "Daddy" Rice in the 1850s. While the Mammy, Sambo, Uncle Tom, Tragic Mulatto, and Exotic Primitive stereotypes inherent in minstrelsy prevailed at the beginning of the century, they diminished, while not vanishing, as the century closed.

Black community theatres emerged from the beginning of the century to offset the 1910–20 Exile from Broadway exacted by the Theatrical Syndicate, which barred all black performers except Bert Williams, a famous pantomimist, from The Great White Way. "Never let a nigger say a line!" was the mantra. Loften Mitchell, an African American theatre historian, explained:

> In 1896 the Theatrical Syndicate was organized. This syndicate was spearheaded by Marc Klaw, Abraham Erlanger, Charles Frohman, Al Hyman, Sam Nixon and J. Fred Zimmerman. Its control of the theatre lasted for sixteen years.
> The syndicate had good intentions. It originally sought to do away with theatrical wastage, to prevent exploitation and to bring organization into the theatre. . . . The syndicate set out to control all bookings, hirings and firings.
> The desire for money ruined the syndicate's esthetic values and caused it to fight healthy competition. . . .
> During its reign, the Syndicate noted, too, the rising tide of reaction against the Negro (54–55).

Taking its cue from other businessmen, the Theatrical Syndicate imposed its exile on all black performers except one. As an antidote to this exile, African Americans established their own dramatic groups. The Lafayette Players were among the more prestigious black community theatres, with branches on both coasts. Such famous actors as Evelyn Preer, Anita Bush, Edna Thomas, and Dooley Wilson were a part of the group. They often presented white plays. Sister Francesca Thompson wrote:

> The original Lafayette Players was the first major professional Black dramatic company in America. Making a significant stride forward, this

ambitious band of Black actors performed over a seventeen-year period from 1915 to 1932 (13).

Other groups, such as the Pekin Players emerged in the second decade, but few had the visibility of the Lafayette Players.

Gender was also a factor within the color line. Opportunities for black male actors were greater than those for black females. But the sexual threat of the black male put him in constant jeopardy. Several black actors who dated or married white women had their careers destroyed, although this was seldom the reason given for the destruction. Management favored fairer-skinned females over darker complexioned ones, although Gershwin considered Anne Wiggins Brown to be too light to play Bess. This did not prevent his choosing her to play the role. The Negro also danced about alienation.

> Whirl! Whirl! Fly. Fly. Zoom!
> Tap. Tap. Tap. Tap. Tap.

Kariamu Welsh Asante speaks of Josephine Baker who danced for joy:

> Josephine Baker was the first and greatest Black dancer to emerge in the genre now called performance art. She epitomized through dance what freedom of expression and artistic expression really meant for generations of artists worldwide. Baker was one of the few artists in the world who were acclaimed and awarded for being themselves. Her genius resided in her conception of music, dance and comedy. . . . Not merely an entertainer, Baker was in every sense of the word an artist, and it was as an artist that she made her mark on the world (75).

Not only did she dance almost entirely nude in the Folies-Bergère, but Baker was daring in her activism and her humanitarian efforts. She adopted her "rainbow tribe" of 12 children, worked for civil rights, and died in poverty, but she lived a life of constant risks and adventure.

La Baker strolled down the Champs Elysées with her cheetah. She made love to a Swedish prince in his private railroad car. So enamored with her was a raja that he offered to banish his entire harem if she would marry him. Thousands of proposals came in to this dancer who tied a string of bananas around her waist in 1925 and became a sensation. Maurice Chevalier visited her one day and suddenly saw her descending the stairs wearing only a few flowers in the right spots. She had been baking bread and did not hear his knock. Baker's life was lived with such extravagance that when she died in Paris at age 68, Princess Grace of Monaco had to pay for the funeral.

What Shall the Negro Dance About?   9

At the time that Baker was leaving for Paris in 1925, white playwrights and their producers were also entranced by the "exotic primitive" mystique she exuded, and capitalized on this stereotype. Eugene O'Neill, Paul Green, and Elmer Rice, white playwrights, wrote plays for black actors and fought for their being able to get on the mainstage. The "exotic primitive" stereotype was obvious in the work of all three. O'Neill's plays that included parts for black actors—*The Iceman Cometh, The Emperor Jones, All God's Chillun Got Wings,* and *One Act Plays of the Sea*—showed frustrated, power-drunk, lost, and hollow people of all races. Carl Van Vechten, a white Negrophile and photographer from Cedar Rapids, Iowa, captured a number of "exotic primitive" images of African Americans with his camera from 1924 to 1963.

> Geoffrey Holder.
> Zoom! Zoom!
> Carmen deLavallade.
> Zing! Jump! Glide!!!

Paul Green, with good intentions and a strong social conscience similar to Van Vechten's, captured the essence of rural North Carolina Negroes for the stage. He won the Pulitzer Prize in 1927 for *In Abraham's Bosom,* a play about a black man who cannot educate his people. Green wrote ten plays that included black actors in the early part of the twentieth century, including *The House of Connelly* and *Hymn to the Rising Sun,* the latter on a chain gang.

Green was once at a garden party in his native Chapel Hill, North Carolina, where nothing stronger than cucumber sandwiches was expected. He rose and talked about the plight of the prisoner, much to the shock of the ladies in fancy hats under the southern heat. Elmer Rice's *Street Scene,* about a racially mixed group of New York City tenement dwellers, has been on PBS in the 1990s and is still produced on rare occasion on college campuses. But these representations were limited and not necessarily authentic representations of Negroes beyond the region with which Green and Rice were familiar.

> Tap. Tap. Tap. Whirl. Bend. Leap!
> Tap! Tap! Tap! Tap! Tap! Tap!

The Negro "danced" on the stage and demanded roles that were not racially designated as early as the second decade of the twentieth century. Only a few actors were permitted nontraditional roles outside of the historically black colleges, which put on Shakespeare and other classics. But, eventually, the greatest change on the theatrical landscape was nontraditional casting. Morgan Freeman, James Earl Jones, and Earle Hyman were among those who got a number of exceptionally strong roles, including many Shakespearean, which debunked the stereotype. Ruby Dee also played Shakespearean and other classical roles, as did several women of color.

Dee believed she could play Amanda Wingfield in Arena Stage's 1989 production of Tennessee Williams's *The Glass Menagerie* because of its universal dimension. Such was also the case with her Cordelia in the 1965 *King Lear* or Kate in *The Taming of the Shrew*. Her identity with Lutiebelle Gussiemae Jenkins in Ossie Davis's 1960 *Purlie Victorious* may have been stronger, but she could feel either role.

> Pilobolus.
> Acrobat.
> Contortionist.

Credibility in non-traditional roles, however, continues to be questioned by the critics. Only on the historically black colleges has this not been so. A drama group existed at Tuskegee Institute at the turn of the century. Howard University, Hampton Institute, and Florida A. and M. University were among the leaders in dramatic activity. Here, most student actors did not expect to go on Broadway or to Hollywood; a few did. Theatre, according to Tom Pawley of Lincoln University in Jefferson City, Missouri, was a good liberal arts education.

Many historically black college theatre groups produced only plays by white playwrights until the early 1960s. Winona L. Fletcher, retired professor of theatre at Indiana University, wrote me one reason:

> I guess it comes down to the ugly fact that we were successfully brainwashed! It took a second World War to jolt many of us into an awareness of our own worth. Then some of us saw the need to pass on our own heritage.

Participation in drama by white playwrights on historically black campuses gave black actors, in many instances, their only opportunities to be on stage, especially in roles from the classics.

James T. Guines, for example, played the plum role of Creon, in Anouilh's *Antigone*, with the Alabama A. and M. Thespians in 1954. He recalled in a telephone conversation with me on 4 July 1993:

> Alabama A. and M. was like the Harlem Renaissance during that time period of the 1940s and 1950s. Powerful stuff was going on—there was a theatrical network with Owen Dodson at Howard and Lillian Voorhees at Fisk.

What Shall the Negro Dance About?   11

And of his plight in Chattanooga, Tennessee, before William Days, a mentor, put the young Guines in his car and drove him to Alabama A. and M. in 1950:

> I literally carried pistols when I was 12—on my bicycle—got them from my Uncle Bob, a numbers runner, who had them in a suitcase where he had his loose cash, which I stole. Some kids had an allowance. I had my uncle's suitcase.

Guines worked for Brock Candy Company after he got out of high school, having been tracked into the vocational education courses by black teachers at an all-black high school. He lifted very heavy bags of sugar over steaming vats. And in reflection in his retirement, after earning a doctorate from the University of Tennessee in Knoxville and serving as Acting Superintendent of the Washington, D.C., schools for a significant portion of his adult life, Guines said:

> Much of my cultural experience—my broadening—came out of those [drama] experiences. . . . I was a street thug, but a friend of mine and I went to college and college turned us into gentlemen and scholars.

Guines credits his transformation from "street thug to a gentleman" to acting in three plays. He was Mortimer in *Arsenic and Old Lace*, Beresford in *The Bat*, and Creon in *Antigone*. Guines also credits J. Preston Cochran, director of the Alabama A. and M. Thespians from 1949–54, and William Days, the mentor who drove him to Alabama A. and M. in his car. What shall the Negro dance about?

This "dance" was often serious. Patricia Roberts Harris (1924–85) played Lavinia Mannon in O'Neill's *The Homecoming* in the trilogy *Mourning Becomes Electra*, at Howard University in the 1940s. (Owen Dodson directed and Sadie Brown was Christine.) It was, according to Jim Hatch, the "first non-professional production of the trilogy" (121). Gordon Heath, the Brett of *Deep Are the Roots* fame, played Adam Brant. Dodson was himself the gardener. Lyndon Johnson appointed Harris to be Ambassador to Luxembourg in 1965, and in 1977 President Jimmy Carter appointed her to be U.S. Secretary of Housing and Urban Development. Drama played a role in her success.

Historically, black colleges brought all kinds of artists to their campuses in the twentieth century, including dancer and choreographer, Talley Beatty. "Beatty's choreography was rooted in classical ballet and American modern dance techniques and required highly trained and virtuosic dancers to perform it" (Dunning B-11). Beatty created his own troupe,

Tropicana, which performed at Alabama A. and M. College in 1949. "Mourner's Bench," a solo, became his signature piece. Beatty danced and choreographed works about urban strife in such compositions as his 1959 "Road of the Phoebe Snow," and the 1982 "The Stack Up," which he created for the Alvin Ailey group.

Jennifer Dunning stated:

> Mr. Beatty had the wry humor and sizzling temper of a man who had weathered history. He came to modern dance in the late 1930s, a time of hectic growth in that discipline in America and a time when black dancers and choreographers were slowly beginning to establish themselves. Mr. Beatty was one of the first black modern-dance choreographers to become well-known, but somehow never had the acclaim to which many thought he was entitled, eclipsed, perhaps, by the dazzling commercial success of Alvin Ailey (B-11).

I witnessed Beatty work with students at the American Dance Festival at Duke in the summer of 1991, where he granted me a personal interview about Ethel Waters with whom he performed in *Cabin in the Sky*. It is unfortunate that Ailey eclipsed the underrated Beatty.

Katherine Dunham was among the great pioneer dancers appearing at this time. She, like most, struggled with finances even more than some actors or singers, since dance seems among the more marginalized of the fine arts. Dunham is reputed to have even fed and housed her dancers. With her troupe, she performed throughout the world in the 1940s and 1950s, including in *Cabin in the Sky*. Joyce Aschenbrenner observed:

> Her concerts were visually and kinesthetically exciting and appealing; they were also based on a profound understanding of the peoples and cultures represented as well as a keen knowledge of social values and human psychology. Her achievements as anthropologist, teacher and social activist are less well known (363–364).

But Dunham was an activist, who, among her many creations, presented a ballet, *Southland,* on lynching, while on an international tour, following the murder of Emmett Till, a 14-year-old black male accused (circa 1955) of "reckless eyeballing" of a white woman in Mississippi. The U.S. State Department tried to stop the performance (Aschenbrenner 365). It could not.

Whirl. Leap! Zoom!
Slide! Jump! Jump Jim Crow!

What Shall the Negro Dance About?

In 1959, Lorraine Hansberry's *A Raisin in the Sun* went to Broadway. Ruby Dee was in that cast as well, along with Sidney Poitier, Diana Sands, Claudia McNeil, and Louis Gossett, Jr. Lloyd Richards, an African American, directed. The play opened 11 March 1959, at the Ethel Barrymore Theater. It was a major hit. Until that evening, Broadway had never seen a play written by a black woman, nor a play with a black director, nor a commercially produced drama about black life, rather than musicals or comedy. The Broadway premiere of *A Raisin in the Sun* was as much a milestone in the nation's social history as it was in American theater (Anderson 7). But *A Raisin in the Sun* had astronomical difficulty getting funded as well as getting a theatre on Broadway.

Christopher M. Webb, a graduate student at Michigan Tech, in reviewing the Anderson essay wrote about the financial struggles of the producer of the 1959 play and 1961 film, Philip Rose:

> Anderson outlines the struggles Rose faced raising the money for the show. Traditional financial backers shied away from *Raisin in the Sun* because they were unconvinced that it would bring in large crowds. Racism played a strong role in this analysis. Potential financial supporters were unconvinced that whites would want to watch a play about a black family. They refused even to consider audiences of black theater-goers. Anderson quotes from a Hansberry letter in which she writes, "Nobody was going to pay those prices to see a bunch of Negroes emoting."
>
> When the money eventually fell into place, Rose faced similar barriers from Broadway theaters. None wanted to offer the play a home. Rose was forced to take the play to New Haven . . . and Philadelphia for brief runs and hope that the play would be such a huge success that Broadway could not ignore it (Webb 1–2).

Webb also points out that he was struck by the fact that almost 50 per cent of a review of a black play such as *A Raisin in the Sun* contained a summary, assuming reader ignorance, but that a review of Sophocles's *Antigone* had virtually no summary, in spite of a decline in American culture of reading the classics.

What shall the Negro dance about? Alvin Ailey, with 200 pieces in his repertoire, including his 1960 signature piece, *Revelations,* danced about alienation, joy, and spiritual renewal. The 1960s were a generally turbulent time for the African American on the stage. Dramatic actors had a great deal in common with the dancers.

The turbulence of the 1960s was reflected with such violent and moving pieces as Amiri Baraka's *Dutchman,* a 30-minute one-act, which takes place on a New York subway. A literal dance takes place between Lula, the white temptress, and Clay, the malleable middle-class Ivy League-trained black male. Ultimately, she stabs him to death after they insult one another unmercifully. The play is based on Wagner's *Flying Dutchman*, which indicated, in Baraka's opinion, at least, that the black man is doomed forever to sail the tempestuous seas of racial strife in the subterranean ocean of life. The 1960s saw some in this book—Ruby Dee, Ossie Davis, and James Earl Jones—in dramas about African Americans equally thought-provoking.

Dancers provoked thought about pain, as well. Bill T. Jones, a 1994 recipient of the MacArthur Genius Fellowship, danced about AIDS, a major concern of the latter two decades of the twentieth century. His ten-member company traveled nationally and internationally, with one of their most famous works being "Still Here." Jack E. White wrote:

> Few black artists exploit the cultural styles of blacks and whites as brashly as Bill T. Jones. The dances he creates for his New York City-based troupe are closer in spirit to the works of white choreographers like Mark Morris than to those of Alvin Ailey (66).

White continued:

> The most versatile and inventive of America's black dancer-choreographers is Bill T. Jones, 42, the son of impoverished farm workers from upstate New York. In 1988 his longtime lover and collaborator, Arnie Zane, died of AIDS. Jones himself was diagnosed as HIV-positive in 1985; today, he works with the intensity of someone who knows his time is running out (68).

Another innovative dancer/choreographer was Judith Jamison, who became artistic director of the Alvin Ailey American Dance Theater in 1990, and expanded the Alvin Ailey dancers to all colors of the rainbow. According to Kariamu Welsh Asante, Jamison

> has been a vital force in the dance community for over twenty years. Although her early training was in ballet, she went on to become an international symbol of American modern dance and provided inspiration for generations of aspiring young African-American female dancers.
>
> ... She helped to redefine the image of a dancer with her African appearance and carriage. In the tradition of Katherine Dunham and Pearl Primus, she proudly acknowledged her heritage through her own choreography.... *Cry*, the *magnum opus* created by the late choreographer Alvin Ailey for Jamison, epitomized the struggle of Black women in America and symbolized for the world the dignity and strength of Black women through four hundred years of oppression and victory.
>
> ... Jamison is the first African-American woman to direct a major modern dance company (631–632).

What Shall the Negro Dance About?

Jamison, as a cultural icon of the 1960s and 1970s, created inspiration for several black female playwrights who emerged in those years, including Ntozake Shange whose famed *For Colored Girls Who Have Considered Suicide When the Rainbow Is Enuf* caused black men in the balcony of the audience to talk back to the seven female actors on the stage in a never-ending exchange at Winston-Salem State University in the 1980s, and to walk out of the Broadway theatres where it played in the 1970s. Critics could be as difficult as audiences.

Critical reception of the dramatic black actor in the twentieth century by such white critics as John Simon, Alexander Woollcott, John Mason Brown, Brooks Atkinson, Rosamond Gilder, and Mel Gussow brought strong reactions from actors and audiences. Most critics have the power to sink or swim a play, and the black actor faced the peril, often, of being reviewed by non-comprehending, but often well-intentioned, white critics. John Simon, for example, believed that African American actors putting on *Coriolanus* in 1979 at the New York Public Theater's Anspacher, with Morgan Freeman in the title role "ranked as 'advanced dementia'."

One white critic was very objective: Rosamond Gilder, a woman of privilege whose father, Richard Watson Gilder, supported Tuskegee Institute and was a personal friend of Booker T. Washington. She gave an extremely favorable, yet unbiased, review of Canada Lee's portrayal of Bigger Thomas in the 1940 production of Richard Wright and Paul Green's *Native Son*. She wrote for *Theatre Arts Monthly*, a journal about theatre that was very different from the major newspaper dailies. (See my "Rosamond Gilder: Influential Talisman for African American Performers," *Theatre Survey*, vol. 37, no. 1, May 1996, 99–117, which contains a personal interview with Ms. Gilder, and 17 letters I received from her before her death.)

A few white critics were outright cruel, such as Percy Hammond of *The New York Herald Tribune* who called the all-black *Macbeth* of 1936 a "deluxe boondoggle." He also suggested that Lee and others acted as if they were delivering oratory. A witch doctor and voodoo drummers of that production allegedly killed Hammond after three days of drumming and chanting in the basement of Harlem's Lafayette Theatre, so incensed were they about his review.

Black drama critics such as Langston Hughes of *The Chicago Defender*, Abram Hill, Roi Ottley, and Saint Clair Bourne of *The New York Amsterdam News* brought balance, often, and on occasion, hagiography. This still leavened the bitter bread many actors had to eat from the critics. No black drama critic served on a major white newspaper until 1995. Paul Robeson and Canada Lee often had hostile critical and audience reception as well as laudatory kudos from audiences and critics across racial lines.

Audiences in the late 1960s were, according to Deborah Kaplan,

> notably homogeneous—white, affluent, and well educated. Theatre historians and critics were lamenting the absence of multi-class audiences by the mid-1960s, and though some theatres, often with the help of government and foundation support, sought out new, more diverse audiences in that and subsequent decades, they had little success. Audiences did become somewhat more racially diverse over the course of the 1980s, but the multi-class audience remained an unattainable goal.... In 1965 Richard Schechner enumerated the stultifying effect that resulted from resident theatres addressing the interests of middle-class subscribers—"A resident theatre that has systematically retreated into the middle class is doomed to a monotony equivalent to an Ohio highway," he complained (310–311).

Black audiences, conversely, in the 1960s often attended black theatre, little of which could be considered monotonous.

> Do the slide.
> The Electric Slide!
> Rent!

The Negro Ensemble Company, with a Ford Foundation grant of $1.2 million emerged in 1967, following an inundation of black revolutionary theatre in black communities. Lonnie Elder III's *Ceremonies in Dark Old Men*, Wole Soyinka's *Kongi's Harvest*, Phillip Hayes Dean's *The Sty of the Blind Pig*, Joseph Walker's *The River Niger*, Paul Carter Harrison's *The Great McDaddy*, Charles Fuller's *Home, Zooman and the Sign*, and *A Soldier's Play* were among their better known productions under the leadership of Douglass Turner Ward. Ford's grant marked one of the first times since the government invested $46 million in the 1935–39 Federal Theatre Project that white money had been heavily invested in African Americans on the stage.

The Wiz, a black production of *The Wizard of Oz*, *Purlie*, a musical based on Ossie Davis's *Purlie Victorious*, and Charles Gordone's *No Place To Be Somebody* were celebrated and recognized in the 1970s, Gordone's work with a Pulitzer Prize. John Houseman and Margot Harley's The Acting Company, formed in 1972, accepted classically trained black actors who toured in major Shakespearean productions and other classics. Thespians of color in the 1970s became more accepted in the American theatre.

The acceptance of black actors in the 1970s was a far cry from what Paul Robeson and Canada Lee experienced between 1924 and 1952. Both demanded roles that gave them dignity. Both were blacklisted by the House Un-American Activities Committee and both were destroyed by it, in terms of health, reputation, and finances. How the Negro was to be represented on the stage was a major struggle of the black artist during the twentieth century.

What, indeed, shall the Negro dance about? The five interpreters of *Porgy and Bess* discussed in this book—Anne Wiggins Brown, Todd Duncan, Leontyne Price, William Warfield and Maya Angelou—concerned themselves with how the denizens of Catfish Row would be portrayed, not as low-class, low-life, watermelon eating, gin-guzzling, fried chicken-loving caricatures, but as real people.

Those in this book never gave up. Through their incessant struggle, their strong sense of identity, their resistance against racism, and their unrelenting demands that African Americans be represented authentically, they paved a smoother way for the African American performing artists of the twenty-first century.

Works Cited

American Dance Festival. *The Black Tradition in American Modern Dance.* Essays compiled by Gerald E. Meyers and Stephanie Reinhart (distributed in 1991 to National Endowment for the Humanities participants in the American Dance Festival activities at Duke University in "Interpreting the African American Experience Through the Performing Arts, 1890–1990").

Anderson, Michael. "A Landmark Lesson in Being Black," *The New York Times,* 7 March 1999, 7 and 28.

Asante, Kariamu Welsh. Entry on Judith Jamison in *Black Women in America: An Historical Encyclopedia.* Brooklyn: Carlson Publishing Company, 1993, 631–632. Entry on Josephine Baker in the same book, 75–78.

Aschenbrenner, Joyce. Entry on Katherine Dunham in *Black Women in America: An Historical Encyclopedia.* Brooklyn: Carlson Publishing Company, 1993, 363–367.

Cose, Ellis. "The Good News About Black America (And Why Many Blacks Aren't Celebrating)," *Newsweek,* 7 June 1999, 28–40.

Dunning, Jennifer. "Talley Beatty, Who Depicted Inner City Life in Dance, Dies," *The New York Times,* 1 May 1995, B-11.

Estrada, Ric. "Pearl Primus," *Dance Magazine,* Nov. 1968, n. p.

Fletcher, Winona Lee. Letter to author. 11 Feb. 1994.

Gill, Glenda E. "A History of the American Negro Theatre, 1940–1949," *Class,* Feb. 1987, 30–32.

———. "The Alabama A. and M. Thespians, 1944–1963: Triumph of the Human Spirit," *The Drama Review,* winter 1994, 48–70.

Guines, James T. Telephone interview with author. 4 July 1993.

http://www.pbs.org/ktea/alive/prodbios.html#bill [Bill T. Jones]

Hall, Stuart. *Representation: Cultural Representations and Signifying Practices.* London: Sage Publications, 1997.

Hatch, James V. *Sorrow Is the Only Faithful One: The Life of Owen Dodson.* Urbana: University of Illinois Press, 1993.

"Josephine Baker Is Dead in Paris at 68," *The New York Times Biographical Service,* Apr. 1975, 410–411.

Kaplan, Deborah. "Learning 'to Speak the English Language': *The Way of the World* on the Twentieth Century American Stage," *Theatre Journal* 49, 1997, 301–321.

Krasner, David. *Resistance, Parody and Double Consciousness in African American Theatre, 1895–1910.* New York: St. Martin's Press, 1997 (courtesy of Michael Flamini).

Mitchell, Loften. *Black Drama.* San Francisco: Leswing Press, 1967.

O'Neal, Frederick Douglass. Personal interview with author. 24 June 1980.

Ploski, Harry, and Warren Marr. *The Afro-American.* New York: The Bellwether Company, 1977.

Rule, Sheila. "Frederick O'Neal, 86, Actor and Equity President," *The New York Times,* 27 Aug. 1992, B8.

Stearns, David Patrick. "Ailey Troupe Stays in Step at 40," *USA Today,* 31 Dec. 1999, 8D.

Thompson, Sister M. Francesca. "The Lafayette Players, 1917–1932," in *The Theater of Black Americans,* vol. II., ed. Errol Hill. Englewood Cliffs, New Jersey: Prentice-Hall, 1980, 13–32.

Webb, Christopher M. "Staging the Classics: A Survey of Reviews," final examination submitted for HU531 Reading Literature: Slaves of Passion, Winter Quarter, 1998–1999, 8 Apr. 1999.

White, Jack E. "The Beauty of Black Art," *Time,* 10 Oct. 1994, 66–73.

N.B. I use the term Negro in this chapter because it is historically appropriate.

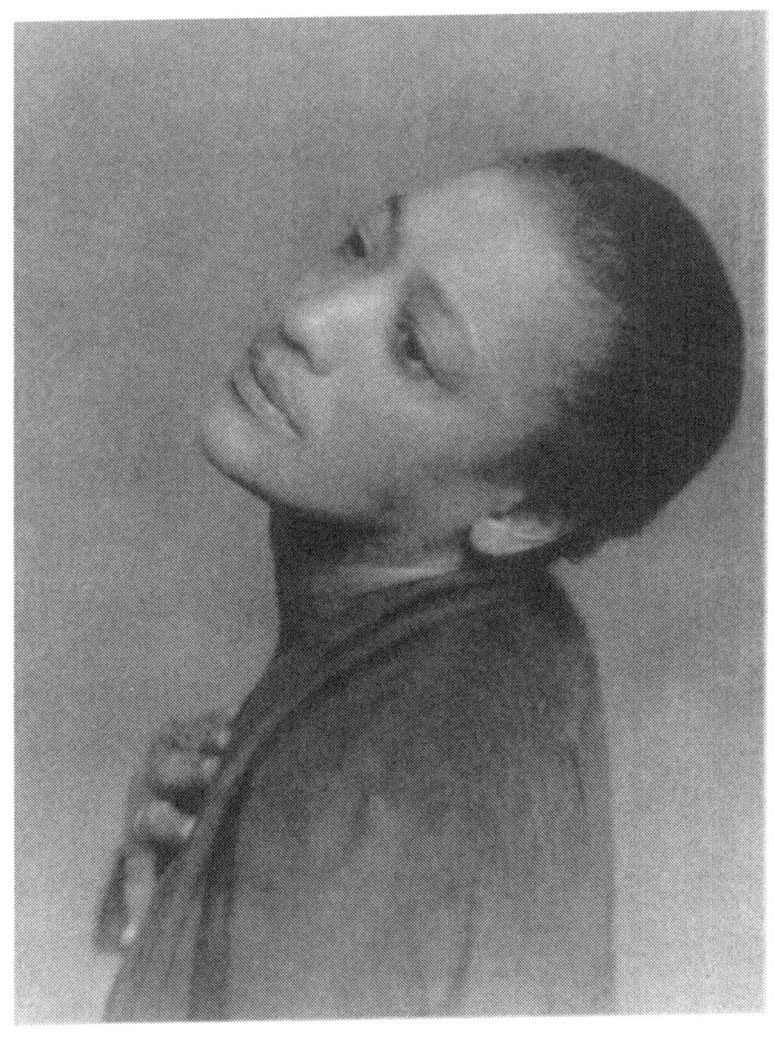
Rose McClendon, *Theatre Magazine,* August, 1927.

Chapter II

Crucible and Community:
The Vision of Rose McClendon

"Her voice was ever soft, Gentle, and low, an excellent thing in woman"

(King Lear *Act V, scene. iii, 246–247).*

Rose McClendon, like Cordelia, was one of the quiet but determined women of her time. Critics extolled her "sweetness," "majesty," and "queenly" dignity. Her frail, small body and demeanor belied her strong commitment to her vision. An actor and visionary, Rose McClendon created a Negro People's Theatre that accurately reflects varied black experiences, with a diverse group of actors playing a wide range of roles.

Lisa M. Anderson, in her groundbreaking work, *Mammies No More*, examines three stereotypes of black women: the Mammy, the Tragic Mulatto, and the Jezebel. McClendon's career consisted, almost exclusively, of these three stereotypes. Through dogged persistence, courage, and naturally endowed talent, with her Negro People's Theatre, she helped to change the image of African Americans on the American stage.

In August 1936, *Opportunity* wrote:

> It was Rose McClendon's great ambition to establish a Negro theatre—a theatre that would "develop not an isolated Robeson, an occasional Bledsoe or Gilpin, but a long line of first-rate actors" (228).

While her dream was never fully realized, African American participation in the Works Progress Administration (WPA) Federal Theatre of 1935–39 came, in great measure, because of her influence. Many black Federal Theatre actors played heroes for four brief years. With $46 million of government money spread out across America, 13,000 people crossed the boards of the Federal Theatre Project, 851 of them black. McClendon died a year after the Federal Theatre opened, but her influence on the inclusion of black actors cannot be denied.

In spite of Rose McClendon paving the way for others, her own career was filled with disappointment in the limited kinds of roles she obtained and in the way she was treated. Dick Campbell, a close friend of McClendon's, and her professional partner in her vision, recalled in a 20 May 1988 interview:

> It was the dream of Rose McClendon to have a theatre group that could do any kind of plays—plays that were actually something that expressed black life as it existed.... I recall about 1930 or 1931, we used to go by Dr. McClendon's [Rose McClendon's husband] apartment and a group of us would sit and she would read things from the *Medea* ... and we would applaud just like we were in the theatre.

With the exception of Langston Hughes's *Mulatto*, in which McClendon starred on Broadway in 1935, most of the other work in which she performed was written by white playwrights: Dorothy and DuBose Heyward, Paul Green, and Laurence Stallings.

McClendon's dream of a Negro People's Theatre, however, was not an artistic one, alone. Theatre is an art and a business. Broadway invests millions, and the simplest venues cost. Two years before the Great Crash of 1929, Eva LeGallienne solicited $1, each, from thousands of potential subscribers for the Civic Repertory Theatre.

While many Americans stood in soup and bread lines during the Great Depression, Rose McClendon wrote Dick Campbell on 28 June 1935 about her efforts:

> Dear Dick: You can see by this leaflet that we are working like mad. I have contacted all of the active theatre groups and find them eager to work for and with us, so we must carry on. Our greatest concern is now to raise $150.00 ... by next Friday to pay for the house before we go in it. I don't know where it's coming from, but I do know we will have it. That is just how much faith I have in what we are doing. Will write after the 30th to tell you the results. Keep your fingers crossed until then. Yours up to my ears in work. P.S. Best to the wife. Rose.

McClendon never gave up.

Born on 27 August 1884, in Greenville, North Carolina, to Sandy and Tena (Jenkins) Scott, Rosalie Virginia Scott McClendon was a woman of the South: gracious, refined, polished. Her parents were domestics—a coachman and a housekeeper—for a wealthy family in New York City. They were a part of the early 1890 field-to-factory migration. McClendon was about six when her family moved to New York City, where she attended Public School No. 40 on East 28th Street, and took part in Sunday school plays.

Active in the St. Mark's Methodist Episcopal Church, one rich with ritual and ceremony, she had seen some programs done poorly. In an article called "Dramatis Personae," in the April 1927 issue of *Crisis*, McClendon said, "I cannot say all my life I wanted to act. I had seen so many things badly done in churches that I wanted to teach children what to do and how to do it" (55).

Unlike many in theatre, however, McClendon seemed to have had a successful traditional marriage. On 27 October 1904, Miss Rosalie Scott married Henry Pruden McClendon, a chiropractor and Pullman porter for the Pennsylvania railroad. They moved to Harlem where they set up residence at 133 West 138th Street. There were no children. But McClendon was a mentor who, according to the 18 July 1936 *New York Amsterdam News*, "was never too tired or too busy to give unstinted time to amateur productions in the community and to give advice to young aspirants in the theatre" (18).

While the woman of color on stage has, since the time of the Greeks, been portrayed mainly through the stereotype, Rose McClendon was seeking to change the image of her race and gender. The black man on the American stage has consistently been portrayed as a ne'er-do-well, shiftless, immoral, untrustworthy, intellectually inferior, dialect speaking, chicken eating, gin guzzling, razor toting brute, buffoon, buck, Sambo, or Uncle Tom. McClendon, through prudence, cultivated such diverse and influential friends as Carl Van Vechten, John Houseman, and Dick Campbell, all of whom also desired more authentic representations on the stage.

McClendon's involvement with the theatre, and possibly her vision, began in 1916, at the age of 31, when she received a scholarship to study at the American Academy of Dramatic Art in Carnegie Hall. Franklin Sargent taught her there for three years, and in 1919, she made her debut in the Bramhall Players' production of Butler Davenport's *Justice*. Frank Wilson had the other leading role. From that moment on, McClendon was involved in virtually every significant play that included African Americans, as well as a number of other kinds of drama, until her untimely death at the age of 51.

Although the 1920s and 1930s were a fertile period for the American theatre, not only were stereotypes pervasive, but there was a separate booking agency for black people, the Theatre Owners Booking Association, better known as Tough on Black Actors. Hollywood reinforced the images. Currier and Ives painted them. Radio gave credence to their thought. Management consistently reneged on black contracts. White theatre groups included black actors, but virtually always in demeaning roles, and touring was a massive problem in terms of segregated conditions in theatres, commercial travel, and hotels. McClendon sought to assuage some of these problems, including reducing the stereotype, by creating her own group in Harlem.

Catherine Clinton, in *Black Women in America: An Historical Encyclopedia,* wrote:

> The Mammy figure remains a staple of plantation legend and continues as a powerful icon well into the present. . . . Most scholars agree that her role in popular culture reflects a deliberate manipulation of stereotype for racial exploitation and commercial gain. . . . They appear not only in fiction, but in films and television, advertising and other media. . . . [I]t was perhaps no accident that until 1991 no black female screen performance *except* the Mammy was singled out for American film's highest accolade [Hattie McDaniel won for her excellent portrayal of Mammy in the 1939 film version of Margaret Mitchell's *Gone With the Wind.*] (744–746).

What appeared on the stage was not typically true in real life for the vast majority of people of color. Even now, television and the theatre often portray the black family as less than cohesive. McClendon, as a woman in a stable marriage, knew that many black families stayed together. James V. Hatch and Ted Shine argued:

> Following the Civil War, freedmen throughout the South began a frantic search for family members, loved ones, and friends separated by slavery or by war. They legalized their marriages. . . . They sought land. . . . They sought educations for their children. By 1890, more than 90 percent of African families lived in the South. . . . At the center of these large extended families were married couples. . . . Less than a hundred years later, 90 percent of all African-American families lived in urban areas scattered in all parts of the country. . . . From the end of the Civil War up to 1960, there was a remarkable degree of stability in the structure of Black family life. Divorce was rare, and 78 percent of the homes were headed by married couples (65).

Major crucibles of the African American were economic marginality and a lack of formal education, not a lack of cohesive families. According to Elizabeth Clark-Lewis, also in *Black Women in America: An Historical Encyclopedia:*

By 1925, the growth in the number of African-American women domestics [in the North] was a natural phenomenon. The majority of these household servants did not live in the homes of their employers . . ., In Pittsburgh, 90 percent of African-American women worked as dayworkers, washerwomen or live-in servants. . . . They averaged about $5 per week in the North and this was more than five times what they were paid in the rural South. . . . During the Depression, the situation deteriorated greatly. White women who had lost their jobs in factories began to compete for domestic work and were generally preferred (341–342).

Most African Americans who attended college at all studied at one of the 110 historically black colleges, the only choice for many. Most faculty members were also African American. (Nepotism was generally ignored and husbands brought their wives with formal training to the campuses where the men, often, but not always, had jobs already.)

Not all black women college professors held college degrees, such as singer/actor Abbie Mitchell who headed the vocal department at Tuskegee Institute from 1931 to 1934 (see Tanner 120). She taught with only a high school education. McClendon wished to showcase this element of society, too.

Black women playwrights were also writing between 1916 and 1928: Angelina Grimke, Alice Dunbar-Nelson, Mary Burrill, Myrtle Smith Livingston, Ruth Gaines-Shelton, Eulalie Spence, and Marita Odette Bonner, but their works were often too realistic for the major stages. Black male playwrights were at work as well in the 1920s and 1930s: Garland Anderson, Willis Richardson, Jean Toomer, John Matheus, and Randolph Edmonds (see Hatch and Shine, vol I). Getting their work produced or published was difficult. McClendon was not unmindful of these barriers. She and other actors wanted a balance.

Many other major African-American female stars in the pantheon of this era on Broadway, in black community theatre and supper clubs, functioned within the stereotype. Gilbert Seldes wrote about Florence Mills, for example: "Merely to watch her walk out on the stage with her long, free stride and superb, shameless swing, is an aesthetic pleasure" (quoted in Isaacs 68). Several women performers of color may have felt that their only opportunity on the stage came via their revealing their feminine pulchritude.

McClendon, nevertheless, played her roles only with great dignity. Edna Lewis Thomas, Abbie Mitchell, and Laura Bowman were also neither flamboyant nor lacking in dignity. Bowman, Thomas, and Mitchell were part of the Lafayette Players, a distinguished black community theatre that had a vision similar to McClendon's. In spite of the success of many black musicals, vaudeville, and serious dramatic theatre, the black female actor was, generally, reduced to being a servant, slut, or Tragic Mulatto.

A physical description of Rose McClendon was that she was "Five feet or a little more," according to Dick Campbell, "she probably weighed about 115 pounds or so. Very thin" (20 May 1988). But, she had regal serenity, humor, and balance. Those qualities, however, did not change her opportunities.

The Lafayette Players offered McClendon the chance to play in its 1924 production of white playwright Nan Bagby Stevens's *Roseanne*. White actors, using burnt cork, had performed the roles in December of 1923 at the Greenwich Village Theatre for 42 performances. Charles S. Gilpin played the role of the preacher, Cicero Brown, who seduces a young girl entrusted to him. McClendon played the girl's mother. *The New York Times* observed:

> The play, of course, is more interesting with a cast of negroes [sic], although one who did not see the first production suspects that it is not quite so well played on the whole. The honors of the evening went to Rose McClendon, whose performance was uneven, but frequently moving in the extreme (11 Mar. 1924, 16:3).

Fannin Belcher, in his mammoth 1945 dissertation, wrote of *Roseanne:* "The heroine of the story is Roseanne Lee, a hard working and devout church-goer who discovers too late to save her runaway young sister from death that the preacher, whom all idolize, has betrayed them both" (204). As a result of McClendon's visibility in this moving drama, she attracted major critics to her work two years later in Laurence Stalling's 1926 *Deep River.*

Achieving legendary status in this play, she played a madam. Opening at the Shubert on 4 October 1926, in New York City, *Deep River* cast white actors, primarily, in a "native opera," which explored life in New Orleans in 1835. African-American actors included Julius Bledsoe as Tirzan, Rose McClendon as Octavie, and Charlotte Murray as The Queen. Major critics flocked to Broadway. Alexander Woollcott wrote of McClendon:

> In the third act of *Deep River,* when, for a moment, the vast stage was emptied and one heard only the murmur of unseen choruses, saw only the lazy tracery of the tree shadows upon the gray-green jalousies of the old New Orleans house, the door opened on the high balcony and down the winding stone steps came an aging mulatto actress who played, in black taffeta and diamonds, the procuress of the quadroon ball. She stood there for a mo-

ment, serene, silent, queenly and I could think only of the lost loveliness that was Duse. The noble head, carved in pain, was Duse's (55).

Critics often compared Rose McClendon with Eleonora Duse, the great Italian actress of the 19th century.

But Duse played in the classics, and McClendon did not. Although she continually played the mammy, mulatto, or madam, white actors came to learn from her performances. While *Deep River* was having its trial flight in Philadelphia, Ethel Barrymore came to watch what moments she could. According to the April 1927 *Crisis*, in an article titled "Dramatis Personae," Arthur Hopkins, the famous producer, whispered to her, "Stay 'till the last act if you can, and watch Rose McClendon come down those stairs. She can teach some of our most hoity-toity actresses distinction" (55).

Reputedly, according to the same *Crisis* article, Miss Barrymore replied, "She can teach them all distinction" (55). McClendon's "innate aristocracy and poise" were the kudos Gilbert Gabriel heaped on her (66), also reported in the April 1927 issue of *Crisis*. John Anderson of *The New York Evening Post* wrote of McClendon as one who "created out of a few wisps of material an unforgettable picture of a proudly withered madam in the house of the quadroon women. Hers was a faded, but imperious beauty, the faintly tragical grandeur of stately ruins" (*The Crisis* April 1927 66). McClendon had found fame, if not satisfaction, in her part.

White playwrights all too often wrote parts for the African American in dialect, as if all blacks lacked formal education. In 1926, McClendon was cast as Goldie McAllister, who spoke in a thick southern dialect. The vehicle was Paul Green's Pulitzer Prize- winning *In Abraham's Bosom*. Frank Wilson and Julius Bledsoe played Abraham, and Abbie Mitchell, Muh Mack. Many African Americans, including the late Darwin T. Turner, have criticized Green for his narrow regionalism.

In a telephone conversation (24 October 1980) and correspondence with Paul Green, I sensed that he was more informed and comprehending about the North Carolina rural African American than many, the main group to which he had been exposed since childhood. I think that he wrote accurately and extremely sympathetically in his ten plays for black actors, more than any other white playwright of his era. McClendon benefited in visibility and exposure, in spite of the regionality and class limitation of the role.

While black critics were incensed by *In Abraham's Bosom*, Caucasian critic Brooks Atkinson wrote on 30 December 1926, in *The New York Times* that Rose McClendon, in the very last moment of the play, was "fine indeed, although she only looked it" (22:4). Positively, he called *In Abraham's Bosom* "powerful." In addition to winning the Pulitzer, the play also afforded McClendon an acting award from *The Morning Telegraph*. The drama ran for 116 performances, unfortunately continuing to reinforce the stereotype of African Americans as violent and resisting education.

McClendon played Serena, the wife of Robbins, whom the Bully, Crown, kills in a street brawl on Catfish Row in Dorothy and DuBose Heyward's famed *Porgy*, the 1927 play on which the opera *Porgy and Bess* is based. Few plays have excited the theatre as much as *Porgy* did. The Theatre Guild produced it. A stellar cast played the roles. Norman Nadel reflected: "Well before the music was added and the script was rewritten as a libretto, this story captured the imagination and heart of almost everyone who encountered it" (70 and 72). *Porgy* showcased the lower depths of black America, although the action and characters excited many.

The play toured Europe and the United States. James Weldon Johnson believed:

> [*Porgy*] did not run along on a monotonous level; at times it rose to heights of ecstasy and tragedy; and always it was suffused with Negro humour. Not only was the play well written, but it was remarkably mounted and staged. In the closing scene of the first act—in which the company is gathered in Serena's room holding the wake over her murdered husband; singing and singing until they rise and break into religious frenzy, their swaying bodies and uplifted hands suddenly thrown in black shadows against the background of the white-washed walls of the room; singing and singing—there have been few scenes in New York theatre to equal it in emotional power. *Porgy* loomed high above every Negro drama that had ever been produced (211).

Richmond Barthé, the distinguished black sculptor, was so touched with McClendon in this role that he did a full bust of her as Serena. Frank Lloyd Wright placed it in his garden.

In spite of the success McClendon enjoyed in the role of Serena, all was not well with the economic conditions in the United States. America tottered on the brink of economic collapse. Seventy-five percent of African Americans became unemployed in the 1930s, as the Great Depression hit. The Harlem Renaissance waned along with all its fertility, joy, and excitement. The theatre changed its mood to mirror the mind set of America: anxious, fearful, ready to fight and judge the have-nots as inferior or unworthy.

In 1931, Rose McClendon played yet another Mammy, the stereotype of one who lives to nurture white children while neglecting her own. The vehicle was Paul Green's *The House of Connelly* put on by The Group Theatre. The Martin Beck Theatre in New York City was the venue. McClendon was Big Sue, a watchful Negro who "won't allow no white trash" to take over Connelly Hall. Thus, she strangles Patsy Tate who sets out to win the aristocratic and weak Will Connelly.

At this juncture, McClendon, weary of playing roles that did not please her, met Dick Campbell, a tenor singer/actor, with whom she formed the theatrical partnership of The Negro People's Theatre. Her chances to break the shackles of the stereotype, however, seemed elusive.

Again, she was cast as a Mammy in James Knox Millen's 1932 drama, *Never No More*. Mammy was literally the name of the character. This was the first in a series of lynch dramas. Leigh Whipper played the son who strangles a white girl in panic early in the play; in the second act, a white mob burns him alive. Brooks Atkinson wrote in *The New York Times* on 8 January 1932:

> It is the most torturing scene this chronicler has ever seen on the stage. Still a little shaken by the grim reality of that lynching inferno, he hopes never to see another . . . As the mother Miss McClendon is both majestic and humble, if such a thing is possible. She acts from the inside out. The emotion she conveys is interior; it has pride, dignity and sweetness and confirms the high esteem in which she has long been held (27:1).

In spite of her disappointment with her roles, McClendon, according to Dick Campbell, "was not bitter and she was not an activist in the sense that she was fighting for everything. She tried to rectify conditions" (1988).

The Mammy role lingered for her when she took the part of Phyllis opposite Juano Hernandez, a respected craftsman in Annie Nathan Meyer's *Black Souls* in 1932. She was also a woman who worked the fields, Sudie Wilson, in Paul Green's symphonic drama, *Roll, Sweet Chariot* in 1934. A different kind of role was that of Carrie Washington in John Charles Brownelle's 1934 *Brainsweat,* an attempt at showing a middle-class figure. She played an old woman in 1935 in Archibald McLeish's *Panic* at the Imperial.

Meanwhile, McClendon became a supporter of The Scottsboro Boys in the famed Scottsboro Case where, in 1932, nine young blacks, the youngest of whom was 13, were accused of raping two white women on a freight train. It became a *cause célèbre*.

At this critical time in history, McClendon's dream of The Negro People's Theatre was being minimally realized. Her group performed Caucasian playwright Clifford Odets's *Waiting for Lefty,* under Communist sponsorship, according to Dick Campbell (5 Jan. 1978). "We did not select that play as being representative of the Negro People's Theatre, but we had no money and no help," Campbell recalled. This short *tour de force* about striking taxi workers who are waiting for their leader, Lefty, played to over 5,000 people at the Rockland Palace Dance Hall at 155th Street and 8th Avenue (5 Jan. 1978). But this shoestring effort could not compete with white producers such as Martin Jones.

Unfortunately, Jones gave McClendon the greatest role of her career. Ironically, it was also a Mammy, and it came within less than a year of her death. Rose McClendon was Cora in Langston Hughes's 1935 Broadway play, *Mulatto*, a vehicle Jones sensationalized with scenes Hughes had neither written nor authorized. Jones's purpose was to make money.

Opening on 11 November 1935 at the Vanderbilt Theatre, the play told a story about a black woman who worked in a home for a white colonel by whom she bore five "yard" children. The oldest son, Robert, demanded that he be given recognition as his father's child, and takes his father's hand in the yard, one day, calling him "Poppa" in front of guests who are there for supper. The white father spurns him and the mulatto son kills the colonel. The play ends with a posse coming for Robert, who commits suicide as he hears the mob nearing. Critics and audience, alike, were uncomfortable. Martin Jones created a melodrama out of the play. (See Jay Plum.)

Rose McClendon as Cora, in one of the most powerful scenes in the American theatre, loses her mind near the end of the drama, and tells the dead colonel: "You said he was ma boy—my bastard boy . . . but he's yours, too. . . . I borned you five chilluns, and now one of 'em is out dere in de dark runnin from yo' people" (Smalley 26 and 27). She demands that the dead colonel rise and protect his son.

In the meantime, McClendon's health began to fade and in December of 1935 she had to withdraw from the cast. Arnold Rampersad wrote:

> [Langston Hughes] visited the seriously ill Rose McClendon, who had been forced by her doctors to leave the show. Langston sent her roses from Thorley's, where he had worked as a delivery boy in 1922. He was bitter about Jones' treatment of a gracious woman and a fine actress who had been cheated by racism of the recognition and rewards she deserved; which other Broadway star rode the subway home at night, as she had done each night after her performances in *Mulatto* (328)?

Martin Jones deliberately snubbed McClendon by not inviting her to a buffet supper he hosted for the cast of *Mulatto*.

Her struggle during the last months of her life was intense. She battled cancer, gallantly performed in *Mulatto,* and sought, successfully, to see African American inclusion in the Federal Theatre. On 12 July 1936, Rose McClendon died. Hundreds paid their respects.

Opportunity, in August 1936, wrote:

> Rose McClendon is no more. She, who held enthralled thousands of theatregoers by the startling fidelity of her character delineations, she who gave to the American theatre its first real, authentic depiction of the Negro woman has

made her exit from the stage of this world. ... There can be no doubt that Rose McClendon must be ranked among the great actresses of her generation. Not only by her rare gifts, but by her dream, Rose McClendon has attained immortality (228).

In 1937, Dick Campbell and Muriel Rahn, his first wife, set up the Rose McClendon Players in her honor. (Ossie Davis was one of the members.) Carl Van Vechten, in 1946, gave to Howard University a collection of 100 of his photographs known as the Rose McClendon Collection.

Rose McClendon struggled against the odds of sexism, racism, and capitalism. The black female actor of today still plays in the shadows of the stereotype. Sidney Poitier, on 22 February 1988 in *Newsweek*, asserted, "There is still a complete shutout of the black actress" (73). And there are still far too few produced plays written by black playwrights.

Perhaps the thought in Langston Hughes's "Note on Commercial Theatre" offers a consoling benediction and lament. He bemoaned the fact that whites had "taken my blues and gone," but fervently believed that someone would "put on plays about me," and it would probably be Hughes, himself. It was the gifted actress and visionary, Rose McClendon, a prime mover in the American theatre, a force for creating a theatre that would represent African Americans authentically, who helped bring about Hughes's poetic dream.

When Lisa M. Anderson wrote her 1997 book, *Mammies No More: The Changing Image of Black Women on Stage and Screen*, she was writing about work begun by the gentle, but principled, Rose McClendon.

Works Cited

Anderson, Lisa M. *Mammies No More: The Changing Image of Black Women on Stage and Screen.* Lanham, MD: Rowman and Littlefield Publishers, 1997.

Atkinson, Brooks. *The New York Times*, 30 Dec. 1926, 22:4. [*In Abraham's Bosom*] 8 Jan. 1932. 27:1. [*Never No More*]

Belcher, Fannin. *The Place of the Negro in the Evolution of the American Theatre, 1767 to 1940.* Ph.D. Diss., Yale, 1945.

"Brainsweat," program, Apr. 1934. (courtesy of Dick Campbell)

Campbell, Dick. Letter to author. 5 Jan. 1978.

———. Personal interview with author. 8 July 1985.

———. Personal interview with author. 27 Mar. 1986.

———. Personal interview with author. 20 May 1988.

Clark-Lewis, Elizabeth. "Domestic Workers in the North," in *Black Women in America: An Historical Encyclopedia*, ed. Darlene Clark Hine. Brooklyn: Carlson Publishing Company, 1993, 340–342.

Clinton, Catherine. "Mammy" in *Black Women in America: An Historical Encyclopedia*, ed. Darlene Clark Hine. Brooklyn: Carlson Publishing Company, 1993, 744–747.

Cornwell, Byrd Green. Personal interview with author. 30 Nov. 1984.

"Dramatis Personae," [Rose McClendon] *The Crisis*, April 1927, 55.

DuBois, W. E. B. "The Creative Impulse," in *The Crisis Writings*, ed. Daniel Walden. New York: Fawcett, 1972, 275–299.

"Final Services Held for Rose McClendon," *The New York Amsterdam News*, 18 July 1936, 1 and 18.

Green, Paul. "In Abraham's Bosom: The Pulitzer Prize Play," *Theatre Magazine*, Aug. 1927, 24–26, 54.

———. Telephone interview with author. 24 Oct. 1980.

Hatch, James V. and Ted Shine. *Black Theatre USA, Expanded and Revised*, vols. I and II. New York: The Free Press, 1996.

Houseman, John. *Run-Through: A Memoir*. New York: Simon & Schuster, 1972.

Isaacs, Edith J. R. *The Negro in the American Theatre*. New York: Theatre Arts, 1947.

Jefferson, Annetta. "Rose McClendon," in *Black Women in America: An Historical Encyclopedia*, ed. Darlene Clark Hine, Brooklyn: Carlson Publishing, 1993, 765–766.

Johns, Robert L. "Rosalie 'Rose' McClendon (1884–1936), Actress," in *Notable Black American Women*, ed. Jessie Carney Smith. Detroit: Gale Research, 1992, 695–699.

Johnson, James Weldon. *Black Manhattan*. New York: Atheneum, 1930.

Journal of Negro History, Jan. 1937, 130–131.

Kellner, Bruce. *The Harlem Renaissance: A Historical Dictionary for the Era*. Westport, CT: Greenwood Press, 1984.

Le Gallienne, Eva. *The Mystic in the Theatre: Eleonora Duse*. New York: Farrar, Straus, and Giroux, 1966.

McClendon, Rose. Letter to Dick Campbell, 28 Jun. 1935. (courtesy of Dick Campbell)

———. Letter to potential subscribers of the Negro People's Theatre, 19 Jun. 1935. (courtesy of Dick Campbell)

Mitchell, Loften. *Black Drama: The Story of the American Negro in the Theatre*. San Francisco: Leswing Press, 1967.

Nadel, Norman. *A Pictorial History of the Theatre Guild*. New York: Crown Publishers, 1969, 70 and 72.

New York Times, The, 11 Mar. 1924, 16:3.

Newsweek, 22 Feb. 1988. 73.

Opportunity, Aug. 1936, 228. [Rose McClendon]

"Passing of Rose McClendon Leaves Another Vacancy In Ranks of American Theatre," *The Journal and Guide*, 25 Jul. 1936, n.p.

Plum, Jay. "Accounting for the Audience In Historical Reconstruction: Martin Jones's Production of Langston Hughes's *Mulatto*," *Theatre Survey*, vol. 36, no. 1, May 1995, 5–19.

———. "Rose McClendon and the Black Units of the Federal Theatre Project: A Lost Contribution," *Theatre Survey*, Vol. 33, No. 2, Nov. 1992, 144–153.

Rampersad, Arnold. *The Life of Langston Hughes.* New York: Oxford University Press, 1986, 328–329.
"Rose McClendon, 51, Negro Actress, Dies," *The New York Times,* 14 July 1936, 20.
Smalley, Webster. *Five Plays By Langston Hughes.* Bloomington: Indiana University Press, 1963.
Tanner, Jo A. *Dusky Maidens: The Odyssey of the Early Black Dramatic Actress.* Westport, CT: Greenwood Press, 1992.
Voorhees, Lillian W. "Rose McClendon," In *Notable American Women 1607–1950,* ed. Edward T. James, et al. Cambridge: Harvard University Press, 1971, 449–50.
"Waiting for Lefty," directed by Rose McClendon and Chick McKinney, program, n.d. (courtesy of Dick Campbell)
Woll, Allen. *Dictionary of the Black Theatre.* Westport, CT: Greenwood Press, 1983.
Wollcott, Alexander, quoted in *The Crisis,* Apr. 1937, 55.

Paul Robeson as Othello in the Brattle Street production, 1942, Cambridge, Massachusetts. The Harvard Theatre Collection, The Houghton Library.

Chapter III

The Silencing of Paul Robeson

I'm goin' to tell God all of my troubles when I get home.

These words—from a Negro spiritual Paul Leroy Bustill Robeson sang and recorded in New York City on 10 May 1927—epitomize a gifted but tormented life. Robeson rose to the pinnacle of fame as an actor/singer, but fell to the nadir as an activist. On 23 January 1976, age 77, Robeson died, but *Ebony* asserted, in quoting Coretta Scott King, that he had been "buried alive" long before his funeral (Douglas 33). Many people today do not know his name, in spite of the 1998 Centennial Celebration of his 100th birthday. The curtain of silence had come down for too long.

Bart Lanier Stafford, III wrote me in a 16 September 1976, letter:

> I ran into Paul Robeson many times when we lived around the corner from each other in New York City. By then he was old and battered and well-nigh penniless, but the dignity and stature were still there, though I could tell that it was a supreme effort for him merely to hold himself together in the face of overwhelming adversity and the "slings and arrows of outrageous fortune." A great man walked the earth and few of us recognized him.

Once the best known black actor/singer in the world, Robeson lived in virtual obscurity the last 15 years of his life. Many things contributed to the silencing of this great man. In addition to the fact that America did not permit him to be an outspoken activist, as well as an artist, there were factors beyond Robeson's actions that exacerbated conditions: the development of the Cold War between Russia and the United States following World War II, McCarthyism and the Red Scare, the entire House Un-American Activities Committee (HUAC) syndrome, which helped destroy many lives, the hearings involving the Hollywood Ten, and the conviction of Alger Hiss for perjury.

Paul Robeson was the only man in the history of this country who was "never once permitted to appear on American television," according to *Variety* in a "Statement of Conscience," published on 11 January 1978. Such has not happened today to Louis Farrakhan, for example, a man perceived by many to be less palatable to many whites than Robeson. Part of the reason for Robeson's suffering was the era in which he lived.

Born in Princeton, New Jersey, on 9 April 1898, the son of an escaped slave and minister, William Drew Robeson, and Anna Louisa (Bustill) Robeson, a schoolteacher, Paul Robeson arrived in this life at one of the most difficult times to be black. The unfortunate and adverse Dred Scott Decision, handed down by Supreme Court Justice Roger B. Taney in 1857, said that a black man was property and a slave, even if his master had taken him to a free state. *Plessy v. Ferguson*, the "separate but equal" doctrine, became another negative Supreme Court decision in 1896. The greatest number of lynchings in America occurred, as well, between 1896 and 1917, the beginning of World War I.

Whatever may be said of Robeson, one must acknowledge that he had a great deal to endure simply because he was black. Throughout most of his life, as a traveling artist he could not stay at many hotels or eat in their dining rooms. When his son chose to intermarry, hordes of people wrote hate mail to Robeson and his wife. On occasion, men hurled racial epithets at him. One woman spat in the face of Uta Hagen when she saw her with Robeson. Some directors insulted him during rehearsals, demanding very peculiar stage business that only added, often, to negative images of African Americans. Robeson did not take insults lightly and spoke out loudly and often.

Donald Bogle declared:

> It is one of the less pleasant aspects of the American way that when a black artist is successful and silent, he remains a national favorite. But when a black artist becomes important enough to want better roles (usually those with more dignity and less racism inherent in them) or when the artist makes some comment against the social-political climate of the country, he becomes a doomed man. When Robeson became associated with the Communist Party in the mid-1930s, when he spoke out against American discrimination and segregation, when he began making trips to the Soviet Union, he was singled out and finally silenced (94–95).

The silencing of Paul Robeson is a tragedy of the American theatre.

Like Richard Wright and James Baldwin, Paul Robeson was an intellectual who became discouraged by his treatment in America and lived abroad a great deal. *The New York Times* wrote: "It was often pointed out that, spending so much of his life abroad, he had relatively few profound associations with the black community in this country" (24 Jan. 1976, 30).

He entered Rutgers in New Brunswick, New Jersey in 1915, and took his B.A. there in 1919. *Current Biography 1941* reported:

> The minister's son attended Rutgers College on a scholarship and made a remarkable record there: won the freshman prize in oratory and the sophomore and junior prizes in extemporaneous speaking, was a member of the glee club [some sources differ as to whether or not Robeson was denied membership in the glee club] and the debating team, and a speaker at commencement. In addition he was a "four-letter" man—winning, in all, twelve letters in track, football, basketball and baseball—and was chosen All-American end by Walter Camp in 1918 and 1919. His academic record was equally good. . . . In his junior year he was elected to Phi Beta Kappa (716).

While his extraordinary success at Rutgers was remarkable, it was marred by fellow football players who intentionally dislocated one of his shoulders, and with the cleats in their shoes saw to it that he had no fingernails. Robeson never gave up, however, and sought an advanced degree, as well.

Fascinated, initially, with the law and probably hoping to make a difference in conditions for his people, Robeson began the pursuit of his LL.B. at Columbia in 1920. Financing his studies by playing professional football on weekends, Robeson even entertained the notion of becoming a professional boxer. But fate determined otherwise. It was at Columbia that he met the theatre critic Alexander Woollcott who was quite acerbic, in general, about black actors, referring to them as "darkies," and other negative terms, in spite of being well-intentioned.

Woollcott had an affinity for Robeson. As a result of Robeson's connection with Woollcott and other major theatre personalities, he was cast in the Broadway chorus of the famed work of Miller and Lyles, *Shuffle Along*, in 1921. It ran for 504 performances and catapulted many unknowns to fame.

Robeson also met at Columbia his future wife, Eslanda Cardozo Goode, a chemistry student he married on 17 August 1921. At her insistence, he took part in an amateur production of Ridgeley Torrence's *Simon the Cyrenian* at the Harlem Young Men's Christian Association. He remembered, fondly, "Even then, I never meant to [become an actor], I just said yes to get her to quit pestering me," (*The New York Times,* 24 Jan. 1976, 30). Eugene O'Neill was in the audience and offered him the title role in *The Emperor Jones*. At the time, Robeson refused, but made his professional debut in 1921 at Harlem's Lafayette Theatre in another production of *Simon the Cyrenian,* Simon being the black man who bore Christ's cross.

Still networking, and with his wife's help, the actor obtained another early role, that of Jim in Mary Wiborg's *Taboo* at the Sam Harris Theatre in 1922, opposite Margaret Wycherly in America, and Mrs. Patrick Campbell in London. A great deal of tension existed in the American production, since Ms. Wycherly got bad reviews and the playwright wanted a stronger actress. In London, the play did extremely well, except that Robeson dominated, much to the displeasure of the renowned Mrs. Campbell. Abroad, Robeson and his wife were not subjected to the Jim Crow railroad cars of his native land, a refreshing change for him. But disappointment loomed around the corner.

Robeson completed his law degree in 1923, earning, mainly, the "gentleman's C." Law was not an obsession with him. He worked briefly in a law firm, but Robeson's size—240 pounds and six feet, three inches—gave many people pause. One secretary said that she simply could not take dictation from a nigger. The actor also realized that he would never be able to sit on the Supreme Court, a dream he at one time entertained. Robeson found this, among many other discouraging matters, intolerable. With his wife's encouragement, he gave up the law and went into the theatre, film, and the concert stage.

However, as Martin Duberman stated:

> When the Provincetown Players encouraged Robeson to act, black performers in Robeson's day were largely confined (as the historian Donald Bogle has amply documented) to playing loyal, subservient Uncle or Auntie Toms, goggle-eyed buffoons; tragic mulattoes; primitive, violent, African savages; rotund and devoted mammies; or mostly in the 70s, powerfully muscled, sexually threatening, cunningly criminal big black bucks (Duberman *The New York Times* 38).

Robeson struggled mightily against these stereotypes. One group that meant to be helpful in this direction was The Provincetown Players, an experimental group in Greenwich Village. In May of 1924, Paul Robeson performed roles in two of their plays: Jim Harris, a dialect-speaking black lawyer in love with a demented white woman in O'Neill's *All God's Chillun Got Wings,* and the power-drunk, Pullman porter in O'Neill's *The Emperor Jones.* Both parts were still galling stereotypes, an ironic occurrence for a well-intentioned white playwright and theatre group that wanted desperately to include African American actors in their plays.

O'Neill had fought tenaciously for Robeson to play Jim Harris, after falling out with the then better known and more experienced black actor, Charles Gilpin, who created the title role of *The Emperor Jones* in 1920. Gilpin's unfortunate heavy drinking often caused him to behave in a way displeasing to many, especially O'Neill. The actor once boasted, "I created the role of the Emperor. That role belongs to me. That Irishman, he just wrote the play" (Gelb 450).

Robeson was certainly able to match Gilpin. *The New York Telegraph* wrote on 7 May 1924:

> For one hour and a half, with only a few minutes for scene-shifting, the atmosphere kept alive by the steady throb, throb of a tom-tom, Robeson held his audience—enthralled is the word. He was dragged before the curtain by men and women who rose to their feet and applauded. When the ache in the arms stopped their hands, they used their voices, shouted meaningless words, gave hoarse throaty cries. Canes were thumped on the boards of the floor. The power of the play had much to do with the emotion fired—that must be admitted—but the ovation was for Robeson, for his emotional strength, for his superb acting (quoted in Hill 121).

George Jean Nathan, a highly respected critic, described Robeson as "one of the most thoroughly eloquent, impressive and convincing actors" he had ever come upon (*The New York Times*, 24 Jan. 1976, 30). These kudos led to an almost instant recognition of Robeson's talent and charisma, and another O'Neill vehicle that very month.

Because of the interracial love affair in O'Neill's *All God's Chillun Got Wings*, pandemonium broke loose before Robeson ever saw opening night. The controversial vehicle created the self-effacing Jim Harris, played by the 26-year-old Paul Robeson at the Provincetown Playhouse. Mary Blair was Ella Downey, the white wife. Jim wants desperately to assimilate, to turn white, to be a lawyer and to intermarry for the sake of intermarriage.

The distinguished black theatre historian Loften Mitchell wrote:

> The most notorious theatrical event of 1924 was the Provincetown's production of Eugene O'Neill's *All God's Chillun Got Wings* . . . The script, published prior to production in the *American Mercury*, dealt with a Negro intellectual who married a "lost" white woman. Yellow journalism blazed. Headlines, editorials and news stories sought to destroy the work. . . . The critics disliked the work. They were many steps behind Negroes, who hated it (83).

Critical and audience reception of the play created a firestorm. The Hearst newspapers launched a campaign of hysteria against it. The Ku Klux

Klan issued death threats. Audiences threatened to tear down MacDougal Street, on which the Provincetown Playhouse stood, if Robeson kissed Blair on stage. Newspaper reports indicate that Ella was supposed to kiss Jim on the hand, but pre-production publicity caused such public furor that it is uncertain whether or not they kissed at all.

On 16 May 1924, John Corbin of *The New York Times* reported, "MacDougal Street stands where it stood. So, presumably do Plymouth Rock and the Congo . . . (22:3). Fearing that he might be misunderstood as overly sympathetic to the play, Corbin hastened to clarify his thoughts by writing yet another review in *The New York Times* on 18 May 1924:

> Let me add with all possible emphasis that I do not believe in mixed marriages, especially between races as different as the white and the black. Common observation tells us that in many respects, both mental and moral, the average negro [sic] is inferior to the average white, and the army tests have strongly confirmed it. Biologists from Darwin and Spencer down have said the same. Many of them add that wide outbreeding, like hybridization, tends to develop the less desirable traits of both stocks (1:1).

Errol Hill believes:

> This public expression of bigotry coming so early in his theatrical career might well have helped to set Robeson on a course that would make him, for most of his adult life, the victim of political harassment in his home country, notwithstanding his distinguished international career on stage and screen (121).

In spite of mixed reviews and considerable furor, Robeson had the extraordinary opportunity of playing in two highly touted productions, a rare opportunity for an actor of color in the early 1920s. This led to his first film appearance with an equally remarkable black independent filmmaker, Oscar Micheaux, who produced *Body and Soul* (1924). Thomas Cripps wrote:

> The picture represented the highest level of achievement for Micheaux. For the first time he wrestled with the nature of the black community, without recourse to shoddy devices . . . or sensationalism. . . . To his stable of new stars he added Paul Robeson. . . . The result was a rich black imagery that never materialized in other survivals of the 1920s and a modest accommodation with black intellectuals. . . . In *Body and Soul* Micheaux not only exposed cultist parasites but also advertised the promise that blacks could organize against the bootleggers and gamblers in their midst (191).

Robeson played preacher Isaiah T. Jenkins of Tatesville, Georgia, who is paid to "tone down his temperance sermons" (Cripps 192).

The Silencing of Paul Robeson

Robeson, himself, according to Loften Mitchell in *Voices of the Black Theatre*, believed:

> I thought I could do something for the Negro race in films, show the truth about them and other people, too. I used to do my part and go away feeling satisfied, thought everything was o.k. Well, it wasn't. The industry was not prepared to permit me to portray the life or express the living interests, hopes and aspirations of the struggling people from whom I come (156).

More fortunate than many black actors, Robeson delved into film. But, more importantly, he also had the concert stage where he could more accurately and authentically depict the Negro.

Another first for him as a black soloist was Robeson's singing of Negro spirituals and hymns in concert on 19 April 1925. Robeson was not the first to artfully sing the Negro spiritual or work song. Before Robeson, George L. White, in 1866, began training the extraordinary Fisk Jubilee Singers of Nashville, Tennessee, a group of African American singers of spirituals and work songs (Clark 435). Catherine King Clark reported: "In 1871, the Jubilee Singers began a . . . singing tour to save Fisk School from imminent closing due to financial difficulties. They toured . . . England, Scotland, Ireland, Holland and Switzerland . . ." (436). The Tuskegee Institute Choir, under the direction of William L. Dawson, also sang at Radio City Music Hall in the 1930s.

Robeson's son, Paul Jr., born in 1927, wrote on the back of the record album *Paul Robeson in Live Performance*, "In 1925, he gave his first concert, with Lawrence Brown, in New York City. It was an historic concert. . . ." Lawrence Brown had once been the accompanist for the great Negro tenor Roland Hayes (1887–1976), a well-trained singer who excelled in German lieder. "Brown remained Robeson's pianist for 35 years" (*The New York Times* 24 Jan. 1976, 30). Robeson eschewed a great deal of formal training, although he did study. Singing lessons he took only to learn control, not how to sing. He preferred to say that he learned his style from singing in his father's church.

Through the efforts of Negrophile Carl Van Vechten, a wealthy Caucasian from Cedar Rapids, Iowa, and Walter White, the fair-skinned African American President of the National NAACP, Robeson and Brown had a full house. The Provincetown Players' Greenwich Theater was the venue, offered without charge to Robeson. He rendered 16 numbers. So successful was the concert that Howard Kropf offered Robeson exclusive management with a $10,000 signing bonus. Robeson declined, since he and Brown preferred James B. Pond, whom they trusted.

The concert of spirituals opened doors of which Robeson had not dreamed. While Robeson enjoyed overwhelming support from many white and black people, he constantly ran into dehumanizing incidents. Like so many other black people who toured or traveled, Robeson was constantly subjected to indignities. He did not bear them well.

The actor did enjoy a 1925 London production of *The Emperor Jones*, and during that European stay, entertained and was entertained both in private homes and in night clubs. He and his wife went not only to London, but to Paris and the Riviera. They took in *La Revue Négre* with Josephine Baker in Paris in 1925. As Robeson's reputation steadily grew, he also had the lead in the 1926 Broadway production of *Black Boy* by Frank Dazey and Jim Tully. Fredi Washington, later of *Imitation of Life* fame, co-starred. Robeson played the bully, Crown, in DuBose Heyward's *Porgy*, the play on which Gershwin based his opera, *Porgy and Bess*.

A major occasion in Robeson's life was that of playing Joe in Jerome Kern's *Show Boat*, the seminal work, which played in 1928 at the Drury Lane Theatre in London, and on Broadway in 1932. Robeson is, perhaps, other than for his role in *Othello*, most remembered for his spine-chilling rendition of "Ol' Man River."

Michael C. Browning of *The Florida Times Union* reported:

> He assumed the role of the philosophical Negro, Riverboat Joe, in the Broadway musical, *Show Boat*. Composer Jerome Kern said that he had written the song "Ol' Man River" with Robeson in mind.
>
> Edna Ferber, who wrote the novel on which the musical was based, attended the New York premiere of *Show Boat* in 1932, and described the wild, glad furor that greeted Robeson's rendition of "Ol' Man River."
>
> "Robeson, a few minutes later, finished singing "Ol' Man River." The show stopped. They called him back again and again. Other actors came out and made motions and their lips moved, and the bravos of the audience drowned out all other sounds (A6).

Robeson's visibility in *Show Boat* led to his going to Switzerland in 1929 for *Borderline*, directed by Kenneth MacPherson, which also included Robeson's wife, Eslanda. His continuing popularity abroad led to a return to London for his first performance in the title role of *Othello*. He played the jealous Moor on 19 May 1930, at the Savoy Theatre. Peggy Ashcroft was the gentle Desdemona; Maurice Brown, the villainous Iago, and his wife, Nellie Van Volkenburg, director. Sybil Thorndike was Desdemona's fearless handmaiden, Emilia, and Ralph Richardson, the gullible Roderigo. Errol Hill wrote, "On opening night, Robeson took twenty curtain calls" (123). He was 32. While London audiences were often ecstatic about Robeson, Nellie Van Volkenburg shouted at Robeson from a megaphone during rehearsals, ordering him about the stage with considerable disrespect, often staging the play with movements that added to the stereotype of Othello, the man and the army general.

Unfortunately, also, Robeson became enamored of Peggy Ashcroft and they had an affair, one of many for Robeson. Nancy Caldwell Sorel discovered it: "Later, she admitted, without specifics, that 'what happened between Paul and myself' was 'possibly inevitable.' Although both were married, she made no apology for falling in love." (105). In America, Robeson could not play Othello, yet. The threat of riots attended the very notion of mixed casting. But Robeson never gave up. Meanwhile, Eugene O'Neill wanted him for the film *The Emperor Jones*.

It was in *The Emperor Jones* (1933), directed by Dudley Murphy, that Robeson had his greatest moment in film, according to several film historians. Shot in one week on a budget of $10,000 in Queens, New York, the film had two eager promoters, John Krimsky and Gifford Cochran. Rex Ingram, Fredi Washington, Dudley Diggs, and Frank Wilson were among the stars in the cast.

Thomas Cripps discerns:

> Robeson's [Brutus] Jones overawes the picture and gives it heroic dimensions. The crapshooters and pretentious, overdressed courtiers who are named for the rail stops on Jones's old run, the voodoo drummers, and the 'bush niggers' surrounding the court appear as plausible figures rather than extreme stereotypes. . . . When Jones dies in a revolt, he is a black king dying in pain and rage at his demeaning fall (216–217).

Robeson left New York, however, for European shores, once more. He moved again to London where he made *Sanders of the River* (1935), which co-starred beautiful Nina Mae McKinney. It was produced by Alexander and Zoltan Korda.

> Since the plot revolved around the character played by Robeson, *Bosambo* is a far more fitting title than *Sanders of the River*. Hoping to portray the role of an African leader with some cultural integrity and accuracy, the actor was disillusioned with the final edited movie which presented Bosambo as merely a loyal servant of British colonialism. It is rumored that Robeson attempted to buy every print of the film to prevent its distribution (Kisch and Mapp 42).

American posters focused on the *Sanders of the River* title, while Argentinian and Belgian versions used *Bosambo*. Robeson's struggle to play dignified roles was constant. *Song of Freedom* (1936), directed by J. Elder Wills in England, cast Paul Robeson as a "dockworker turned opera singer and a long-lost royal heir to a small kingdom in Africa" (41).

Unfortunately, Bogle thinks: "In most of his other European motion pictures... Robeson was cast as an 'undercover servant,' exploited in much the same way Sidney Poitier was to be some twenty-five years later" (95–97). Exploitation notwithstanding, Robeson made some significant achievement in film, and tried to give dignity to the most demeaning roles. He played in *King Solomon's Mines* in 1937, *Jericho* (or *Dark Sands*) also in 1937, *Big Fella* in 1938, and *Proud Valley* in 1939. In 1998, the Black Arts Festival in Atlanta showed three of Robeson's films; his films are still viewed among the avant garde and most are available on video. It is ironic that only two of Robeson's films were made by Hollywood, *Show Boat* (1936), and *Tales of Manhattan* (1942). Gary Null observes:

> ...although Hattie McDaniel, for instance, made twenty films in the thirties, Robeson made his reputation on a mere handful, of which his last [in Hollywood, i.e.], *Show Boat* (1936), put him in the kind of 'singing nigger' role of which he later complained (75).

Donald Bogle further states: "Robeson's greatest contribution to black film history—and the aspect of his work that most disturbed American white moviegoers—was his proud, defiant portrait of the black man" (98). Hollywood was committed to maintaining the status quo, with few exceptions. Africans were portrayed as savages, and African Americans spoke in dialect, keeping white audiences comfortable. This, too, was a form of silencing.

Twelve years after his European stint in *Othello,* amidst great fear because of the interracial marriage and the domestic violence in Shakespeare's *Othello,* Robeson got a chance to play the title role on the American boards. He was the first black to play the Moor on American soil. (Ira Aldridge had crossed the Atlantic in the early 1800s, but had never been permitted to play Othello in America.) Margaret Webster persuaded the powerful Theatre Guild to put the play on. Robert Edmond Jones, who had worked with the Provincetown Players, designed. Uta Hagen played Desdemona; her husband, José Ferrer, was Iago, and Margaret Webster directed and played Emilia.

In August of 1942, they opened at the Brattle Street Theatre in Cambridge, Massachusetts. The audience went wild. Before finally coming to Broadway, the show also tested in Princeton, New Haven, and Boston. Finally, it reached New York's Shubert Theatre on 19 October 1943. It broke records for a Broadway Shakespearean play, with 296 performances! It was also the first Broadway play with a black Othello and an all-white cast. Conversely, in 1998, Patrick Stewart played a white Othello with a predominantly black cast in Washington, D. C.

Gordon Heath, the black intellectual actor who played the Moor for BBC television in 1955, attended one of Robeson's Broadway productions of *Othello*. He and Owen Dodson, another black intellectual director of distinction on historically black college campuses, could get standing room only. Heath observed:

> Paul was a great-souled man but he had not yet a technique to project the shades of madness and obsession that possessed the Moor. He was hamstrung and muscle-bound. "Roar" he did, but it was a hollow sound. . . . His body did not cooperate with the tremors, the collapse, the twisted rage. . . . We were sick at heart (135).

Heath admitted that it was arrogant of him to disagree with much of the public and many of the critics who believed Robeson to be splendid indeed. Major mainstream critics and virtually all of the black press spoke of Robeson in superlatives. George Jean Nathan called him the greatest Othello of the century. Edith Isaacs reported that he was so great that he was frequently compared with Ira Aldridge and Edmund Kean, and consequently movie offers still came, although few roles worthy of his talent.

Tales of Manhattan (1942) featured Robeson, Eddie Anderson, and Ethel Waters. It was considered a film of poor quality, in that it also stereotyped African Americans, and stereotyped very badly. Thomas Cripps wrote:

> Julien Duvivier's *Tales of Manhattan* . . . was a string of gemlike stories held together by the presence of a money-stuffed coat and its impact on the lives of its possessors. In the end, it falls from the grasp of an effete group of airplane passengers and into the rough hands of a village of Southern Negro farmers. Their enclave is sketched in stylized, almost hillbilly, imagery—as though Duvivier had reached the limits of French capacity for comprehending Southern American racial arrangements. The dramatic conflict was symbolized by Robeson's open-handed communal vision of a black sharecropper as opposed to Eddie Anderson's raspy-comic venal preacher. . . . (383–384).

Bogle stated:

> In *Tales of Manhattan*, . . . Robeson portrays a backwoods Southern coon who discovers a satchel of money that has been dropped into his cotton field from an airplane. Immediately, he and Waters thank de almighty Gawd in the hebben above. Throughout the film the blacks sing in the fields, dance in the churches, clap their hands in joy, and stand tremblin' 'fore de power and de glory above (99).

Some groups picketed the film and Robeson did not blame them.

The completion of the three-year run of the Broadway *Othello* (1942–45) ended Robeson's mainly artistic career, since his heavy involvement with politics coincided with the death of Franklin Delano Roosevelt.

Roosevelt died in 1945, the year that *Othello* ended its run. Roosevelt and his wife, Eleanor, had made the United States a more congenial place for the person of color. In 1944, Robeson and his wife campaigned for Roosevelt. Robeson, during the 1930s and early 1940s had traveled to Moscow, Berlin, and other world cities. He constantly spoke out, especially for the dispossessed, and by now J. Edgar Hoover was convinced that Robeson was "undoubtedly 100% Communist" (quoted in Duberman *Paul Robeson* 280). Hoover began to build a file on Robeson, and FBI surveillance became something Robeson had to contend with for the rest of his life.

In addition to speaking out at rallies, singing for labor unions, and issuing pro-Communist statements to the press, Robeson was highly indelicate with his personal affairs. All of these alienated him with some in the white press and many in the United States government. He and his wife had been in a troubled marriage for many years. But Essie had no intention of giving Robeson a divorce. Two of the better known affairs occurred abroad, but Robeson not only courted Uta Hagen in the presence of her husband, José Ferrer, but seemed to set up an arrangement where the three of them were constantly together in what could only be called a brazen boldness.

Martin Duberman reported in his biography *Paul Robeson:*

> Hagen had not initially thought of Robeson romantically or sexually—"I thought of him as a fabulous older friend," she later recalled. Then one night they were standing in the wings waiting for an entrance and joking together. Suddenly, with total boldness and confidence, Robeson "took his *enormous* hand—costume and all—and put it between my legs. I thought, What *happened* to me? It was being assaulted in the most phenomenal way, and I thought, What the hell, and I got unbelievably excited. I was flying" (286).

Ultimately, Ferrer denounced Robeson before the House Un-American Activities Committee, in what could only be perceived of as revenge. The Machiavellian stage villain, Iago, played his role off stage, as well.

Near the end of the *Othello* Broadway triumph, and partially because of it, the NAACP awarded Robeson its highest honor, the Spingarn Award, in 1945. The NAACP, since its inception at the turn of the century, has been categorized as a conservative group, which struggled for civil rights through the courts and through pressure not associated with violence or any other means perceived to be lacking in political savvy. Walter White, National President of the NAACP, who eventually denounced Robeson,

considered the Spingarn Banquet an august event. Robeson, however, now a millionaire according to Edwin Embree, in addition to insisting on a downtown hotel, which deprived the poor from attending, also used the event to give a highly political speech. Many were shocked.
The *New York Times* reported:

> Meanwhile, Mr. Robeson stepped up his political activity by leading a delegation that urged Baseball Commissioner Kenesaw Mountain Landis to drop the racial bars in baseball; and by calling on President Harry S. Truman to widen blacks' civil rights in the South. He became a founder and chairman of the Progressive Party, which nominated former Vice President Henry A. Wallace in the 1948 Presidential race (24 Jan. 1976, 30).

Hubert Saal declared:

> In the United States, he became a vigorous opponent of racism, picketing the White House, refusing to sing before segregated audiences, starting a crusade against lynching and urging Congress to outlaw racial bars in baseball (73).

It is a bitter irony that, eventually, Jackie Robinson, the first black man to play in the major baseball leagues, and one who profited, somewhat, from Robeson's fight, denounced him before the House Un-American Activities Committee.

Robeson was unusually supportive of labor unions, and sang the famous "Joe Hill," at their gatherings and at his concerts. Matt Fairtlough wrote on the World Wide Web:

> Joe Hill personifies the tradition of political song. Born in Sweden, he migrated to the US and in 1910 joined the Industrial Workers of the World—the "Wobblies." Over the next five years he campaigned for many working class causes. He became a popular song writer with a gift for capturing the meaning of these causes in song. In 1914, during bitter struggles over free speech in Utah, Joe Hill was framed on a murder charge. Despite appeals from President Wilson and the Swedish government, Joe Hill was executed on November 19th 1915. His body was taken to Chicago where over 30,000 people attended his funeral procession and eulogies were read in nine languages.

The eponymous song extolled Joe Hill's virtues. Robeson sang the piece with every fibre of his being.

With Robeson's heavy involvement with labor unions, his inveterate womanizing, and his outspoken political views, he was considered a dangerous man. Some in the public and in power labeled him a Communist. The California State Legislature called him before a committee in 1946; he testified that he was not. The Communist label, until recent years, was virtually always a label attached to African Americans and others, especially in the theatre, who went against the grain. Hysteria reigned in the late 1930s through the 1950s as madness and fear permeated much of America. Rutgers University removed Robeson's name from the alumni rolls and athletic records. They withdrew his honorary degree. Robeson was now a pariah in his own country.

Not helping Robeson's plight was the concurrent activity regarding the Hollywood Ten. All were white: Alvah Bessie, a novelist; Herbert Biberman, a writer/director; Lester Cole, author of screen plays; Edward Dmytryk, a film director; Ring Lardner, Jr., screenwriter; John Howard Lawson, a highly controversial playwright; Albert Maltz, novelist and screenwriter; Samuel Ornitz, novelist; Adrian Scott, producer; and Dalton Trumbo, a very famous novelist and screenwriter. Between 1947 and 1948, they were subpoenaed by the House Un-American Activities Committee to answer questions about their alleged left-wing writing and the Communist influence on the motion picture industry. Some were convicted, jailed, and all were blacklisted. Any number of people involved committed suicide.

Bart Stafford wrote me in a letter of 24 September 1976, the year of Robeson's death:

> I would ask you to remember the case of the Hollywood Ten who were blacklisted for many years due to the tiniest suspicion of communist or leftwing taint in their makeup. And not one black among them! . . . Robeson's blackness was only the contributing factor in his plight. He would have been hit hard if he had been white, but not as hard as he was when he was a black.

The framing of Alger Hiss also added to the crescendo of alarm and activity surrounding Robeson. According to Lisa Pease, in 1948, Hiss, a high-level worker in the State Department, was framed as a result of the HUAC hearings. Whittaker Chambers, a Senior Editor at *Time*, indicated that Hiss had been a member of the Communist party for 20 years. Eventually, Hiss was convicted of perjury, although it was never proven that he was a Communist. Richard Nixon was heavily involved in Hiss's demise, although Nixon's motives have never been clear. It is clear that the political climate was not at all favorable to anyone who chose to speak out. Some very innocent, non-political people were destroyed by HUAC in the hysteria (www.webcom.com/1pease/hiss.html).

Meanwhile, Robeson was also concerned about black men who fought in America's wars, who died in disproportionate numbers on the front lines of the battlefield, only to return to a segregated home where often even decent housing, hotels, restaurants, water fountains, or a non-segregated movie seat were denied them. Public accommodations did not

The Silencing of Paul Robeson

open until the advent of Martin Luther King, Jr., mainly after his 1968 assassination.

Robeson was also highly vocal about the lack of public accommodations from which he suffered in his vast travels, and certainly about black military men, in particular. At the World Peace Conference in Paris in 1949, attended by the great scholar/activist, W. E. B. DuBois, Robeson said,

> It is unthinkable that American Negroes will go to war on behalf of those who have oppressed us for generations against a country [the Soviet Union] which in one generation has raised our people to the full dignity of mankind (*New York Times*, 24 Jan. 1976, 30).

Veterans groups were incensed. Until Harry Truman became President, virtually every black unit in the armed forces was segregated, with very few highly qualified men of color ever making the ranks of Lieutenant Colonel, Colonel, or the several ranks of General. Robeson was painfully aware of this.

He toured eight European countries during the March-June months of 1949. As he stepped off the plane, a police squad met him. *Time*, on 27 June 1949, reported that this was "standard New York City procedure for celebrities likely to draw a crowd" (36). Robeson was upset by the police escort.

He denounced not only the police, but also the press for giving broad coverage to the wedding of his son, Paul Jr., and Marilyn Greenberg, a white Cornell classmate. Interracial marriages in 1949 were rare indeed and often occurred only between celebrities. Moreover, laws in Wisconsin, Iowa, Virginia, Alabama, and Mississippi forbade miscegenation, a derogatory legal term used in laws dealing with intermarriage and interracial dating.

Robeson further announced that he would prefer to talk to papers like *The Daily Worker*, a newspaper with Communist leanings. Communist organizations were widely supportive of financially impoverished black theatre, and *The Daily Worker* gave coverage to a number of liberal causes, including African American theatre.

However, the more Robeson refused to shut up, the more his life worsened. His and his wife's health deteriorated as he became more and more preoccupied with social conditions, while still managing some concert work. Robeson attempted to give a concert in Peekskill, New York, on 28 August 1949, at the Lakelands Area Picnic Ground. Anatol Schlosser wrote:

> The press of Peekskill, the Peekskill Chamber of Commerce, and Veterans' groups protested Robeson's presence. On the day of the concert, busloads of protesters arrived at the grounds and blocked the entrance so that the audience could not leave (376).

Riots erupted instead, with the Ku Klux Klan burning crosses. There was no concert. A second concert was scheduled for 4 September 1949, with the illusion of police protection. There were 25,000 people to hear Robeson sing. Protesters beat the concert-goers and Robeson got out by lying down on the floor of an automobile, as police stood idly by.

The Nation reported:

> In the second Battle of Peekskill at least 140 persons were injured, some seriously; hundreds were bruised; innumerable cars were wrecked; violence raged over a ten mile area; and for hours no car was safe from volleys of flying rocks. Radio commentators, broadcasting from the scene, asked in horrified tones whether this could be the United States in the year 1949.
>
> ... Paul Robeson's recent statements have been stupid and uncalled for, if not deliberately inflammatory, but the explosion at Peekskill was not merely anti-Communist. It was anti-Negro and anti-Semitic as well, charged with indiscriminate hatred (244).

After the Peekskill concert, other cities were afraid that the same might occur in their towns. Eighty managers canceled Robeson's concerts, according to Schlosser.

On 19 September 1949, *The New Yorker* decried:

> Mr. Robeson strayed from the field of song a few years ago and wandered into politics. ... The sound he makes is neither pure song nor pure argument, but a subtle blend of the two, and when he mixes Ol' Man River with Ol' Man Marx he is being unfair to the Mississippi and is playing fast and loose with the Negro race, for whom he purports to speak (23).

The press combined forces with the government to destroy Paul Robeson.

Events gained momentum. All were part of the dynamics affecting Robeson. Late January of 1950, a New York court convicted Alger Hiss of perjury, even though they could not prove that he was a Communist. The McCarthy hearings were alarming in their frequency, their breadth, and the fear they generated. Many dreaded the question, "Are you now, or have you ever been a member of the Communist Party?" José Ferrer testified against Robeson; otherwise, friends of HUAC would have picketed Ferrer's new film, *Moulin Rouge*. Ferrer's was a scathing denunciation of the black actor.

Robeson, himself, appeared before the HUAC committee, once when his health was failing exceedingly and against the advice of his physician. Robeson seemed to improve after he had gone in and spoken out. Perhaps the most frequently quoted testimony by Robeson went:

Mr. Schrerer: Why do you not stay in Russia?

Mr. Robeson: Because my father was a slave, and my people died to build this country and I am going to stay here and have a part of it just like you. And no Fascist-minded people will drive me from it. Is that clear? (www.cs.uchicago.edu/cpst/robeson/)

Meanwhile, according to Duberman in his biography of Robeson,

> In the midst of this crescendo of alarm, Eleanor Roosevelt's son Elliot announced that Paul Robeson would appear on his mother's Sunday afternoon television show, "Today with Mrs. Roosevelt," to debate with Representative Adam Clayton Powell, Jr. and the black Mississippi Republican committeeman Perry Howard on "the role of the Negro in American political life." He might just as well have announced the imminent appearance of the devil (384).

NBC hastened to make announcements that Mrs. Roosevelt had been premature and that Robeson would not appear—in fact would *never* be on NBC (384). The silencing was now intensifying in frantic fury. Many of Robeson's friends deserted him, lest they, too, might become damaged—Walter White, Carl Van Vechten, and Josh White, a well-known folk singer.

In 1950, also, the United States State Department revoked Robeson's passport as a way of further silencing and financially enslaving him. Robeson filed suit. On 1 January 1951, *Newsweek* reported in an article called "Robeson's Plea":

> For a long time, the people and the government suffered him gladly because of his artistic gifts. But in a period of undeclared war and rising conflict between the democratic and the Communist world, it was inevitable that he should come up against the government he decried. When he applied for a passport . . . the State Department refused to issue the necessary papers. It canceled his old passport.
>
> Last week, Paul Robeson filed a suit in Washington Federal Court against Secretary of State Dean Acheson, asking the court to lift the passport ban (13–14).

It was felt by those in the State Department, according to *Newsweek,* that Robeson was not just going to Europe to sing, but to wage a propaganda war "if past performance were a gauge" (13).

Hubert Saal reported,

> . . . his outspoken admiration for the Soviet Union, which culminated in his acceptance of a Stalin Peace Prize in 1952, inflamed public opinion during the Cold War and eventually wiped out his career. Summoned before

House and Senate committees, he refused to say whether or not he was a Communist (privately he maintained he was not).... He was blacklisted by concert managers—his income, which had been $104,000 in 1947, fell to $2,000 ... (73).

Eventually, Robeson had to sell his home in Enfield, Connecticut. It had such luxuries as its own bowling alley. He moved, alone, into his brother Ben's parsonage. As a gesture of help, the Soviet Union awarded him the Stalin Peace Prize in 1952, amounting to $25,000. The U.S. government immediately taxed it, with Robeson hastily noting that the Nobel Prize was not taxable (*Ebony*, 16 Apr. 1976).

Meanwhile, a landmark Supreme Court Decision, *Brown v. Topeka*, occurred in 1954, one that had impact on virtually every American. Thanks to the courage of Attorney Thurgood Marshall and others, the ruling reversed *Plessy v. Ferguson* and said that "separate but equal" was unlawful because segregation was damaging. Kenneth Clark, the famous psychologist, was a major force in establishing this. He brought in black and white dolls to prove his point. In a test case, black children chose white dolls instead of black, signifying low self-esteem based on color and the hostile environment black children had to endure.

Such a change in the attitude of the highest court in the land, combined with the 1955 Montgomery Bus Boycott, may have helped Robeson. Meanwhile, Black citizens were demanding their rights as the century grew to its mid-point. The Little Rock Crisis, where nine black children had to be assisted by the National Guard to enter Central High School, occurred in 1957. Orval Faubus, then governor of Arkansas, defied the order of President Eisenhower to integrate the school. The Little Rock saga was one of the most tense of racial incidents of the twentieth century.

Most white schools were closed to blacks. Theatres were either closed to African Americans or rigidly segregated. Blacks could sit in the "buzzard roost," or the balcony, but seldom, if ever, in the orchestra seats. Bathrooms, if they existed at all for citizens of color, were labeled "white men," "white women," and "colored." In spite of unbearable oppression, the Supreme Court, as a result of a law suit Robeson filed, returned his passport in 1958, and the actor/singer set out to restore his career.

On 1 June 1958, he gave a poignant sold-out concert at Mother A.M.E. Zion Church in New York City. His brother, Rev. Benjamin C. Robeson, was pastor. Accompanied by Lawrence Brown and Alan Booth, Robeson sang "Swing Low, Sweet Chariot," "No More Auction Block," "Water Boy," "Chinese Children's Song," "The House I Live In," "Sometimes I Feel Like A Motherless Child," and "We Are Climbing Jacob's Ladder."

Of that concert, Paul Robeson Jr., wrote:

The Silencing of Paul Robeson

Among other remarks made at that concert, my father said: "I want the folks of Mother Zion to know that a lot of hard struggle is over and that my concert career has practically been reestablished all over this country.... This could not have happened without the strength and the courage and the help and the prayers of you not only here in Mother Zion but also in many parts of America.... I hope soon that it will be possible to travel all over the world to accept many invitations.... (back of recording, *Paul Robeson in Live Performance*).

Robeson was well received and his wish to travel all over the world was soon granted.

On 10 August 1958, accompanied by Lawrence Brown and Bruno Raikin, Robeson sang "Every Time I Feel the Spirit," "Ezekiel Saw The Wheel," "I'll Hear the Trumpet Sound," "Get On Board, Little Children," "L'Amour De Moi," "Volga Boatman," "Joe Hill," and "Ol' Man River" at the Royal Albert Hall in London. Robeson changed the words of "Ol' Man River," from "I gets weary and sick of trying," to "I must keep fighting until I'm dying." The British could not contain themselves. There was a never-ending hot wall of emotion between singer and audience. They made requests as if sitting in their living room with a personal and amiable house guest. The applause was thunderous, often interrupting the gifted bass-baritone as he was just beginning.

It was very clear that the nine years since Robeson had sung on British soil had not diminished the respect and awe with which he was held. Unfortunately, his health began to fail, in spite of his still being in very good voice. His last tour to Australia and New Zealand ended in 1960.

In 1961, Robeson fell ill in Europe with arteriosclerosis and was forced to retire from the stage. At points, he suffered from a bipolar illness (manic depression), as well as a serious prostate cancer condition. His wife, who had battled cancer for some time, died in 1965. Shortly thereafter, Robeson moved to Philadelphia with his sister, Marian Forsythe, where he declined interviews and became a virtual recluse.

After a serious stroke on 28 December 1975, he entered the hospital in Philadelphia and died on 23 January 1976. Drenched in rain, a largely African American gathering filed into Mother A. M. E. Zion Church. An overflow crowd, which could not get into the church, filled the streets for a 75-minute funeral service. Robeson's surviving family, friends, unionizers, and a number of colleagues in the theatre came. Robeson's own recorded voice sang spirituals and work songs. Several friends spoke, and Robeson's son paid his father a moving tribute.

Ebony indicated: "Bishop J. C. Hoggard had closed with words from a labor anthem Robeson had made famous. The song concerned a union man framed for murder and executed in Utah. His name was Joe Hill and in the song he said, 'Don't mourn for me. Organize!'" (Douglas 42).

Paul Robeson is, arguably, the only great man in the history of America whom it took an entire government and many members of the press to silence. That silencing may have been only temporary, for the eminence and power of the man may be greater than that of all of his detractors. Julianne Malveaux asserts:

> Although there will never be another Paul Robeson, his audacity and principle not only leave a legacy but also an image of African American manhood that is the antithesis of current images. It is for this reason, if no other, that his legacy must be both embraced and deconstructed (28).

Robeson's image as an actor/singer/fighter, in the long run, is no longer darkly tarnished. The Rutgers that disowned their son in the 1950s now claims him proudly. Robeson's career is being viewed through a new repertory of lenses.

The epitaph on his grave at Ferncliff Cemetery, New York, reads simply,

> Paul Robeson
> April 9, 1898–January 23, 1976
> "The Artist Must Elect to Fight
> for Freedom or Slavery. I
> Have Made My Choice. I Had
> No Alternative."

Works Cited

Beatty, Jerome. "America's No. l. Negro," *American Magazine,* May 1944.

Bentley, Eric. *Are You Now or Have You Ever Been: The Investigation of Show Business By the Un-American Activities Committee 1947–1958.* New York: Harper and Row, 1972.

Bogle, Donald. "Paul Robeson: The Black Colossus," in *Toms, Coons, Mulattoes, Mammies and Bucks,* by Donald Bogle. New York: Continuum, 1996.

Bontemps, Alex. "Culture," *Ebony,* Aug. 1975.

Browning, Michael. "Robeson: A Man of His Times," *Florida Times Union,* 26 June 1978, A1-A6.

"Burden of Proof," *Time,* 27 June 1949.

Campbell, Colin. "Robeson's Return," *Horizon,* May 1978, 35–37.

Clark, Catherine King. Entry on the Fisk Jubilee Singers in *Black Women in America: An Historical Encyclopedia,* ed. Darlene Clark Hine. Brooklyn: Carlson Publishing, 1993, 434–436.

Corbin, John. Review of *All God's Chillun Got Wings, The New York Times,* 16 May 1924, 22:3.

―――. "Mixed Marriages: A Word to the Unco Guid-Law Fields as a Classic Composer—A Not Too Wonderful Visit," *The New York Times*, 18 May 1924, VII, 1:1.
Cripps, Thomas. *Slow Fade to Black: The Negro in American Film, 1900–1942.* London: Oxford University Press, 1977.
Current Biography Yearbook 1941. ed. Maxine Block. New York: H. W. Wilson, Reissued 1971, 716–718.
Current Biography Yearbook 1976. ed. Charles Moritz. New York: H. W. Wilson, 1976, 345–348.
"Declaration of War," *Time,* 25 July 1949.
Douglas, Carlyle. "Farewell to a Fighter," *Ebony,* Apr. 1976, 33–42.
Duberman, Martin. "A Giant Denied His Rightful Stature in Film," *The New York Times,* Arts and Leisure Section, 29 Mar. 1998, 1 and 38.
―――. *Paul Robeson.* New York: Knopf, 1988.
Embree, Edwin R. "Voice of Freedom," in *Thirteen against the Odds.* New York: Viking Press, 1944.
Emperor Jones and Paul Robeson, The: Tribute to an Artist. (Narrated by Sidney Poitier) Home Vision Cinema. Video. (gift of Sarah W. Hruska)
Fairtlough, Matt. http://www:8000/~matt/ [brief biography of Joe Hill].
Fast, Howard. *Peekskill: USA.* New York: Civil Rights Congress, 1951.
Franklin, John Hope. *From Slavery to Freedom: A History of Negro Americans.* New York: Alfred A. Knopf, 1947.
Gelb, Barbara and Arthur. *O'Neill.* New York: Harper & Row, 1960.
Graham, Shirley. *Paul Robeson, Citizen of the World.* New York: Julian Messner, 1946.
Hayman, Robert L., Jr. *The Smart Culture: Society, Intelligence and the Law.* New York University Press, 1998. (courtesy of Eunice Carlson)
Heath, Gordon. *Deep Are The Roots: Memoirs of a Black Expatriate.* Amherst: University of Massachusetts Press, 1992.
Hill, Errol. *Shakespeare in Sable: A History of Black Shakespearean Actors.* Amherst: University of Massachusetts Press, 1984.
Hughes, Langston. Review of *Paul Robeson, Negro* by Eslanda Goode Robeson, in *The New York Herald Tribune Books,* 29 June 1930, 1 and 6.
Isaacs, Edith J. R. *The Negro in the American Theatre.* New York: Theatre Arts, 1947.
"Journey's End," *Time,* 14 Aug. 1950, 12.
Kisch, John and Edward Mapp. "A Film Anachronism: Paul Robeson," in *A Separate Cinema.* ed. Kisch and Mapp. New York: Farrar, Straus and Giroux, 1992. (gift of Ed Hancock)
Kroll, Jack. "Robeson's Tragedy," *Newsweek.* 30 Jan. 1978.
"Lonesome Road, A," Paul Robeson. Living Era Recording. (gift of Gloria Melton)
Malveaux, Julianne. "Reflecting on Robeson's Artistic and Sociopolitical Legacy," *Black Issues in Higher Education,* 30 Apr. 1998, 28.
Mason, Theodore O., Jr. Entry on Paul Robeson in *The Oxford Companion to African American Literature,* ed. William Andrews, Frances Smith Foster, and Trudier Harris. New York: Oxford University Press, 1997, 634.
Mitchell, Loften. *Black Drama.* New York: Hawthorn Books, 1967.

———. *Voices of the Black Theatre.* Clifton, New Jersey: James T. White & Company, 1975.

"Mr. Robeson and Democracy," *Commonweal,* 9 Sept. 1949, 524.

Myrdal, Gunnar. *An American Dilemma.* New York: McGraw-Hill, 1944.

"Nightmare in Peekskill," *Nation,* 10 Sept. 1949, 243–44.

Notes and Comment from "The Talk of the Town," *New Yorker,* 19 Sept. 1949, 23.

Null, Gary. *Black Hollywood: The Negro in Motion Pictures.* Secaucus, New Jersey: Citadel Press, 1975.

"Open Letter to the Entertainment Industry," *Variety,* 11 Jan. 1978.

Ovington, Mary White. *Portraits in Color.* New York: Viking Press, 1927.

"Paul Robeson," Atlas Artists, n.d. (gift of Bart Lanier Stafford III)

"Paul Robeson Centennial, The," *Ebony,* May 1998, 110–112.

Paul Robeson Centennial Website <www.cs.uchicago.edu/cpst/robeson>

"Paul Robeson in Live Performance," Columbia Records, 1958. (gift of Eunice Carlson)

Paul Bustill Robeson's Grave. <http://www.findagrave.com/pictures/robeson.html>

Pease, Lisa, "The Framing of Alger Hiss," <http://www.webcom.com/lpease/hiss.html>

"Robeson Demands Violence Inquiry," *The New York Times,* 29 Aug. 1949, 19–23.

Robeson, Eslanda Goode. *Paul Robeson, Negro.* New York: Harper and Brothers, 1950.

Robeson, Paul. *Here I Stand.* New York: Othello Associates, 1958.

Robeson, Susan. *The Whole World in His Hands.* Secaucus, New Jersey: Citadel Press, 1981.

"Robeson's Plea," *Newsweek,* 1 Jan. 1951, 13–14.

"Robeson's Ruckus," *Newsweek,* 12 Sept. 1949, 23.

Saal, Hubert. "Tragic Hero," *Newsweek,* 2 Feb. 1976, 73.

Schlosser, Anatol. "Paul Robeson: His Career in the Theatre, in Motion Pictures and on the Concert Stage." (Ph.D. diss. New York University, 1970).

Sergeant, Elizabeth Shepley. "The Man with His Home in a Rock: Paul Robeson," *New Republic,* 3 Mar. 1926, 40–44.

"Solid Rock: Favorite Hymns of My People," by Paul Robeson. Othello Records, 1953 (gift of Eunice Carlson).

Sorel, Nancy Caldwell. "Paul Robeson and Peggy Ashcroft (First Encounters)," *The Atlantic,* May 1992, vol. 269, no. 5, 105. (courtesy of Andy Thomas)

Stafford, Bart Lanier. Letters to author. 16 Sept. 1976 and 24 Sept. 1976.

"A Statement of Conscience," *Variety,* 11 Jan. 1978, n.p. (courtesy of Rob Rotman)

Stewart, Jeffrey C., ed. *Paul Robeson: Artist and Citizen.* Piscataway, New Jersey: Rutgers University Press, 1998.

Whitman, Alden. "Paul Robeson Dead at 77; Singer, Actor and Activist," *The New York Times,* 24 Jan. 1976, 1 and 30.

Woll, Allen. *Black Musical Theatre: From Coontown to Dreamgirls.* Baton Rouge: Louisiana State University Press, 1989.

Ethel Waters as Hagar in Dorothy and Dubose Heyward's *Mamba's Daughters,* 1939. Alfred Bendiner, 1899–1964. The National Portrait Gallery, Smithsonian Institution.

Ethel Waters singing "Heat Wave," in "As Thousands Cheer," 1933; photo by Anton Bruel and first appeared in *Vanity Fair*. Prints and Photographs Collection, Moorland-Spingard Research Center, Howard University.

Chapter IV

Measure Her Right: The Tragedy of Ethel Waters

When you starts measuring somebody, measure him right, child, measure him right. Make sure you done taken into account what hills and valleys he come through before he got to wherever he is.

—A Raisin in the Sun, *Lorraine Hansberry*

These ungrammatical but powerful words of Mama Younger admonish all who would criticize the singer/dramatic actor Ethel Waters. I saw her in person only once. It was 1972 in El Paso, Texas, at the First Baptist Church on Montana Street. The Billy Graham Crusade was in town. By then, she toured with Graham as a singer. She was 75 and looked a lot older. Her soft and bountiful snow-white hair formed a gentle halo around the head of a woman who was no saint. Her body was, by then, trapped in 350 pounds of flesh. Her finances were strained, and her health clearly frail with the illnesses—cancer, high blood pressure, and diabetes—that ultimately claimed her. A gifted singer and a dramatic actor many praised, Ethel Waters lived a tragic life.

The sun mercilessly pierced the arid desert air that summer day in El Paso, but Waters's spirit was undaunted; her stage presence, reflective and resigned. She sang "His Eye Is On the Sparrow," which had become her trademark. Many know only the Waters of the Graham Crusade. Some know nothing of the slimmer "Sweet Mama Stringbean"—the young, gorgeous Ethel Waters—who rocked the house all night long at Edmonds's Cellar in New York City with "You Can't Do What The Last Man Did," "Handy Man," "The St. Louis Blues," and "Organ Grinder." So beautiful was she in her youth that Antonio Salemni asked for the privilege of sculpting her head in bronze (Johnson 210). This was irrelevant that 1972 evening in El Paso.

Five years later, on 1 September 1977, Ethel Waters died, penniless and in broken health. I was a doctoral student at the University of Iowa at the time. The *Iowa City Press-Citizen* carried the death as headlines. So did every major newspaper in the United States. A legend was gone, a legend who could hold an audience spellbound and a legend who was one of the first interpreters of a number of ballads. The triumphs and tragedies of Waters were the grist of news. Her life was one of amazing accomplishments and astonishing mistakes—a lot of both. Her life and career both had been affected by phenomenal racial, gender, and class oppression, especially given the pervasiveness of the Mammy stereotype for the African American woman in most of the twentieth century.

Ethel Waters came from the lower depths. By her own admission, she could out curse a stevedore. She had a sixth grade education. She made a fortune and lost it all, admitting that she was unaccustomed to money. She loved and lost, always unwisely, at least three times. Giving men lots of money was a major weakness for her. And she made a great deal. During the Great Depression, while others stood in soup lines, Waters was the highest paid woman on Broadway, earning $5,000 a week. She knew fame, fortune, and a number of fickle friends.

On 31 October 1896, as a result of a rape at knifepoint by a white man, 13-year-old Louisa Tar Anderson gave birth, out of wedlock, to Ethel Waters in a slum section of Chester, Pennsylvania. John Wesley Waters was the father. As a result, all of her life, Ethel Waters felt unwanted. In her mid-50s, she joined the Graham Crusade, but publicly disassociated herself from the civil rights movement and, in later years, the women's movement. She said God would take care of everything.

From 1917 to 1952, Ethel Waters was a rising, but volatile star who appeared on stage, screen, records, radio, and eventually television. From 1952 on, she could not get work on a sustained basis, and remained in financial quicksand the rest of her life with the Internal Revenue Service. Her life was a series of contradictions. Thomas Anderson, an actor who played one of Satan's henchmen with her in Lynn Root's *Cabin in the Sky,* said that she was "able to pray one minute and curse the next" (11 Nov. 1977). Waters grew up with prostitutes, procurers, and thieves, and ran errands for them.

Talley Beatty, a renowned dancer/choreographer, who performed with the Katherine Dunham troupe in *Cabin in the Sky,* said that Waters "abused her power" (26 June 1991). Only one person that I knew spoke well of Waters. It was Frederick O'Neal, former President of Actors Equity, who played opposite Ethel Waters as Jake in the 1949 film *Pinky*. O'Neal spoke well of everyone. "I liked Ethel," he said; "She was very talented" (24 June 1980). Leonard dePaur of the dePaur Infantry Chorus, said she was "mean, violent, opinionated, and obstreperous" (29 Mar. 1982). Talley Beatty remembered her "excessive religiosity and meanness" (26 June 1991).

Knowledge of Waters's behavior was not limited to those in the performing arts. Joseph Comprone, Head of the Humanities Department at Michigan Technological University, 1989–92, and a native Philadelphian, mentioned to me that his father used to drive him by the speakeasies where Ethel Waters sang to show him where this tough woman entertained (15 June 1992). Dick Campbell (also one of Satan's henchmen in the Broadway version of *Cabin in the Sky*) recalled how he "had to assure 'The Waters' in the wings that she was as good as Katherine Dunham" (27 Mar. 1986). Waters's violence was a major contributing factor in her economic woes and in her romantic liaisons.

A judgment of Ethel Waters as being only talented and difficult, however, misses the mark. The singer/actor was born during the nadir in African American history. From 1896 to 1917, America experienced more lynchings than at any other time in its history. Booker T. Washington, "America's most powerful Negro," preached social separation and accommodation in his Atlanta Exposition Address of 1895. *Plessy v. Ferguson*, the "separate but equal" doctrine, originated in 1896, and its impact lasted well past *Brown v. Topeka* in 1954.

Women did not have the right to vote during the first 26 years of Waters's life. They lacked many other rights, as well. Waters had many battles to fight—a poignantly sad childhood, and a world torn by racial terror and formal segregation. There was also gender oppression. Marriage to someone—anyone—was expected. Ethel Waters was no exception.

In 1909, she married Merritt "Buddy" Purnsley, who was 23 years old. She was 13. To obtain the marriage license, Purnsley took another woman with him, inasmuch as Waters was under age. Purnsley demanded control in every way. He beat Ethel Waters and humiliated her frequently. He played the old game of isolation and alienation, demanding that she give up everything she liked—dancing, roller skating, and her friends. Purnsley worked for the Pennsylvania Steel Casting Company, earning only a few dollars a week. Waters dreaded the sexual relationship. Her "wedding dress" was a skirt and a blouse.

In *His Eye Is on the Sparrow*, Waters says that the community of Chester believed that men were czars, and women, their serfs (60). Since many black women worked outside of the home most of the twentieth century, Waters worked as a maid, often for as little as $3 to $5 a week; her absences from home provided her husband with an excuse to accuse her of infidelity. The singer, fed up with abuse, separated from Purnsley by the time she was 14.

Having begun to sing when she was around five, Waters became known as "Baby Star." She entered competitions and by 1917 made her professional debut at the Lincoln Theatre in Baltimore, Maryland for $9 a week. She sought the permission of W. C. Handy to sing "The St. Louis Blues" when it was a new song. Unlike the fairer skinned black women, the darker sisters were not as much in demand on stage or elsewhere. Waters and Josephine Baker were both rejected for the 1921 Broadway musical *Shuffle Along,* which ran for 504 performances (Woll 72). Waters resented this all of her life.

Baker finally worked her way into the chorus and clowned her way into acceptance. "Every night she rolled her eyes, purposely got out of step, and mugged to the audience" (75). Waters sulked and became bitter. Edmonds's Cellar at 132nd Street and Fifth in New York City, became Waters's domain; it seated around 200 patrons, many of them sporting men; Waters sang from dusk until dawn. Happy customers threw money on the floor and when Waters sang, money rained. Her undulating hips were also part of the wild attraction. But the hours were too long and this was the beginning of her exhaustion. Management was often cruel.

While a number of white managers reneged on contracts with impunity, Waters also had friends with integrity in management. Milton Starr of Nashville was an original officer of the Theatre Owners Booking Association (T.O.B.A.), a separate booking agency for black performers only. Organized in Chattanooga, Tennessee, in 1920, the T.O.B.A. came about through the efforts of an influential group of theatre owners in the South and Midwest. The circuit grew to over 80 theatres and could book African American employees for a full season.

Although the organization provided booking for a large number of black performers, unfair treatment on the part of management reigned, and black performers were not unionized at this time. Waters and many others often rehearsed without pay and did not get money if a show closed on the road. Frequently, they were denied hot or cold running water and other amenities in dressing rooms. More than once, Waters dressed under a staircase, without even a curtain for privacy.

In one of many incidents, Milton Starr came to Waters's rescue. Charles P. Bailey of Atlanta ran a vaudeville theatre in the heart of the Negro section. Conflict rapidly ensued between Waters and Bailey. She asked to have the piano tuned and offered to pay for it. Bailey interpreted her request as telling him how to run his theatre. She interpreted his refusal as telling her how to run her act. Bailey set out to destroy Waters, possibly to lynch her.

Securing a police guard, his own black chauffeur, and the train ticket agent to keep the singer in her place, Bailey set his plan in action. Thwarted by the agent when she attempted to buy a train ticket, Waters escaped just in time on horse and buggy. By the time she reached Nashville, Bailey had called Milton Starr, head of the T.O.B.A. Fortunately, Waters was able to defend herself from being blacklisted at that time.

On another T.O.B.A. tour, this time through Alabama, some of the men with Waters secured a white man's car for a "joy ride." An accident ensued, and Waters's leg was permanently injured. Confined to the black wing of an Anniston, Alabama, hospital, Waters was ignored and her bandages were not changed for days at a time. When the leg began to emit a powerful odor, she feared that gangrene might set in. Not too long thereafter, a physician, mercifully, cut out the poisoned contents as well as oil, dirt and gravel, but prior to this, the only treatment she received were lectures on the evils of car theft.

For much of the 1920s and all of the 1930s, Waters sang at popular night spots and recorded. She was with Fletcher Henderson and Duke Ellington's bands. The Cotton Club, the Plantation Club and many other elegant establishments were her venues. It was Earl Dancer who implored Waters to leave the "colored time" and try the white clubs. This gave her more visibility, touring the Keith-Orpheum vaudeville circuit with Dancer as her manager.

The year 1925 marked a watershed for the singer. Having had to compete with the sexual energy of Josephine Baker, Waters priced herself out of a Paris possibility. She relinquished the opportunity to Josephine Baker who starred in *La Revue Nègre*. Baker walked down the Champs Elysées with leopards and swans, and went to the opera with her cheetah. She made her entry on the stage entirely nude except for a pink flamingo feather ("Black Venus"). A raja offered to abolish his harem if she would marry him, and it was rumored that she had made love to a Swedish prince in his personal railroad car. Over 2,000 men proposed marriage.

In contrast, Waters could not have performed nude if the Lord had required it of her: she had been abused as a child; nuns had taught her Catholic values. Waters was very straight-laced. She was not on level playing ground, did not have the same sexual appeal as Baker, although she was highly sexed and very sexually active.

Waters also had to compete with the image of the beloved Florence Mills whom she replaced in 1925 at Sam Salvin's Plantation Club at Broadway and 50th Street in New York City. Gilbert Seldes wrote about Florence Mills, "Merely to watch her walk out on the stage with her long, free stride and superb, shameless swing, is an aesthetic pleasure" (quoted in Isaacs 68). Mills was small and "darling size." Waters was lanky and lean.

When Mills died of an appendicitis attack two years later, 150,000 people lined the streets of Harlem to say farewell. At no point in her career did Waters ever have the adulation given to Baker and Mills. Nor was she as beloved as Lena Horne. But she did appeal to a multiracial audience.

G. R. F. Key spoke of Waters's multiracial appeal. Born in 1896 also, he saw Waters perform at the Howard Theater in Washington, D. C. Her risqué singing attracted a diverse audience. Keys reflected, when I interviewed him at the Washingtoniana Collection in the D.C. Public Library: "Some white patrons came to the Howard Theater. Ethel Waters was *par excellence* with me. She was accepted by everyone" (28 June 1990).

Unfortunately, though, Waters permitted herself to be cast in a stereotyped role. Her low self-image drove her to embarrassing behavior. By 1927, she had her first Broadway role, that of Miss Calico in *Africana*. Slim and 31, Waters desired the trappings of material success. Unable to drive, she nevertheless purchased a Locomobile, as she called it. Waters rode in taxis; her boyfriend drove the car. One day as Waters was winding down the street in the back of a hired car, she spotted her own automobile parked outside the apartment of one of the *Africana* cast members. Asking the driver to stop, Waters, pretending to be Western Union, proceeded upstairs. A roommate of the other woman answered the door. Waters announced that "our boyfriend," was there and she just wanted her car keys. Strong denial occurred. Finally, Waters saw a closed door, which she promptly struck open with force. There in the bed with an *Africana* cast member was Waters's beau. Assuring him she would "get" him later, she demanded the car keys, put them into the ignition, and deliberately wrecked the car. A few days later, Waters discovered the other woman in a rest room in a local night spot and, according to Waters, herself, "I locked the door, then just beat the living hell out of her" (Waters *Sparrow* 193).

Following Mills's death, Waters's career continued upward as she performed in Lew Leslie's *Blackbirds* in 1927 and 1928. She also went to Europe on the *Ile de France* with Clyde Matthews, whom she married in 1928. On this tour was Algretta Holmes, an adopted daughter. Waters said of her second husband, "In Philadelphia, Clyde Edward Matthews appeared out of nowhere. I'd met him in Cleveland . . . he slithered back into my life" (198).

Still on the edge financially, and with throat trouble, Waters had taken the advice of her physician who had recommended rest. Waters had surgery in Europe for the removal of a nodule that was on her throat. The operation cost $750, so she sang at the Cafe de Paris in order to earn the money. By 1929, with the Great Crash, Waters, like many others, declared bankruptcy. She owed $143,812, and had assets of $40 (*Journal and Guide,* n. p.).

In that year, she also appeared in the film *On with the Show*, clad in a bandana and carrying a large basket of cotton. She began to recover from her bankruptcy by getting employment in *Rhapsody in Black*, a revue at the Belasco Theatre in Washington, D. C. Several New York City theatres picked it up in 1930, as well. By 1931, Waters was a star. The revue ran through some of the roughest days of the Great Depression, bringing in from $22,000 to $24,000 a week. No week was bad for Waters. Lew Leslie's revue, *Blackbirds*, continued to enjoy favorable audience reception as well.

One evening, at The Cotton Club, Waters sang the story of her marriage in the song "Stormy Weather," using a lamp post as prop. Duke Ellington's band accompanied her. As she belted out "Don't know why there's no sun up in the sky, stormy weather, since my man and I ain't together," Irving Berlin heard her and cast her in the famous *As Thousands Cheer* at The Music Box. Waters sang four songs, and was extricated from the plot. The stars, Marilyn Miller, Clifton Webb, and Helen Broderick, got top billing; Waters did not. But the audience and critical reception were unusually positive.

Four years out of devastating bankruptcy, Waters became the highest paid woman on Broadway. Each night, after the show ended, Waters worked a second job after *As Thousands Cheer*. She sang for a night club's late show. The singer had little regard for her health and often worked from dusk to dawn when it was no longer required. Her legendary "Suppertime" evoked a sad spirit of a woman preparing supper for a man who was not coming home; he had just been lynched. Waters's "Heat Wave," showed her openly parodying Josephine Baker with a fancy headdress of fruit. Waters comforted an America in economic collapse.

The year 1933 was a frightening one for most Americans. The banks closed. Franklin Delano Roosevelt gave his famous inaugural address: "The only thing we have to fear is fear itself," and it was the year that marked the first anniversary of the Scottsboro Case where nine young black men were jailed in Scottsboro, Alabama, for the alleged rape of a white woman. Tensions erupted, but Waters, except for the unhappiness of her marriage, lived royally. The money from *As Thousands Cheer* permitted the star to live lavishly—an apartment on Harlem's "Sugar Hill," clothes, furs, a vast collection of earrings, a Lincoln towncar with a chauffeur, servants for the ten-room apartment, and "sweet men" to occupy it. In 1934, she divorced Matthews, remarking that it was the toughest of all good-byes. Divorced a second time, she lived on the edge. Unable to save money, she was more often than not hard pressed. By September of 1935, she worked on Broadway again, this time in *At Home Abroad* with Beatrice Lillie. Waters sang with vim and humor according to *The New York Times*. But money was almost impossible for her to keep.

Waters's lack of education was a factor in preventing her from developing many genuine friendships, because her work often brought her into contact with those better trained than she. One of the relationships that she cultivated in the 1930s was with Zora Neale Hurston, the novelist of *Their Eyes Were Watching God*. The author defended Waters. Too timid to go backstage, Hurston wrote Waters letters, which she ignored. Hurston, upon succeeding with the friendship, finally, wrote in *Dust Tracks on the Road*, "I sensed a great humanness and depth about her" (177). Hurston had a college education from Barnard, and was a major literary figure. Waters wrote very poorly; she may have just wanted to hide her marginal literacy, but created the impression of rudeness by not responding.

She did write a few people, however, including a large notebook of letters to her secretary, Floretta Howard, and to philanthropist and Waters supporter, Carl Van Vechten. To the latter, she penned:

> Darling Pal, . . . Well darling love to Fania and I'll be seeing you when I get home and I'm praying I get to California. Oh, yes, I'm still enroute and help me pray that I get a chance to show my ability and not my shape—Ethel.

This letter, written 3 October 1936, shows Waters being aware of the weight gain that was to plague her all her life.

In 1939, as the Great Depression waned and World War II approached, Waters became the first woman of color to star in a dramatic role on Broadway. The vehicle was Dorothy and DuBose Heyward's *Mamba's Daughters;* Waters was Hagar; Georgette Harvey, Mamba; Fredi Washington, Lissa; and Willie Bryant, Gilly Bluton. Canada Lee gave a cameo appearance as Drayton. Hagar was a violent, dull, cigar-smoking "stupid wench" who worked on a South Carolina plantation. Alfred Bendiner did a caricature of Waters in the play, emphasizing the Mammy stereotype. In spite of the Bendiner sketch, the caricature signaled Waters's growing stature in the American theatre.

During this time, white philanthropist Carl Van Vechten, writer, *bon vivant*, and photographer, went to great lengths to support Ethel Waters. In the February 1939 issue of *Opportunity*, he compared Waters with the great Sarah Bernhardt who had played, among many great roles, the title one in *Hamlet*. Van Vechten also compared Ethel Waters to Ellen Terry, who had been Lady Macbeth in the late 1800s (46–47). Van Vechten added that Waters might well play the vindictive Medea who killed Jason's younger bride and Medea and Jason's own two sons. Van Vechten carried on in the most lavish accolades (47).

Waters's opening night audience for *Mamba's Daughters* gave her 17 curtain calls. Brooks Atkinson was not so enthralled. Referring to Waters's style as "personally earnest and magnetic... but... limp, plodding.... [S]he seems unable to vary" (6 Jan. 1939, 24:2). The critic gave, at best, a lukewarm review. Many of Waters's friends were incensed. Several took out a full page in the Sunday *New York Times* demanding that Atkinson retract his statement. Burgess Meredith, Tallulah Bankhead, and a host of others signed. Saying that he had a virus on the first viewing, Atkinson went again and relented.

Mamba's Daughters continued to build Waters's reputation as a violent woman. In a scene with Gilly Bluton, played by Willie Bryant, Waters came close to killing him, so involved did she become in playing the role. Legend says that Waters was not merely acting: she became Hagar. Hagar was an unfortunate stereotype. Perhaps Waters was typecast, but in the late 1930s, it is not inconceivable that she might have been given more favorable roles. Lena Horne, for example, with a similar career of more singing than dramatic roles, obtained positive parts. Yet, Horne was not one who failed to show some anger when mistreated. In a restaurant someone asked as it was learned that she was inside, "Where is the nigger, anyway?" "Here I am," she shouted, sending a water glass with her answer. It is not expected from reasonable people that a public figure should take every insult. Not even Harry Truman, President of the United States did that, when someone suggested that his daughter's piano playing was less than desirable. Even if he was President, Truman expressed his anger, but not on a regular basis.

With the closing of *Mamba's Daughters,* America found itself at war, and Ethel Waters entertaining at a stage door canteen. More than three million Negro men registered for service in the armed forces. During the course of World War II, roughly one million men and women of color served their country. African Americans, who had begun the Great Migration north from field to factory in 1915, were still pouring into New York, St. Louis, and Chicago. Americans of any color sought fantasy in their entertainment, and Waters helped to provide it.

In 1940, she starred as Petunia, the wife of Little Joe, in Lynn Root's *Cabin in the Sky* at the Martin Beck in New York City. The play focused on a God-fearing woman whose husband enjoyed gambling and women; Dooley Wilson, who had been Sam, the piano player in *Casablanca,* played Little Joe. Satan, portrayed by Rex Ingram, battled with the Lord General, performed by Todd Duncan, for Joe's soul. Katherine Dunham, the dancer, was "Sweet" Georgia Brown, the hussy of the play. Her dance troupe appeared, directed by George Balanchine. Reviewers came in droves. Audiences danced in the aisles, and theatre-goers left humming "Taking a Chance on Love," Waters's centerpiece.

During the *Cabin* production, Waters lived with Eddie Mallory, a good-looking trumpet player. Once, she removed him from her car and relegated him to the bus, when on a tour she discovered that he had been looking at other women. In spite of Mallory's behavior, as well as Ethel Waters's public humiliation of her man, she showered him with a large chunk of her savings, set him up in his business, Fat Man's Place, and helped to sponsor his musical career. Gaining weight and age, Waters became desperate.

Talley Beatty witnessed Waters remove Katherine Dunham from two dance numbers, including a cabaret scene, so that she might dance with the younger Archie Savage (26 June 1991). Savage and Dunham had danced together in "Pins and Needles." Arguably, Dunham was the greatest dancer of color in the world. But it made no difference to Waters. She was the better known at the time, and the powers bowed to her wishes. The Mallory affair was in trouble, and Waters took Savage as her protégé, or so she said. Beatty believes that Waters was romantically attracted to Savage (26 June 1991). This was the beginning of her undoing.

Meanwhile, Waters had quite an explosion with Lena Horne, whom Waters, by all accounts, resented greatly. Horne was 21 years younger, believed to be one of the world's most beautiful women, and truly in her prime. After the success of the play *Cabin*, Hollywood rushed to do the film. MGM sought Horne for the part of "Sweet" Georgia Brown. Gail Lumet Buckley, Horne's daughter, wrote that Waters envied light-complexioned, formally educated African Americans. On the set of the film *Cabin*, Waters accused Horne of parodying her "Honey in the Honeycomb," and she and Horne never spoke again (Buckley 165).

Waters had reason to resent Lena Horne, over and above her youth. Horne was the darling of Vincent Minelli, who directed the film. Although not yet married to Lennie Hayton when the film came out, Horne was the object of many a man's eye. She was a pin-up girl for soldiers in World War II, and entertained the troops. Her father protected her from sexual abuse; Waters never had the protection of a father or a good husband. Horne came from a middle-class family with a long history of achievement.

In the midst of the filming of *Cabin*, Waters toured, with Hattie McDaniel, working military bases throughout California. Waters also appeared with USO Camp Shows for Negroes on network radio. She starred in the film *Tales of Manhattan* with Paul Robeson, in a work where he found the stereotypes offensive. Waters disagreed. She also was in the film *Stage Door Canteen*, and went on tour with *Laugh Time*, in 1943, the year *Cabin In The Sky* was released.

Meanwhile, Waters had purchased a home on Hobart Street in Los Angeles. Being sensitive to the dilemma of people of color who often had to live in private homes and houses of prostitution because hotels barred them, Waters permitted the dancer Archie Savage to live in her house while she toured in *Laugh Time*. Savage stayed rent free. Upon her return, she learned that Savage had stolen $10,000 in cash and $30,000 worth of jewelry (*People v. Savage*). The dancer had called a locksmith.

According to Waters in *Sparrow*, he bragged that there was nothing she could do. She filed suit in the California courts, and in 1944, the California Appellate Courts recorded that Savage was sentenced to a year and a day in San Quentin. Such a public display of her revenge and poor judgment did not help her career. Additional negative images surfaced, including explosions on the set of *Cabin in the Sky*, where she is said to have uttered strong anti-Semitic epithets.

Consequently, for six long years, Waters was unable to get employment except on the *Amos 'n' Andy Show* on NBC radio and a few other brief spots. No sustained employment came her way. By 1949, at the age of 53, Waters secured the leading role of Granny Dysey Johnson, another Mammy role, in Darryl F. Zanuck's *Pinky*. This was one of the three touted films on "passing" for white, the others being *Lost Boundaries* and *Imitation of Life*. Jeanne Crain, a white actress, starred as Pinky, a light-complexioned black nurse who returns to Mississippi after passing for white in Boston.

Crain's grandmother is a black washerwoman, played by Waters, who works for the feisty "Miss" Em, played by Ethel Barrymore. Frederick O'Neal was the unscrupulous Jake, and the voluptuous Nina Mae McKinney, his girlfriend. Pinky has met a handsome white physician in New England, Dr. Thomas Adams, played by William Lundigan, who wishes to marry her. Ultimately, Pinky rejects her white suitor, and opens a nursing school for blacks on the property she inherits from "Miss" Em. Bosley Crowther wrote in *The New York Times:* "By playing the girl's old grandmother in a benign and wistful way, Ethel Waters endows this gentle lady with tremendous warmth and appeal" (30 Sept. 1949 28:2).

In the midst of *Pinky*, Senator Joseph McCarthy of Appleton, Wisconsin, was involved in his highly-publicized search for Communists under every theatrical flat. It was the time of Arthurine Lucy, the first black woman to enroll at the University of Alabama in 1956; students threw tomatoes and rocks at her, but Lucy was accused of disturbing the peace. Waters had reason to be afraid to speak out. Inarticulate, except as an actor or singer, Waters was not outspoken on political issues, yet she still failed to thrive.

Her last great moment came with Carson McCullers's *The Member of the Wedding* in 1950 at New York City's Empire Theatre; she was Berenice Sadie Brown, yet another Mammy role. After considerable negotiating with the producers about a part that showed her as a Christian, Waters played the comforter, Berenice. Frankie Addams, created by Julie Harris, was a 13-year-old lonely adolescent. Brandon de Wilde was the young

John Henry who played cards with Frankie and Berenice, and who ultimately contracts spinal meningitis.

Talley Beatty recalled, "Waters's acting was very shaded. She gave Julie Harris and Brandon de Wilde a run for their money" (26 June 1991). In 1950, Waters gave more than 850 live performances of *Member of the Wedding*. The play ran into 1951, including the 16-month stretch on Broadway, followed by a road tour which included the Cass Theatre in Detroit. Critical reception was wildly enthusiastic. Of all the roles played by Waters, it is the one that is most remembered.

Financial woes seldom left the actor, though. On 8 December 1951, the performer wrote her secretary, Floretta Howard, "It looks as if they [the IRS] are going to make me pay an extra $4,000. . . . They will take $625.00 weekly. . . . They still don't know what I have" (Cache of Waters's handwritten letters to Floretta Howard in a Notebook in the Library of Congress). She signed off, "Your tired weary Boss." On 10 January 1952, Waters wrote Howard, "Mr. Furst called me long distance to tell me the joyful news that I must pay at least $10,000 in January." The IRS claimed back taxes to 1938 and 1939 while Waters was in *Mamba's Daughters*.

Some employment gave the illusion of enough money. The film version of *Member of the Wedding* was released in 1952, with Waters, Julie Harris, and Brandon de Wilde, the three major actors of the stage play. In both, Waters sang her signature song, "His Eye Is on the Sparrow." In 1953, Al Hirschfeld, the renowned caricaturist, recognized Waters in *The New York Times*; it was for *An Evening with Ethel Waters*.

Clearly past her prime, Ethel Waters's career was over. Down, out, bitter, and broke at 56, Waters needed sustenance. Beginning work on the *Beulah* television show, as a maid, in 1950, she played in several episodes of the show with Dooley Wilson as the boyfriend. P. Jay Sidney, who also acted in the series, reported that Waters tolerated no smoking on the set, and that Wilson sustained a stroke during the filming and had to be photographed from the side (15 Apr. 1981). Dooley Wilson died 30 May 1953, and the show was syndicated and withdrawn 22 September of that year.

By 1957, the Billy Graham Crusade was sweeping the world in prairie-fire fashion. The evangelist attracted 200,000 people to Madison Square Garden. After one of her now infrequent one-woman shows with her accompanist, Reginald Beane, Waters went back to her room at the Empire Hotel in Manhattan. She listened to the evangelist on the radio and reflected on how she had not sung in a church since her days back in Chester, Pennsylvania. Lonely and alone, she soon received a call at the hotel desk asking if she would like tickets to the Graham Crusade. She accepted.

Ethel Waters joined the Billy Graham Crusade and remained with it until her death. During those 20 years—20 painful years—the IRS constantly hounded her. They put a lien on her Los Angeles home and attached everything she had. In 1959, she went on the television program *Break the Bank,* to win some money, which only moderately pacified the United States government. One letter to Floretta Howard from Miss Waters was signed, "Miss disgusted with the rotten government Waters."

More employment came in 1959 when Waters took on the role of the Eternal Menial once more—Dilsey, in William Faulkner's *The Sound and the Fury,* opposite Yul Brynner. Most of her work thereafter was with Billy Graham.

She found peace with the Billy Graham Crusade, and was buried at a private service at the Forest Lawn Mortuary in Glendale, California, by friends in whose home she died. *Newsweek* called her a "smoky voiced institution" (74).

Jeanne Noble of Hunter College wrote that Waters died a misfit who was at home with neither whites nor blacks (48). Ethel Waters embraced, with zeal, Graham, but took no notice of Martin Luther King, Jr., who by 1955 was equally as popular. She was also friendly with President Richard Nixon, who invited the star to the White House to Julie Nixon Eisenhower's Rose Garden wedding.

If Waters had friends of color in her twilight years, the media failed to cover the camaraderie. However "mean" Waters was, her childhood, her treatment on the T.O.B.A., her Mammy roles, her segregated world, her bout with the IRS, and her men gave her reason to be. Beautiful and fiery in her youth, vivacious in her middle age, poignant in her twilight years, Waters knew victory and defeat. A different set of choices, in some instances, and perhaps a different class of men might have provided her with more reliable support. Her life was tragic, but her power as a performer is a significant legacy.

Works Cited

"Actress-singer Ethel Waters Dies," *The Chicago Tribune,* 2 Sept. 1977, I:5:2.

"Africana, A Swift Negro Musical Revue: Ethel Waters Leads in Show with Champion Cake Walker and Amusing Sketches," *New York Times Theatre Review,* 12 July 1927, 29:2.

Adams, Russell L. *Great Negroes Past and Present.* Chicago: Afro-American Publishing Company, 1969.

Anderson, Lisa M. *Mammies No More: The Changing Image of Black Women on Stage and Screen.* Oxford: Rowman and Littlefield Publishers, 1997.

Anderson, Thomas. Personal interview with author. 11 Nov. 1977.

Atkinson, Brooks. "Mamba's Daughters," *The New York Times,* 6 Jan. 1939, 26:6.

Barretto, Larry. *Bookman.* Apr. 1926, 215–216.

Beatty, Talley. Personal interview with author. 26 June 1991.

"Black Venus," *Newsweek*, 31 Oct. 1977, n.p. [Josephine Baker]

"Blues Singer Ethel Waters Dies," *Iowa City Press Citizen*, 2 Sept. 1977, 1.

Blum, Daniel. *Great Stars of the American Stage*. New York: Grosset and Dunlap, 1952 (Courtesy of Richard Goldstein).

Bogle, Donald. *Blacks in American Film and Television*. New York: Garland Publishing, 1988.

———. *Brown Sugar: Eighty Years of America's Black Female Superstars*. New York: Harmony Books, 1980.

———. *Toms, Coons, Mulattoes, Mammies and Bucks: An Interpretive History of Blacks in American Films*. New York: Viking Press, 1973.

Buckley, Gail Lumet. *The Hornes: An American Family*. New York: New American Library, 1986.

Campbell, Dick. Actor/Manager. Letter to the author. 5 Jan. 1978.

———. Personal interview with author. 27 Mar. 1986.

Comprone, Joseph. Personal interview with author. 15 June 1992.

Crowther, Bosley. A review of *Pinky*, *The New York Times*, 30 Sept. 1949. 28:2.

dePaur, Leonard. Personal interview with author. 29 Mar. 1982.

Drake, Anne Q. Telephone interview with author. 5 Jan. 1991.

"Ethel Waters Conquers the Devil in *Cabin in the Sky*," *Life*, 9 Dec. 1940, 63–66.

"Ethel Waters in Big Money." Chicago Historical Society clipping,

———. Associated Negro Press, 10 June 1935.

"Ethel Waters Recalls Being Stranded in 1931," *Cleveland Call and Post*, 25 Nov. 1939, n.p.

"Ethel Waters—Torch Singer to Dramatic Actress," *The New York Post*, 6 Dec. 1940, 337.

Feather, Leonard. "Remembering Ethel Waters," *Los Angeles Times*, 3 Sept. 1977, II, 9:1.

Frazier, C. Gerald. "Ethel Waters Is Dead at 80," *The New York Times*, 2 Sept. 1977, 1 and D 12:1.

Gilder, Rosamond. "In The Groove," *Theatre Arts Monthly*, 24:841–2, Dec. 1940. [*Cabin in the Sky*]

Hurston, Zora Neale. *Dust Tracks on the Road*. New York: Harper, 1942.

Isaacs, Edith J. R. *The Negro in the American Theatre*. New York: Theatre Arts, 1947.

Johnson, James Weldon. *Black Manhattan*. New York: Atheneum Press, 1930.

Journal and Guide, "Ethel Waters's Rise Saga of the Theatre," 25 Mar. 1939, Tuskegee University Archives clipping file, n.p.

Kazan, Elia. *A Life*. New York: Knopf, 1988.

Key, G. R. F. Personal interview with author. 28 June 1990.

Knaack, Twila. *Ethel Waters: I Touched a Sparrow*. Waco, Texas: Word Books, 1978.

Lee, Chauncey. "USO Camp Shows and the Soldier," *The Crisis*, Feb. 1944, 50–61.

"Member of the Wedding, The," *Ebony*. Apr. 1959, 108.

"Miss Waters Regrets: Theater's First Ebony Lady Is Broke and Bitter at 56," *Ebony*, Feb. 1957, 56–60.

Morse, Evan, "Ethel Waters," in *Black Women in America: An Historical Encyclopedia*. ed. Darlene Clark Hine. Brooklyn: Carlson Publishing Company, 1993, 1236–1238.

Newsweek, 12 Sept. 1977, 74 (Transition section).

Noble, Jeanne. *Beautiful, Also, Are the Souls of My Black Sisters: A History of the Black Woman in America.* Englewood Cliffs, New Jersey: Prentice-Hall, 1978.

Null, Gary. *Black Hollywood.* Secaucus, New Jersey: Citadel Press, 1977.

O'Neal, Frederick. Personal interview with author. 24 Jun. 1980.

Patton, Gerald. *War and Race: The Black Officer in the United States Military, 1915–1941.* Westport, CT: Greenwood Press, 1981.

People v. Savage. 66 Cal. App. 2d 237 152 2d 240 (Cal. App. 2d Dist, 1944).

"Pinky," *Ebony*, Sept. 1949, 23–25.

Robeson, Susan. *The Whole World in His Hands.* Secaucus, New New Jersey: Citadel Press, 1981 (on Paul Robeson).

Sidney, P. Jay. Telephone interview with author. 15 Apr. 1981.

"Singer, Actress Ethel Waters Dies at Age 80," *New Orleans Picayune*, 2 Sept. 1977, II, 5:1.

Thackrey, Jr., Ted. "Ethel Waters, Singer and Actress for 60 Years, Dies," *Los Angeles Times*, 2 Sept. 1977, I:1, 20:1.

Thomas, Edna. Letter to Carl Van Vechten. 16 Jan. 1939.

Van Vechten, Carl. "Mamba's Daughters," *Opportunity*, Feb. 1939, 46–47.

Waters, Ethel. *His Eye Is on the Sparrow.* New York: Harcourt, Brace, Jovanovich, 1980.

———. Letter to Carl Van Vechten. 3 Oct. 1936.

———. Letters to Floretta Howard. 8 Dec. 1951 through 10 Jan. 1952. (Notebook in the Library of Congress).

———. "The Men in My Life," *Ebony*, Jan. 1952, 24–38.

———. *To Me It's Wonderful.* New York: Harper and Row, 1972.

Weil, Martin. "Singer, Stage and Film Actress Ethel Waters Dies," *The Washington Post*, 2 Sept. 1977, C12:1.

Woll, Allen. *Black Musical Theatre: From Coontown to Dreamgirls.* Baton Rouge, Louisiana State University Press, 1989.

Marian Anderson, 1902, singer. Laura Wheeler Waring, 1887–1948. Oil on canvas. National Portrait Gallery, Smithsonian Institution. Gift of the Harmon Foundation.

Chapter V

Marian Anderson: A Serene Spirit

Marian Anderson, arguably the greatest contralto of the twentieth century, had a self-possession under stress that few have. By her own admission, she was "not equipped for hand-to-hand combat" (*The New York Times* 9 Apr. 1993). Born 27 February 1897, in dire poverty, Marian Anderson chose the quiet, regal way. Scrubbing doorsteps in her native Philadelphia, this strong Christian woman knew that God had given her a unique instrument—her voice. To be a black unmarried woman singer meant a struggle: at auditions, with management, with audiences.

In terms of the racial and political divide, her career spanned World War I and II, the 1955 Montgomery Bus Boycott, the 1956 Arthurine Lucy/Thurgood Marshall saga with the University of Alabama, the McCarthy Era, the 1957 Little Rock Crisis, and the 1963 "stand in the doorway" by George Wallace to prevent Vivian Malone and James Hood from entering the University of Alabama. Segregated public accommodations prevailed with hotels, travel, and restaurants. These were times when the lid came off in steamy American racial politics. But Marian Anderson rose above it all.

Any suggestion (and there have been some) that Anderson disassociated herself from either the women's movement or the African American struggle is born in naïveté, and lack of keen perception. Like the slaves who seldom spoke out, Marian Anderson sang her feelings in the Negro spirituals with an emotion and power few could equal. It was her therapy and a way of life. Singing was also her great talent, a talent so immense that Arturo Toscanini declared that a voice like hers came once in a century.

Anderson left most of her battles to others. Sol Hurok, who became her devoted white manager for most of her career, did the combat. Miss Anderson, although marrying in her 40s, eventually had the protection of a genial husband in a marriage that lasted 42 years. Unlike Ethel Waters, Anderson was fortunate to have acquired both a good manager and a good husband. The contralto was also of a very different spirit, perhaps because of having been born in a two-parent home that was nurturing and loving.

In 1954, I heard Marian Anderson sing in the Gymnasium Auditorium at Alabama A. and M. College at Normal. Nothing in my life has impressed me more. It was not just her deeply rich contralto voice that caused me to envision and hear death as she and her accompanist, Franz Rupp, with majestic handling of the lower octaves, rendered Schubert's moving *Der Erlkönig*. It was her silent strength, her humility, her grace under fire. She ended her concert that 13 March night with "He's Got the Whole World in His Hands."

> He's got the whole world
> In His hands.
> He's got the whole world
> In His hands.
> He's got the whole wide world
> In His hands.

I can still see and hear the gambling man "in His hands," and hear her singing about him.

Dr. Henry Bradford, Jr., then Head of the Music Department at Alabama A. and M. College, an ordained minister of more than 50 years and a member of the Lyceum Committee that brought her under the chairmanship of the late Dean Robert A. Carter, remembered:

> When she came here, because of the social restrictions, she had to stay in the home of the President. The Russell Erskine [Hotel] was the epitome of refined living and dining accommodation in Huntsville and could have been available, but was not (16 Sept. 1997).

Mrs. Anne Q. Drake, wife of President Joseph Fanning Drake of Alabama A. and M. College, who died in October 1999 at 104, told me that Miss Anderson insisted on pressing her own evening gown. She carried 15 pieces of luggage with her, only one with clothes. The other had her iron, her sewing machine, and such items as curtains for her farm home in Connecticut.

Marian Anderson was regal in the most literal sense. As she came on stage of the Gymnasium Auditorium that Saturday night, in her long, brown evening gown with a train, I had not then, or now, witnessed anyone with such a stately bearing. She strolled to the piano with the majesty of a queen, kicked her long train in place as she stood, royally, in the neck of the ebony grand piano, and paused. Her strong, feminine hands were striking to look at, as she held them clasped in front of her, nodded to Mr. Rupp, closed her eyes, and began to sing.

Her warm relationship with her white male accompanist culminated with their holding hands as she accepted wildly enthusiastic applause. Miss Anderson endured severe criticism for holding a white man's hand. One manager even told her team that they would not stand for that kind of thing. But, she always insisted on holding her accompanist's hand for the encore. Billy King was her accompanist in the early years, and took over as manager in her early days; he had played for the Negro tenor Roland Hayes. Kosti Vehanen, a Finnish pianist, accompanied Miss Anderson at the piano prior to Rupp. John Motley, an African American, was her last accompanist.

Miss Anderson's warmth was the kind I had not seen in many artists. She also had profound respect not only for her accompanist, but the composers, the people who built the pianos, her family, and Sol Hurok. She was an unusually calm and wise woman. But she demanded respect, as well, for herself.

Dr. Bradford observed on 16 September 1997:

> When Miss Anderson accepted the invitation through Sol Hurok, she demanded that there be no segregated seating in the Gymnasium Auditorium where she performed. People of all cultures, religious persuasions and economic backgrounds came to witness her stellar performance. She sang before a capacity and extremely appreciative audience. They called her back for several encores, one of which was Schubert's *Ave Maria*.
>
> Following the performance that evening, a selected number of students of various academic classifications were invited to share a reception at Councill Hall [a dormitory named for the founder of Alabama A. and M.] in a very elegant drawing room setting.

A look back before that 1954 night is important in understanding her measure of dignity.

In the year 1939, Marian Anderson had toured Paris, the Soviet Union, and other parts of Europe. Her fame had broken international barriers, and Paul Robeson attended a New York dinner in her honor. In America, on tour, she was treated as a second-class citizen in terms of public accommodations. She always traveled with a sleeping bag. If she got hungry on the road, she ate a sandwich obtained from the back door of a restaurant. She took an electric hot plate for tea and boiled eggs. Taxi drivers repeatedly passed her by.

She refused, ever, to make a fuss about public accommodations, saying that this would change, in time. But she was adamant about segregated seating not occurring at her own concerts. At her request, Sol Hurok canceled concerts where segregated seating prevailed.

The most infamous incident, perhaps, in American musical history, occurred in 1939 when the Daughters of the American Revolution (DAR) denied her the right to sing at Constitution Hall in Washington, D. C. Eleanor Roosevelt resigned membership from the group on 27 February 1939, and announced her resignation in her syndicated column, "My Day." Sol Hurok reported: "The front page of her paper in New York, the *World-Telegram*, carried it. Next morning, the front pages of the *Times* and the *Herald Tribune* featured it, and every other paper in New York ran the story (257–258).

By 6 March 1939, *Time,* in an article called "Jim Crow Concert Hall," reported:

> While irate Washingtonians formed a Marian Anderson's Citizens' Committee and held a mass meeting attended by 1,500, violinist Jascha Heifetz, who arrived in Washington on a concert tour, said he was "ashamed" to appear in Constitution Hall under the circumstances (39).

This had truly become a *cause célébrè*.

Further, the wife of the President implored Harold Ickes, Secretary of the Interior, to arrange for Miss Anderson to sing on the steps of the Lincoln Memorial. This she did on Easter Sunday, 1939, before 75,000 people. Patricia Rice of *The St. Louis Post Dispatch* reports: "[This was] the largest public tribute since Charles Lindberg returned from France a decade before" (14A).

Hurok remembered:

> When we took her from Union Station to Governor Pinchot's house, with the sirens of a police escort shrieking through the quiet Sunday-morning streets, she was calm and ready. At the Governor's, she changed to her concert gown and quietly glanced over her music once more, while the police captain stood on the sidewalk nervously counting the seconds ticking by. We drove to the Lincoln Memorial in a trance of hushed expectancy. As she walked beside me along the roped-off aisle and up the steps to the platform, where great men and women of America stood to honor her, the arm I took to steady her was steadier than my own (260).

Anderson relates the categories of people who were in attendance:

> I was led to the platform by Representative Caroline O'Day of New York, who had been born in Georgia, and Oscar Chapman, Assistant Secretary of the Interior, who was a Virginian. On the platform behind me sat Secre-

tary Ickes, Secretary of the Treasury Morgenthau, Supreme Court Justice Black . . . Arthur W. Mitchell of Illinois, a Negro. Mother was there, as were people from Howard University and from churches in Washington and other cities. So was Walter White, then secretary of the National Association for the Advancement of Colored People. It was Mr. White who at one point stepped to the microphone and appealed to the crowd, probably averting serious accidents when my own people tried to reach me (quoted in Austin 206).

The Pittsburgh Courier reported, "Secretary of Interior Harold L. Ickes said of Miss Anderson, 'Genius has touched with the tip of her wing this woman. . . . Genius draws no color line. She has endowed Marian Anderson with such a voice as lifts any individual above his fellows'" (1).

Marian Anderson's own words help convey her emotions of Easter Sunday, 9 April 1939:

> All I knew then as I stepped forward was the overwhelming impact of that vast multitude. There seemed to be people as far as the eye could see. . . . I had a feeling that a great wave of good will poured out from these people, almost engulfing me. And when I stood up to sing our National Anthem I felt for a moment as though I were choking. For a desperate second I thought that the words, well as I know them, would not come.
>
> I sang. I don't know how. There must have been the help of professionalism I had accumulated over the years. Without it, I could not have gone through the program. I sang . . ."America," the aria "O mio Fernando," Schubert's "Ave Maria," and three spirituals—"Gospel Train," "Trampin'," and "My Soul Is Anchored in the Lord" (191).

This was more than just singing, although the *St. Louis Post Dispatch* wrote: "The haunting perfection of her voice stretched more than two octaves" (A14). The artist struck a blow for civil rights in a non-threatening way. This was quiet power.

Time reported on 17 April 1939, in an article titled, "The Anderson Affair,"

> Singer Anderson had waived her $1,700 fee, nobody paid admission . . .
> Democrat John Nance Garner, Republican Henry Cabot Lodge, Jr. ignored or declined invitations to sponsor her appearance.
> In her great singing, there was no politics (23).

On 31 May 1939, Anson Phelps Stokes submitted in *Art and the Color Line:*

> an appeal to the President General and other officers of the Daughters of the American Revolution to modify their rules so as to permit distinguished

Negro Artists such as Miss Marian Anderson to be heard in Constitution Hall (cover of document).

Never an activist, Marian Anderson, through fate, saw the policy at Constitution Hall eventually change. She sang there several times in the 1950s. Members of the DAR attended a later Marian Anderson concert in a Texas city with the purchase of 200 tickets. This confirmed for Miss Anderson that not all in one group can be tarred with the same brush.

It is a sad fact, however, that by the time Marian Anderson sang at The Metropolitan Opera in 1955, one month before her 58th birthday, she was past her singing prime. Burt Folkhart laments in the 9 April 1993, *The Los Angeles Times:*

> Like such other serious black singers as Paul Robeson and Roland Hayes, Miss Anderson was relegated during her vocal prime to occasional appearances in concert halls or churches because many Americans chose to believe that a superior voice could not rise from what was viewed as an inferior race (6).

So embarrassing was the Constitution Hall denial that some have tried to say that racism did not exist, that the hall was already booked. Sol Hurok and Allan Keiler, Professor of Music at Brandeis, refute this. Keiler replied in a letter to *The Wall Street Journal* on 3 April 1997:

> Since the summer of 1938, Anderson had been scheduled for a concert on Easter Sunday, April 9. . . . In early January 1939, Charles Cohen, chairman of the series, asked the DAR for . . . Constitution Hall for Anderson's concert. . . . Anderson could not appear in Constitution Hall on any date because of the ruling of March 23, 1932, which excluded blacks. . . . A request was made to waive the rule for Anderson.
> On Feb. 1, the DAR's Executive Committee met to consider the request; the vote was 39 to 1 in favor of upholding the "white artists only" clause.
> . . . Only Constitution Hall, from 1932 until the 1950s, refused to allow blacks to perform (A 19:2).

Sol Hurok, who offered several alternative dates in the negotiations, stated that he received an answer saying, "The hall is not available for a concert by Miss Anderson" (257). The problem was that Negroes were simply not welcome. Period. Securing the largest performing hall in Washington, D. C. at the time was a clear need for an artist of Anderson's stature.

Marian Anderson was born with several societal strikes against her: African American, financially poor, and female. Her father, John Anderson, sold coal and ice; her mother, Annie Anderson, took in laundry and cleaned at the famous Wanamaker's store. Marian Anderson did not want her mother doing this kind of work. She said that the happiest day of her life was not any of her awards or celebrated moments of achievement, but the day she had enough money to tell her mother that she did not have to clean for others anymore.

The singer was the oldest of three children. On her death, it was learned that she had shaved a few years off her age, in order to appear younger as many performers must.

The *New York Times* reported in its cover page obituary of 9 April 1993:

> During her career, Miss Anderson gave her date of birth as February 17, 1902, but June Goodman, a longtime friend of hers, said that while going through some family papers recently, she found Miss Anderson's birth certificate, which gave the date as February 27, 1897 (A20).

The artist began her astonishing career by singing when she was three. She joined her church choir, Union Baptist at Fitzwater and Martin, when she was six. Handbills on the Philadelphia pavements advertised "The Baby Contralto," and Anderson and her family collected $5 to $10 fees until the singer was around ten years old.

It was Anderson's father who took her to church every Sunday. He bought her a piano from his brother, after having seen her imitating the movements of playing on the dining room table. In 1910, her father died. Marian Anderson was 12. Being a practical person, the contralto studied courses at William Penn High School that would fit her to earn money. Being also an artist, she was bored with these classes, but not with her one hour a week music class. Her school and her church encouraged her with some financial support.

Eileen Southern reports: "Roland Hayes took an interest in Marian Anderson's career and appeared with her in cantatas and oratorios as early as 1916" (422). In 1918, she transferred to the South Philadelphia High School for Girls and immersed herself in college preparatory courses. By 1919, she sang for the Baptist Convention and was, therefore, introduced to thousands. On 18 May 1920, she assisted the great Negro tenor, Roland Hayes, in a concert for the American Academy of Music, including two numbers alone. In 1921, Marian Anderson graduated from high school.

Her church paid $600 for voice lessons with famous Italian voice teacher Giuseppe Boghetti. He taught her breathing and specific classical musicians. *Current Biography 1940* reported:

> Boghetti remembers her first audition well. It came at the end of a long, hard day's teaching when he was weary of singing and singers, and there was a tall calm girl who sang *Deep River* in the twilight and made him cry (18).

Miss Anderson came to modest celebrity as the winner over 300 contestants of a New York Philharmonic voice competition at Lewisohn Stadium in 1924. Boghetti entered her name in the competition. Discouraged, however, that few engagements followed, Marian Anderson toured Europe for several years during the 1920s and early 1930s. Eileen Southern wrote:

> Marian Anderson's debut recital in Berlin in 1933 was followed by two years of successful concertizing in the leading capitals of Europe. At Salzburg in August, 1935, an event took place which decided her future, when she sang a recital before a gathering of the most eminent musicians in the world. As customary, she sang the conventional Bach and Schubert, and ended the program with a group of Negro spirituals (422).

The tribute that followed is known among seasoned professionals. The first reaction was that of stunned silence. Then Toscanini who was present made his famous announcement, "A voice like yours is heard only once in a hundred years."

The singer, in her autobiography, *My Lord, What a Morning*, related, most colorfully, the reaction of Jean Sibelius.

> We [she and accompanist Kosti Vehanen] were greeted warmly by Sibelius and his family. I was surprised to find that he was not so tall as his photographs had indicated, but with his strong head and broad shoulders he looked like a figure chiseled out of granite. I sang one of his songs that had a German text . . . and several other pieces. When I was finished he arose, strode to my side, and threw his arms around me in a hearty embrace. "My roof is too low for you," he said, and then he called out in a loud voice to his wife, "Not coffee, but champagne" (148–149)!

A handwritten note Anderson penned, on exhibit at the University of Pennsylvania in 1997, said that Sibelius had tears in his eyes. Anderson moved many to tears, including Sol Hurok.

In 1935, the distinguished impresario Sol Hurok became her manager and remained so for the balance of her career. He heard her, by chance, one day in Paris as he ambled down the Champs Elysées toward the Salle Gaveau. "A tall, handsome Negro girl came out . . . closed her eyes and sang. Chills danced up my spine and my palms were wet," he recalled (237–238). Hurok chronicled Anderson's trials: "The Berlin manager . . . had a small concert business. He arranged for some recordings—these were later sold in Macy's for 59 cents, some for 29 cents each. He arranged a concert in Berlin which took $500 of her little ($750) fund" (240).

Hurok asked her to cable this manager; the two met with him, and Anderson found a valuable ally in Hurok who worked for her best interest, and freed her from the many mundane tasks essential to the success of a career.Hurok brought her back from Europe, according to historian John Hope Franklin, "in a veritable blaze of glory . . . regarded by many as the greatest living contralto" (390). Hurok arranged a New York City concert. At the invitation of President Franklin Delano Roosevelt, Marian Anderson became, according to the *St. Louis Post Dispatch,* "the first black to entertain at the White House . . . during the 1939 visit of Britain's King George VI" (14A).

The National Association for the Advancement of Colored People (NAACP) awarded her the famous Spingarn Medal for superior achievement. Eileen Southern wrote: "In 1940 she was awarded the Bok Medal and $10,000 by Philadelphia for 'outstanding citizenship and meritorious achievement'" (423). With this, she set up a scholarship fund for other musicians, called the Marian Anderson Award. People from around the world sought her out.

Eileen Southern also stated, "by 1941, she was one of the ten highest paid concert artists in the United States" (423). Hurok declared that she was among the top five. While he opened doors and managed her career extremely well from financial and other standpoints, he did not protect her voice from overuse. This was virtually beyond his control, he said, since she did not want to turn people down. She sang in churches and for school children, later admitting that being overbooked was a major error of judgment in her career. It took its permanent toll on her voice.

She married her childhood sweetheart, architect Orpheus Fisher, in July of 1943. He died in 1985. They had no children. Miss Anderson said: "We both felt that we wanted to raise our own children, not turn them over to nurses. Certainly, I did not want to drag a child with me on my travels . . ."(292). The enormous stresses of having a stellar career and giving children the time, energy, and patience that are so crucial to their development were a combination she did not choose. This was a personal, political, and social decision.

She and her husband lived on a 105-acre farm close to Danbury, Connecticut, called Marianna, named for Marian Anderson and her mother. The estate had two pigs, a separate recording and rehearsal studio, a horse named Brown Jug, a well-stocked kitchen, and an open door for a very few select relatives and friends. The neighbors included Caucasian opera singer Lawrence Tibbett, Lily Pons, and Geraldine Farrar (*Ebony* 1947 9). While these neighbors were her peers and apparently friendly, the contralto had great difficulty buying the farm.

Hurok related that getting the Victorian farmhouse with an 80 by 120-foot swimming pool was an extremely difficult task. Not only did Miss Anderson have to be shown farm after farm by those who had no intention of selling her a place, but she had to pay far in excess of what the farm was worth. She purchased it from a New York Stock Exchange member in 1940, before her 1943 marriage, and her architect husband later refurbished it. It was a refuge from the world, nevertheless. It was her sanctuary from her extremely heavy train travel, and a world with a clear racial divide.

Her husband also provided strong support and a nurturing environment for her. *Ebony* reported in April 1947:

> Marian Anderson has always said that an artist's life belonged to her work until she had reached the top, and before that she would not be free to marry. But she was mistaken; her best concerts were given after her marriage. Critics instantly noted a new warmth and freedom in her singing and attributed it to her marriage (10).

Anderson actually devoted what time she could to personally cooking meals for her husband and close friends, and sewed very regularly.

Her heart was equally in her work. She constantly rehearsed. Close observations of the Marian Anderson Exhibit at the University of Pennsylvania in 1997 reveal that she may not have known German, a language in which she sang or rehearsed almost daily. Had she had an opportunity for a college education, even at a black institution, she could have studied the language. Instead, she wrote the English translation of German lieder, by rote, on her sheet music.

After a great deal of hard work, Marian Anderson finally made her debut at the Metropolitan Opera on 7 January 1955. *The New York Times* reported on 9 April 1993, in her obituary:

> Mr. [Rudolph] Bing invited her to sing Ulrica in Verdi's "Ballo in Maschera." [*The Masked Ball*]. . . .
>
> "The curtain rose on the second scene," Miss Anderson said later about the evening, "and I was there on stage, mixing the witch's brew. I trembled and when the audience applauded and applauded before I could sing a note, I felt myself tightening in a knot."
>
> It did not matter that at 57 she was past her vocal prime. As Howard Taubman noted in his review in *The Times*, "Men as well as women were dabbing at their eyes," during the tumultuous ovation (n.p.).

Her major artistic moment had come too late for real victory.

The State Department sent Miss Anderson on a 10-week tour of India and the Far East between 14 September and 2 December 1957. She trav-

eled 39,000 miles, performing in 24 concerts in 14 countries. CBS television recorded the tour with Edward R. Murrow and "See It Now." ("The Lady from Philadelphia," original soundtrack of "See It Now").
Murrow, famous, also, for his "Harvest of Shame," documentary, wrote:

> In 1957, in collaboration with Fred W. Friendly, I produced a television program titled "The Lady From Philadelphia." We made that documentary . . . because we wanted the American people to know what one woman had accomplished in . . . the field of human communication (inside jacket of *Marian Anderson: He's Got the Whole World in His Hands,* RCA Victor recording 1962).

Anderson returned in virtual triumph.

The politics of her life were captured in the Negro spiritual. It was a political, social, and religious message, including the symbol of the River Jordan as the one a pilgrim crosses into death. Miss Anderson affirmed that she chose to end her programs with spirituals because of their many meanings of importance to Negro people. Over 100 Negro spirituals were in her repertoire. She sang at the inaugurals of Presidents Dwight D. Eisenhower, John F. Kennedy, and Lyndon B. Johnson. She made more than 50 farewell concerts of the world and the United States in 1964 and 1965.

For whatever she lacked in being able to endure "hand-to-hand combat," one need only look at her spirituals sung during the turbulent year of 1964: the plaintive "Lord, How Come Me Here," which questions why African Americans are on these cruel shores; the dramatic "He'll Bring It To Pass," an uplifting number on faith in the midst of adversity, and the absolutely defiant "Ride On, King Jesus!" In the 1960s, when assassinations were a way of life—John F. Kennedy, Medgar Evers, Malcolm X, and Martin Luther King, Jr.—Anderson's choice of spirituals became far more dramatic.

The Crisis offered a comment of wisdom and tribute in celebration of her retirement in its May 1965 issue:

> We salute Marian Anderson, the superbly talented and gracious Lady from Philadelphia. . . .
>
> Miss Anderson's retirement from the concert stage at her Easter recital in New York City's famed Carnegie Hall was a memorable occasion. Tickets for her farewell concert were sold out weeks before the historic event. . . .
>
> In her long career as a concert singer Miss Anderson devoted herself fully to her art but she was never unaware of her obligations to her people and her nation. She has not been one to utilize the concert hall as an overt civil rights platform. Nevertheless as a Negro and as an American, she has recognized the need to support the Fight for Freedom. She has helped raise

money for the National Association for the Advancement of Colored People and other organizations. She has aided young students seeking a career in music. Through her music and personality she has won friends for the cause of equality (281).

Marian Anderson moved the hearts of people. She made men cry. In 1978, the Kennedy Center honored her. In 1997, The University of Pennsylvania mounted an excellent exhibit on her life and work, with Web access. The exhibit quoted a 9 October 1954 comment in *The New York Times*, "Whenever there was discrimination against Miss Anderson, the real suffering was not hers, but ours. It was we who were impoverished, not she" (n.p.). Anderson helped change the world quietly. Hers was not the way of the French Revolution, but one Hurok called "a serene spirit" (4).

When the singer died on 8 April 1993, the world lost not simply one of its greatest singers of the twentieth century. Others vied for that. Marian Anderson, arguably more than any other person of the last 100 years, fought and won, with dignity, and with a series of spiritual, artistic, financial, and personal successes.

When she resigned from the concert stage, she said of her plans to devote time to serving her country in other ways: "A great and concentrated effort is needed to save the potential strength of Americans of both races" (*Pittsburgh Courier* 1). Marian Anderson struck an effective blow for civil rights without ever being offensive or abrasive.

Works Cited

"Anderson Affair, The" *Time*, 17 Apr. 1939, 23.
Anderson, Marian. *My Lord, What a Morning*. Madison: University of Wisconsin Press, 1992 (original copyright registered in 1956).
Arvey, Verna. *In One Lifetime*. Fayetteville: University of Arkansas Press, 1984. (written by the wife of black classical composer William Grant Still)
Austin, Lettie J., Lewis H. Fenderson, and Sophia P. Nelson. *The Black Man and the Promise of America*. Glenview, IL: Scott, Foresman and Company, 1970.
Bing, Sir Rudolph. *5000 Nights at the Opera*. New York: Doubleday, 1972.
Bradford, Henry Jr., Ed.D. Telephone interview with author. 16 Sept. 1997.
Current Biography Yearbook 1940. ed. Maxine Block, New York: H. W. Wilson Company, 1940. [Entry on Marian Anderson, 17–19].
Current Biography Yearbook 1950. ed. Anna Rothe, New York: H. W. Wilson Company, 1950. [Entry on Marian Anderson, 8–10].
"Day at Marian Anderson's Country Hideaway, A," *Ebony*, Apr. 1947, 9–14.
"First Lady of Song Bids Concert World Farewell," *The Pittsburgh Courier*, 7 Nov. 1964, II, 1.
Folkhart, Burt. "Pioneering Singer Marian Anderson Dies," *Los Angeles Times*, 9 Apr. 1993, A, 1:6.

Franklin, John Hope. *From Slavery to Freedom.* New York: Knopf, 1947.

Green, Mildred Denby. Entry on Marian Anderson in *Black Women in America: An Historical Encyclopedia,* ed. Darlene Clark Hine. Brooklyn: Carlson Publishing Company, 1993, 29–33.

Hurok, Sol. <www.library.upenn.edu/special/gallery/anderson/index.html> (in collaboration with Ruth Goode) *Impresario: A Memoir.* New York: Random House, 1946.

"Jim Crow Concert Hall," *Time,* 6 Mar. 1939, 39.

Keiler, Allan. "DAR Ruled in 1932: 'White Artists Only,'"

———. *Wall Street Journal,* 3 Apr. 1997, A, 19:2.

"Lady from Philadelphia, The," *The Crisis,* May. 1965, 281.

Lanker, Brian. *I Dream a World: Portraits of Black Women Who Changed America.* New York: Steward, Tabori, and Chang, 1989, 158–159.

"Marian Anderson: He's Got the Whole World in His Hands and 18 Other Spirituals," RCA Victor recording, 1962 (personal collection of author).

"Marian Anderson Is Dead at 96; Singer Shattered Racial Barriers," *The New York Times,* 9 Apr. 1993, A,1:4. (courtesy of Dave Bezotte)

Program, March 1954 concert at Alabama A. and M. College, Normal. (Personal collection of author.)

Rice, Patricia. "Marian Anderson Dies; Pioneer of Opera, Rights," *St. Louis Post Dispatch,* 9 Apr. 1993, A,1:5.

Sandage, Scott A. Entry on Marian Anderson in *The Oxford Companion to African American Literature,* ed. William Andrews, Frances Smith Foster, and Trudier Harris. New York: Oxford University Press, 1997, 16.

Southern, Eileen. *The Music of Black Americans: A History.* New York: W. W. Norton Company, 1971.

Stokes, Anson Phelps. *Art and The Color Line.* Washington, D. C., Phelps-Stokes Foundation, Oct. 1939.

Tape of Marian Anderson's spirituals, 1961 and 1964 (courtesy of Dr. Gloria Melton).

"The Lady From Philadelphia: Marian Anderson," original soundtrack of "See It Now," by Edward R. Murrow and Fred W. Friendly, RCA Victor recording, 1958 (gift of Bart Lanier Stafford, III).

Leontyne Price as Bess and William Warfield as Porgy. Courtesy of the Billy Rose Theatre Collection, New York Public Library for the Performing Arts. Astor, Lenox and Tilden Foundations.

Maya Angelou at a reception for the Breen European tour of *Porgy and Bess,* circa 1954. Courtesy of the Lawrence and Lee Theatre Research Institute, The Ohio State University.

"Porgy and Bess," October 8, 1941. Todd Duncan as Porgy and Anne Brown as Bess in Cheryl Crawford's production at the Majestic Theatre. Wisconsin Center for Film and Theater Research.

Chapter VI

Five Interpreters of *Porgy and Bess*

Oh, Lord, I'm on my way!

—Porgy

These words, passionately sung by the crippled beggar, Porgy, conclude one of the world's great operas. Porgy heads out for New York, determined to have Bess who has just left him for Sportin' Life. It is a majestic ending.

A great deal of controversy has surrounded DuBose Heyward and George and Ira Gershwin's *Porgy and Bess,* the opera that first exploded on the stage of the Alvin Theatre in New York City on 10 October 1935. One controversy centered on the racial nature of the casting; another, on authorship. Yet another focused on how Negroes were stereotyped. The Theatre Guild produced *Porgy and Bess.* Based on Dorothy and DuBose Heyward's novel-turned-play, *Porgy,* the opera had the good fortune to have been produced by those who also mounted the play in October of 1927. Consistency of experience was valuable, but experience, alone, did not cause the original to be highly successful.

Of the play *Porgy,* Edith J. R. Isaacs wrote in her book, *The Negro in the American Theatre:*

> *Porgy* was produced by the Theatre Guild with Rouben Mamoulian directing. It was the story—panoramic, melodramatic, sordid, but both human and theatrical, of life in the waterside district in Charleston—Catfish Row—once the center of aristocratic life, now down-trodden as only a Southern, urban Negro tenement can be. The leading actors in the play were Frank Wilson as Porgy, Georgette Harvey as Maria, keeper of the cook shop, Jack

Carter as Crown (played in the revival by Paul Robeson), Wesley Hill as Jake, the captain of the fishing fleet, Rose McClendon as Serena, Evelyn Ellis as Bess, Leigh Whipper doubling in the roles of the undertaker and the crab man, A. B. Comathiere as Simon Frazier, the lawyer, Richard Huey as Mingo, and Percy Verwayne as Sporting Life (84).

These were the *crème de la crème* of black actors in the American theatre in 1927. Sixty-six members constituted the cast of the play.

Porgy and Bess came nine years later and attracted a host of celebrities in 1935. "The original production, which cost $17,000 a week to operate, had 124 performances and lost $70,000—the entire production cost" (Atkinson 337). The work was, in the most optimistic reflection, a moderate artistic success, but a financial failure.

William Warfield offers the reason in a personal interview:

> I was told that when Gershwin wrote it, he wanted it done at the Metropolitan Opera, and the Metropolitan Opera was interested, but they did not want to do it with the stipulation that Gershwin made that it had to be an all-black cast. That was before anybody was ready to put blacks into grand opera. They had Helen Jefferson and Lawrence Tibbitt [Caucasian]. They were their big stars. So The Met was very anxious to put it on and had their big stars to put on black face, and the chorus to put on black face. But Gershwin would not permit that—so his recourse was Broadway—and that was heavy fare for Broadway. The crowds were not interested in something like that (28 Feb. 1991).

Caucasian singer Al Jolson, famous for his "Mammy" and burnt cork make-up, wanted to play Porgy in black face. Music and drama critics had their opinions, as well.

Virgil Thomson, a major music critic who had his own *Four Saints in Three Acts* with an all-black cast of 1934 to protect, denounced the 1935 production of *Porgy and Bess:* "It is crooked folklore and halfway opera" (quoted in Alpert 118). Thomson probably resented the three Steinway grand pianos in the Gershwin penthouse. Other major drama critics, including Brooks Atkinson of *The New York Times,* thought the work superb.

Hall Johnson, the distinguished composer/arranger and conductor of the famous Hall Johnson Choir, wrote that the work lacked credibility and authenticity, even though he liked it:

> Now, we can believe that a boastful bully like Crown, in the excitement of a dreadful hurricane, might stalk fearlessly among his panic-stricken brethren and jeer at their prayers to a God who, for the moment, at least, seems to have nothing but scorn for everything weak. It is not easy, how-

ever, to believe that Sportin' Life (a genuine product of Catfish Row, for all his smart talk about New York) could be so entirely liberated from that superstitious awe of Divinity which even the most depraved Negro never quite loses (192).

The work did not sit easy on many hearts and minds.

The controversy surrounding casting extended to authorship. Verna Arvey, the brilliant pianist and wife of black composer William Grant Still, believed:

> Gershwin felt that he was not "borrowing" any musical material exactly. He was listening and absorbing, then transferring the Negro idiom to his own musical speech. Yet we might assume that sometimes there actually was unconscious borrowing, not only in the *I Got Rhythm* episode, but in others. How else can the similarity of the opening notes of his *Summertime* (in *Porgy and Bess*) to the opening notes of the *St. Louis Blues* be explained (Still 25).

George Gershwin died, tragically, in 1937 of a brain tumor and was not able to defend himself against this accusation.

Conversely, William Warfield, a teenager in 1935, was mesmerized by the original:

> I was visiting friends of mine and their relatives in Jersey, and we came to New York that Saturday afternoon. I was strolling on Broadway and looked up and saw *Porgy and Bess* and we had enough money and I went in to see it—Todd Duncan and Anne Brown were in it. I remember afterwards that I just walked away. I heard noises. It sounded like they were all diffuse. I was so tremendously taken by what I had seen, not only the *Porgy and Bess* itself, but the people and the performances and the music and all of that and I've never forgotten that experience (28 Feb. 1991).

Fifty years of struggle went into getting *Porgy and Bess* to the Metropolitan Opera. Cheryl Crawford sponsored a "bargain basement version" in 1942, which was more financially successful and got better reviews than the 1935 original. She cut the length of the work, reduced the number in the orchestra and made other significant changes.

In the 1940s, Dick Campbell took the production on tour through the auspices of the United Service Organization (USO) Camp Shows. He recalled:

> I did the unusual with *Porgy and Bess*. The planes—the C47 planes could not fly that many people at one time. We were only permitted to fly in C47s and they could only have eighteen passengers. So, I produced three companies

of *Porgy and Bess* with only eighteen people each. Each of those companies was directed (the chorus, i.e.) by Eva Jessye who was in the original *Porgy and Bess* (21 Feb. 1991).

Perhaps the government sent Campbell to entertain Negro troops with exotic fare.

The Robert Breen tour of Europe in 1952–56 brought rave reviews. It also brought continued resentment, especially from some black people who continued to bemoan the stereotypes. One African American to sing its praises was a dancer on the tour, Maya Angelou. Early in the opera, Crown, the bully, murders Robbins with a fish-hook in a game of dice. Serena, his widow, rushes to cover his body and place a collection saucer on it for the inhabitants of Catfish Row to help bury him. Of the funeral laments, welling in mounting terror as the hurricane comes, Ms. Angelou remembered:

> There were two or three of those [great choral scenes] which were so grand . . . of course, Serena's soliloquy, that aria, "My man's gone now, ain't no use in listening for his tired footsteps climbing up the stairs . . ." (21 Feb. 1991).

And of those funeral laments, William Warfield recalled:

> I think that one of the very authentic parts of Gershwin's writing was the funeral laments. Gershwin was tremendously taken with the sounds that he heard [on Folly Island near Charleston, South Carolina]—blacks singing together. Gershwin was able to capture a great deal of the ethnic feeling and he superimposed upon that a great deal of very fine writing with that story scene going on while they are singing, "The Lord's Gonna Shake the Heavens and the Earth." I think it is really fantastic what he'd done there. And then later on, "Clara, Clara, Don't You Be Downhearted," that very little plaintive song. That just sets a tremendous mood of quietness after the storm which leads into the return of Crown after the killing (28 Feb. 1991).

Angelou actually spoke of the singing "in those great throats" (21 Feb. 1991).

In 1957, Samuel Goldwyn paid $650,000 cash and ten percent of the gross receipts for the rights to film it (Keyser and Ruszkowski 55). Otto Preminger, considered unsympathetic to African Americans, directed, with Sidney Poitier as Porgy, Dorothy Dandridge as Bess, and Sammy Davis, Jr. as Sportin' Life. In 1974, Clamma Dale and Donnie Ray Albert co-starred in a production of the work at the Houston Grand Opera.

By the time Simon Estes and Grace Bumbry finally stood on the stage of the Metropolitan Opera in Lincoln Center in 1985, under James

Levine's baton, at least five African American pioneers had played significant roles in that miracle: Todd Duncan, Anne Wiggins Brown, Leontyne Price, William Warfield, and Maya Angelou. Many more pioneers could claim credit as well.

Todd Duncan

When Todd Duncan, baritone, died at the age of 95 in 1998, he was still teaching singing. It was he who created the role of Porgy, the crippled beggar on his knees, hopelessly in love with a "wayward" woman in the 1935 production. Sources differ as to whether or not Duncan was 30 or 32. In 1936, the opera went on tour in Philadelphia, Pittsburgh, and Chicago. It was to end in March in Washington, D. C. with a week of performances at Washington's National Theatre, a theatre with a long history of segregated seating as well as no seating of "colored" people. This was common in America at that time. Hollis Alpert wrote of Todd Duncan:

> He announced he had no intention of playing at a theatre he himself would have been unable to attend. When Anne Brown took the same position, a crisis confronted the Theatre Guild and [S. E.] Cochran [manager of the National]. Duncan kept it boiling by hiring a secretary and dashing off letters to such personages as Eleanor Roosevelt and Ralph Bunche (123).

Cochran offered a compromise: Negroes could come for the Wednesday and Saturday matinees. Duncan would not budge. Then Cochran offered that Negroes could occupy the balcony for each performance. Neither was palatable to Duncan.

> The Musicians' Union entered the fray by threatening to fine him $10,000 and suspend him for a year, but Duncan held firm. Nothing would do, he said, other than that black people be allowed to buy tickets for any seat in the house (Alpert 123).

Duncan won and large numbers of African Americans attended *Porgy and Bess* at the National in 1936. This is one of many instances of segregated seating or no seating of blacks that was changed by the sheer will of the two main singers.

Born 12 February 1903, in Danville, Kentucky, Todd Duncan learned piano from his mother. He attended Butler University in Indianapolis, majoring in English, but studying music. He graduated in 1925, landing a job at the Municipal College for Negroes in Louisville (Nash and Turner 67).

In 1930, he earned a master's at Columbia University Teachers College and was named a professor at Howard University in Washington, D. C., where he remained for 15 years. Duncan was in a 1934 production of Mascagni's "Cavalleria Rusticana," with the Aeolian Opera (Kozinn 2 Mar. 1998 n.p.). Olin Downes, a white music critic, was in the audience.

In 1935, George Gershwin selected Duncan, at the suggestion of Olin Downes, to sing the role of Porgy. "Mr. Duncan said that Gershwin offered him the role after hearing him sing 12 bars of an Italian aria, accompanying himself at the piano" (Kozinn n.p.). Ironically, Duncan had no idea of Gershwin's stature. His lack of awareness notwithstanding, the role of Porgy led to Duncan being offered the role of Bosambo in Edgar Wallace's *The Sun Never Sets* at London's Drury Lane Theatre (Nash and Turner 67). From there, he became the Lord's General in Vernon Duke's *Cabin in the Sky*, a play and film, in 1940. In 1949, three years before the movie based on Alan Paton's *Cry the Beloved Country*, Duncan was Stephen Kumalo, in Kurt Weill and Maxwell Anderson's *Lost in the Stars*, an opera based on Paton's novel.

Nash and Turner observe:

> In 1945 Duncan became the first African-American to be hired by a major American opera company, singing Tonio in Leoncavallo's *I Pagliacci* and Escamillo in Bizet's *Carmen* at the New York Opera. In addition, he acted in the films *Syncopation* (1942) and *Unchained* (1955) (67).

Nash and Turner also alluded to Duncan's reaction when one critic in New Mexico asked in the newspaper why he was performing in German and French when he didn't understand what he was singing. Duncan called the critic on the telephone and asked "Wie geht's?" The critic was silent. Duncan further spoke in German for about two minutes, after which the critic admitted: "I don't know what you're talking about." Duncan retorted: "I've been talking to you in German. This is Todd Duncan. I'm the one you said didn't know what I was talking about, and I see *you're* the one who doesn't know German," after which Duncan hung up (Nash and Turner 68).

Duncan's life was filled with many appearances in opera and other musical ventures. He was still teaching when he died.

Anne Wiggins Brown

Gershwin changed the name of his opera from *Porgy* to *Porgy and Bess* when he heard the 20-year-old Anne Wiggins Brown sing in 1935, yet this major player, who created the role of Bess, often has been given only a footnote in the annals of music history. Gershwin was so impressed with his "perfect" Bess that he rewrote Act III of the work in order to have her sing "Summertime," a song written for Clara who has a baby. Gershwin gave Brown equal billing with Todd Duncan.

J. Weldon Norris wrote:

> Currently a citizen of Norway, Anne Wiggins Brown was born to Dr. Harry F. Brown and Mary Wiggins Brown in Baltimore, Maryland, in 1915. (*The New York Times* says 1912.) At an early age, she was obsessed with being a star on the stage, although she realized that Blacks were cast only as servants or in degrading comic roles.... Her mother attempted to enroll Anne in a local private Catholic school.... When school officials discovered that the family was not Spanish, but Black, however, Anne was denied admission even though her father was a prominent Baltimore physician (170).

Of Scottish-Irish, Cherokee Indian, and African American descent, Anne Wiggins Brown has been accused of "passing" for white. Indeed, she left America for Norway in 1948, out of intense frustration, and remained there, taking a Norwegian husband, for 20 years.

Barry Singer observed:

> At 16, Ms. Brown was the first African-American vocalist admitted to the Juilliard School of Music. At 19, in a swipe at her domineering father, she secretly married a young medical student. The marriage didn't last. [It ended after two years.] At 20, she won the Margaret McGill scholarship at Juilliard, presented to the school's finest female singer. Then at 21, as a second-year graduate student in 1933, she read that George Gershwin was writing an opera "about Negroes in South Carolina" (39).

Brown wrote to Gershwin and two days later, Gershwin's secretary phoned. Not wishing to sing a spiritual, Brown carried only classical music to the audition. Gershwin wanted to hear her sing what is now her signature song, "City Called Heaven," which she sang for him *a cappella*. Gershwin was silent he was so stunned. Then he advised her to make that spiritual hers. Gershwin also indicated that Bess was "a very dark woman," but he could accept a "cafe au lait" (McLellan D1). Brown did not escape the color fetish that consumed Broadway, Hollywood, and much of the entire culture, especially the first six decades of the twentieth century.

Brown was an artistic success as Bess, although the financial failure of the 1935 production is legend. Todd Duncan recalled:

> I first met her when she had just finished at Juilliard and we were working together on an all Negro production of "I Pagliacci" in New York. She was

Nedda and I was the Prologue. I thought she was a very intelligent girl, well schooled and an excellent musician with a beautiful soprano voice. The next time we worked together was with George Gershwin. We became very good friends—not close but cordial, a fine relationship onstage and off. She gave a beautiful dinner for me when I came to Norway on a concert tour, and I entertained her when she came to Washington (McLellan D1).

Brown's charm is legendary.

Her second marriage was to a Dr. Jacob Petit, by whom she had a daughter, Paula. Then Brown came back to Broadway for the 1942 *Porgy and Bess*, which Cheryl Crawford mounted. Between 1942 and 1948, Brown appeared at Carnegie Hall and with the Los Angeles Philharmonic (Norris 171). In 1948, she did an exceptionally well received European tour. "Divorced from her second husband, she was married to Norwegian ski jumper Thorlief Schkelderup" (Norris 171). Other sources say that he was also a lawyer. They had a daughter, Vaar, meaning "springtime" in Norwegian. Her third marriage lasted 21 years (McLellan D1).

By 1953, she developed respiratory problems on tour, which affected her singing career. Asthma ended it. She has written her autobiography, *Sang Fra Frossen Gren*, a best-seller that became a Norwegian television documentary (Norris 171 and 172). *The Washington Post* wrote "The best account of her life can be found in *Sang Fra Frossen Gren*" ("Song From a Frozen Branch") . . . which has not been translated into English" (McLellan Dl). Brown has two daughters and four grandchildren. She has rarely returned to the United States, but one of her more celebrated visits came when she and Todd Duncan visited Simon Estes and Grace Bumbry backstage for the 1985 Metropolitan Opera production of *Porgy and Bess*.

William Warfield

According to Ploski and Marr, William Warfield is one of the most distinguished concert baritones in the world today (862). Leonard de Paur who conducted William Warfield and Leontyne Price in the RCA recording of *Porgy and Bess* in 1963 exclaimed: "Leontyne Price was the best Bess, ever, and so acclaimed was Warfield [in the role of Joe] that directors of a moviehouse stopped *Show Boat* [1966] once to allow him to sing a few more bars" (25 Feb. 1991).

Warfield played Porgy in the 1952 Breen production and is, arguably, the best known singer in the role. He appeared in several revivals of the opera and said to me in 1991:

Five Interpreters of *Porgy and Bess* 99

Porgy and Bess had to do with black life and the romance between this beggar and so-called wayward woman and the clash of real love against carnal love. The question that it poses is how can a beautiful, soulful love overcome a carnal passion. Within Bess's statement, she said when they were together she recognized the tremendous beauty of what they had, but she seemed to be completely hopeless, having to do with "when he [Crown] takes hold of me with his hot hands," It was like an obsession or like feelings she had about dope. Everything went out the window. (28 Feb. 1991).

The romance on stage must have been infectious, for William Warfield married Leontyne Price on 31 August 1952. After years of separation, they divorced in 1973 (*Current Biography 1978* 332).

Born in 1920 in West Helena, Arkansas, Warfield received his training in voice and music at the Eastman School of Music at the University of Rochester, where he earned his baccalaureate degree in 1942 (Byrd 130). Ploski and Marr wrote that he received his A.B. while in the army "where he worked in intelligence because of his fluency in Italian, French and German" (862). In 1955, he toured as a singer for the U.S. State Department.

> The following year he made his third such trip—a recital tour through Africa, the Near East and Western Europe. In 1958 concerts took Warfield around the world twice. In between these tours as a cultural emissary, the baritone has won acclaim in countless concerts and recitals throughout the Americas and Europe . . . (inset of the 1963 RCA Victor recording of *Porgy and Bess*).

Warfield also appeared on a number of television shows, including NBC's 1957 televised production of Marc Connelly's *Green Pastures*, where he played "De Lawd." In 1960, he was a soloist in Mendelssohn's *Elijah*.

Byrd continues:

> In 1990 Warfield retired as chair of the department of voice at the University of Illinois at Urbana-Champaign, where he has been a member of the faculty since 1975. Warfield's many honors include the Governor's Award for the State of Illinois, induction into Illinois' Lincoln Academy, and a Grammy Award for his narration of Aaron Copland's *Lincoln Portrait*. He is the author of an autobiography entitled *William Warfield: My Music and My Life* (1991) (130).

Warfield is still active in his retirement.

Leontyne Price

Leontyne Price, who rose to fame as Bess in the Breen production, is frequently referred to as "La Prima Donna Assoluta," the absolute first lady of opera. Others have argued that the title goes to Beverly Sills. Whatever may be one's opinion, it is an indisputable fact that Leontyne Price is one of the finest lyric sopranos of the twentieth century. Audiences stand and cheer when she merely strides on stage. I saw her on 3 October 1981 in Hancher Auditorium at the University of Iowa. Audiences went wild when she sang the aria of Cio-Cio-San from Puccini's *Madame Butterfly*.

Inetta Harris, Assistant Professor of Fine Arts and Choirmaster for the Echoes from Heaven Gospel Choir of Michigan Technological University, who played Maria and Serena in *Porgy and Bess* with the Deutsche Opera in Berlin, and who cited Ms. Price as her mentor, wrote:

> The great Leontyne Price has long shared a profound and definitive relationship with the American masterwork, *Porgy and Bess*. From the very outset of the two-year [Breen] tour, audiences and critics, alike, heralded the arrival of a truly remarkably beautiful voice which seemed to emanate from the very essence of Bess, herself. Miss Price embued the role with a dignity, grace, elegance and sense of style which had heretofore been unheard. She was consistently cited for the dramatic intensity and sincerity which her characterization brought to the role of Bess, thus elevating the opera to a new standard of acceptance in both Europe and America. While we do not have a complete recording, the excerpts originally issued by RCA in 1963 with Leontyne Price and William Warfield set the standard of performance by which this opera is still measured (25 Mar. 1999).

Many agree with Harris.

Also of the Breen production of *Porgy and Bess,* Hollis Alpert stated:

> *Porgy and Bess* looked to be well established at the Ziegfeld, helped by notices such as that of Walter Kerr: "I am surprised that Berlin, Vienna, Paris and London are still standing. For this is surely the most restless, urgent and shatteringly explosive production of the Gershwin masterpiece we have yet had . . .
>
> Leontyne Price was the Bess and it would be lunacy to ask for a better one." (184).

Thomas Anderson, who was on that tour, spoke to me of Price's range and dramatic color.

Dominique-Rene deLerma wrote:

> In April of 1953, Price had, in fact, performed "Summertime" from *Porgy and Bess* in a broadcast gala . . . but her formal debut [at the Metropolitan Opera] came with Verdi's *Il Trovatore* (27 Jan. 1961), when, in the role of Leonora, she won forty-two minutes of cheers from the audience (943).

Born 10 February 1927, in Laurel, Mississippi, Price graduated from high school in 1949, and then studied at Juilliard, after a wealthy patron gave her a scholarship. However, Price's finances were so meager that she thought she would have to leave, due to the high cost of living in New York City. Virgil Thomson, looking for singers for the 1952 Paris revival of his *Four Saints in Three Acts,* with an all-black cast, selected Leontyne Price for Cecelia. "From June 1952 to June 1954, as Bess in a revival of Gershwin's *Porgy and Bess* she appeared before packed houses, both in the United States and under State Department auspices in Europe" *Current Biography 1978* 330). Critical reception for her extraordinary performance was astonishing.

She was the first black to appear in opera on television in 1955 as Floria Tosca in NBC's production of Puccini's *Tosca* (*Current Biography 1978* 330). Thereafter, she appeared frequently on NBC in such works as Mozart's frequently performed *The Magic Flute* and his *Don Giovanni.*

She starred in Verdi's *Aida* with the San Francisco Opera and the Chicago Lyric Opera as well as the American Opera Theater. Price made her debut as Aida at Milan's La Scala in May 1960. "One Italian critic rhapsodized: 'Our great Verdi would have found her the ideal Aida'" (*Current Biography 1978* 330).

Rudolf Bing chose her to open the new Metropolitan Opera House as Cleopatra in Samuel Barber's *Antony and Cleopatra* in 1966; Barber wrote the work especially for Miss Price. Eventually, Leontyne Price gave 118 Metropolitan Opera performances. But, in the 1970s, according to her agent, she reduced her performances on the road to ten a year (telephone conversation with author). Her career lasted almost 25 years. She holds 18 Grammy Awards and the Presidential Medal of Freedom (Lanker 44). She excelled in German, Spanish, French, and Slavic works as well as the Negro spiritual (deLerma 943). Only pure tenacity and God-given talent could have permitted any woman such achievement against the odds.

Maya Angelou

Perhaps best known in the last seven years of the twentieth century as the Presidential Poet because of her participation in President Clinton's 1993 inaugural ceremonies, Maya Angelou's "stage credits . . . included a stint as a featured dancer in a State-department production of George Gershwin's opera *Porgy and Bess,* with which she toured twenty-two nations in Europe and Africa" (*Current Biography Yearbook 1994* 26).

Maya Angelou joined the Breen cast in Venice in 1954. She found dancing and singing every night more like a party than work. She had danced at a night spot, the Purple Onion, when the company had performed in San Francisco. Martha Flowers had seen her and brought others to see her as well (Alpert 189). She was 25 in 1954. Angelou recalls this experience:

> I was overwhelmed by being in the presence of such erudite, sophisticated, talented and trained singer/actors. They had been together so long. They were knit as closely as good tapestry, and they were kind enough to loosen their threads and allow me in. That was enough had we been playing in Lima, Ohio. I would not have been any less taken over by their kindness and their true sophistication. I don't mean snobbery, but true sophistication, but then to add to that the fact that I, me, Maya, was actually in Venice, Italy—that almost immobilized me, with the prior sensation that I could actually walk up and down canals and hear men singing in Italian, and children looking at me with such a mixture of surprise and admiration and fear (21 Feb. 1991.)

Maya Angelou is six feet tall, with a deep bass voice that has had years of training. Most people look at her with admiration and surprise.

Angelou considers *Porgy and Bess* a romance, but in a different sense than Warfield. She elaborates:

> *Porgy and Bess* cannot be gauged alongside other works of similar quality because it is "a romance." It's black. And so it's one-of-a-kind. And it's a cheap out. It says I will not put this beside *La Bohême*. I will not put it beside *Paint Your Wagon*. I will not put this beside *Oklahoma*. This is a one-of-a-kind, being black and all (21 Feb. 1991).

Angelou also takes issue with W. E. B. DuBois that DuBose Heyward would have been drummed out of town for writing such a play about black people, claiming:

> There were white men who subsequently wrote *Tobacco Road,* but white writers did not choose to write about black men and women because we were other. They didn't have the courage to see us as ourselves. And because of that separation, they could write a romance, and I don't mean that positively. *Porgy and Bess* became a romance for Heyward and his wife and for the Gershwins (21 Feb. 1991).

Born in St. Louis, Missouri, on 4 April 1928, with the name Marguerite Johnson, Angelou has overcome many obstacles. Her mother was Vivian Johnson (Baxter) and she and Angelou's father divorced when Maya was three. Reared in Stamps, Arkansas, as a result of her mother's choice, Angelou experienced the pain of dislocation. As a result of many dynamics surrounding a traumatic event in her childhood, Angelou chose to be mute for a number of years. She had voice, as she often tells audiences, but chose not to speak. Her rise to being a major poet, autobiographer, dancer, director, and speaker is a true Horatio Alger story.

The impact of *Porgy and Bess* on world culture is immeasurable. It is an indescribable artistic experience for which many artists deserve credit. It was one that also required dogged struggle. Five of those who never gave up and made *Porgy and Bess* an American masterpiece are Todd Duncan, Anne Wiggins Brown, William Warfield, Leontyne Price, and Maya Angelou. The contributions of the many who were a part of this magnificent opera will last long after the twentieth century.

Endnote

Other pioneers deserve credit: John Bubbles, chosen by George Gershwin to create the role of Sportin' Life, Warren Coleman (Crown), Ruby Elzy (Serena), Cab Calloway (Sportin' Life in the Breen production), Martha Flowers (Bess), McHenry Boatwright (Crown in the RCA recording), Joyce Bryant (Bess), Brock Peters (Crown), Edward Matthews (Jake), Avon Long (Sportin' Life in the 1942 revival), Etta Moten Barnett (Bess in one 1942 production), Abbie Mitchell (Clara) and Leonard de Paur (arranger/composer for the RCA recording). In July of 1986, Glyndebourne, England was the site of a revival of *Porgy and Bess*, an uncut version, directed by Trevor Nunn. Willard White, a Jamaican bass, played Porgy, and Cynthia Haymon was Bess. In 1993, PBS showcased the Nunn version.

Works Cited

Alpert, Hollis. *The Life and Times of Porgy and Bess.* New York: Knopf, 1990.
Angelou, Maya. Telephone interview with author. 21 Feb. 1991.
Atkinson, Brooks. *Broadway.* New York: MacMillan, 1970.
Byrd, Rudolph. *Generations in Black and White* (photographs by Carl Van Vechten from the James Weldon Johnson Memorial Collection). Athens: University of Georgia Press, 1993.
Campbell, Dick. Telephone interview with author. 21 Feb. 1991.
Current Biography Yearbook 1942, ed. Maxine Block. New York: H. W. Wilson Company, 1942 [entry on Todd Duncan 223–224].
Current Biography Yearbook 1961, ed. Charles Moritz. New York: H. W. Wilson Company, 1961 [entry on Leontyne Price 374–375].
Current Biography Yearbook 1978, ed. Charles Moritz. New York: H. W. Wilson Company, 1978 [entry on Leontyne Price 329–332].
Current Biography Yearbook 1994, ed. Judith Graham. New York: H. W. Wilson Company, [entry on Maya Angelou 25–29].
Current Biography Yearbook 1998, ed. Elizabeth Schick. New York: H. W. Wilson Company, 1998 [entry on Todd Duncan 640].
deLerma, Dominique-Rene, entry on Leontyne Price in *Black Women in America: An Historical Encyclopedia,* ed. Darlene Clark Hine. Brooklyn: Carlson Publishing Company, 1993, 941–943.
dePaur, Leonard. Telephone interview with author. 24 Feb. 1991.
Devine, Lawrence. "He's Got Plenty of Something," *Detroit Free Press,* 4 Feb. 1998, 1 and 4C.
"Gershwin's *Porgy and Bess,*" RCA Victor recording, 1963. [Leontyne Price as Bess and William Warfield as Porgy]
Harris, Inetta L. "Here It Is." Personal email. 25 Mar. 1999.
Isaacs, Edith J. R. "The Negro in the American Theatre: A Record of Achievement," *Theatre Arts,* August 1942, 494–541.
———. *The Negro in the American Theatre.* New York: Theatre Arts, 1947.

Johnson, Hall. "Porgy and Bess—A Folk Opera," in *Anthology of the Afro-American in the Theatre,* ed. Lindsay Patterson. Cornwell Heights, Pennsylvania: The Association for the Study of Afro-American Life and History, 1978, 185–196.

Keyser, Lester J. and Andre H. Ruszkowski. *The Cinema of Sidney Poitier: The Black Man's Changing Role on the American Screen.* San Diego: A. S. Barnes, 1980.

Kozinn, Allan. "Todd Duncan, 95; Sang Porgy and Helped Desegregate Opera," *The New York Times,* 2 Mar. 1998, n.p.

Lanker, Brian. *I Dream a World: Portraits of Black Women Who Changed America.* New York: Stewart, Tabori, and Chang, 1989.

McLellan, Joseph. "The Bess Years of Her Life," *Washington Post,* 12 Jan. 1994, D1.

Nash, Elizabeth and Patricia Turner. "The Master Singer: An Interview with Todd Duncan," *American Legacy,* Fall 1998, 67–71 (courtesy of Cecelia Ann Jeffries).

Norris, J. Weldon. Entry on Anne Wiggins Brown in *Black Women in America: An Historical Encyclopedia,* ed. Darlene Clark Hine, et al. Brooklyn: Carlson Publishing Company, 1993, 170–172.

Ploski, Harry A. and Warren Marr II. *The Negro Almanac.* New York: Bellwether Company, 1976.

Singer, Barry. "On Hearing Her Sing, Gershwin Made 'Porgy' 'Porgy and Bess,'" *The New York Times,* 29 Mar. 1998, 39 [on Anne Wiggins Brown].

Still, Judith Anne. *William Grant Still and the Fusion of Cultures in American Music.* Flagstaff, Arizona: the Master-Player Library, 1972 (courtesy of Judith Anne Still).

Warfield, William. Telephone interview with author. 28 Feb. 1991.

"We Loves You, Porgy," *Newsweek,* 18 Feb. 1985, 75.

Woll, Allen. *Black Musical Theatre: From Coontown to Dreamgirls.* Baton Rouge: Louisiana State University Press, 1989.

The Tempest, 1945. Canada Lee as Caliban. Produced by Cheryl Crawford, directed by Margaret Webster, photo by Eileen Darby, N.Y. Wisconsin Center for Film and Theater Research.

Chapter VII

Swifter than a Weaver's Shuttle: The Days of Canada Lee

My days are swifter than a weaver's shuttle.

—*The Book of Job*

Four thousand mourners crowded into Harlem's Salem Methodist Church on 13 May 1952. Six thousand more lined the streets of Seventh Avenue. Canada Lee was dead, dead before his time. Gone at 45, this pioneer actor had given his life as an activist. The working-class man and woman at the funeral sat next to such theatre luminaries as Oscar Hammerstein, II, Noble Sissle, Brooks Atkinson, Dick Campbell, Perry Watkins, Frank Silvera, Sidney Poitier, Frederick O'Neal, and Arnold Moss. Lee's first wife, Juanita Canegata, and Frances Lee, his widow, were in attendance, as well.

It was a fitting tribute for an actor who gave too much to political causes, including his health, his elaborate home, and his finances. What ironic forces contributed to the early death of this pugilist, performer, and politician? Lee demanded roles on stage and screen that gave dignity to the Negro. He fought for soldiers of color and their rights. He attended civil rights rallies. He acted in and produced controversial plays. On 31 January 1946, Lee delivered to Congress 25,000 signatures asking for the ouster of Mississippi senator, Theodore G. Bilbo. As a result of speaking out too many times, the actor was blacklisted.

Fellow actor Kevin O'Morrison remembers Lee's last days:

> I called him to see him regularly . . . to talk with him as he lay under a sheet in the small, dark room to the rear of #235 [a parlor floor apartment on West

4th Street, New York City]. I came by to try to make him laugh, to sing old songs with him and other friends who fell by . . . making the small room seem even smaller, as we watched Canada's once-magnificent body waste under the sheet that covered his nakedness to just above his loins. Sometimes I succeeded in making him laugh—and when I did, the robustness of his laughter made it even more difficult to believe that we were at a death watch (25 Feb. 1980).

A death watch it was in more than one sense. Stefan Kanfer argued: "Overlooked by almost every theatrical or film historian, unmentioned by such retentive and bitter victims as Alvah Bessie and Dalton Trumbo, Lee is the Othello of the blacklist . . . its most afflicted and ignored victim . . ."(179).

Born Leonard Lionel Cornelius Canegata in New York on 3 May 1907, to James Cornelius and Lydia (Whaley) Canegata, Lee sprang from West Indian descent. His grandfather was an importer and ship owner in the West Indies. Lee had extraordinary advantages, including violin lessons, which he began at the age of seven with J. Rosamond Johnson, a distinguished African American composer. At 14, Canada Lee ran away from home to the Saratoga races and became a jockey at Belmont, Aqueduct, Jamaica, and on the Canadian circuit (*Current Biography 1944* 394). Overweight ended his jockey career, and Lee trained to be a prizefighter, winning 90 out of 100 amateur fights, as well as the title of national amateur lightweight.

At the age of 18, the athlete/musician married Juanita Waller, an African American, in December of 1925. Bart Lanier Stafford, III, wrote me:

> It happens that I worked for many years with Juanita Canegata, Canada Lee's wife, in the Department of Welfare [in New York City]. She was a super lady, in the conventional sense of the word, meek and mild and obliging. . . . [T]here was a son who was supposed to be very bright (18 Sept. 1977).

Stafford also remembered in a letter of 6 April 1982:

> Juanita Canegata is truly a genuine lady of the old school. . . . I can imagine her now in hat and gloves and starched little white collar and cuffs on her rather sedate dress . . . softspoken and cultured, she stands out among all of the people with whom I worked in NYC as the most well-bred.

Many have also referred to Canada Lee as an aristocrat.

The son to whom Stafford referred was Carl Vincent Lee who became an actor in his own right as an adult, with many kudos for his role of Blue Haven in Lonne Elder, III's *Ceremonies in Dark Old Men*. Carl Lee also worked in movies. In a personal interview with me at the King Crab Restaurant in New York City on 30 March 1982, Carl Lee said:

> If there was one important thing I remember about my father, it was his courage. The members of the HUAC committee came to him and offered him clearance saying that all he had to do was denounce Paul Robeson. Canada said to me: "I can't do that. Robeson is a great man." But Canada went on to rallies in spite of his high blood pressure. My father died in poverty, but he had integrity. I remember our being followed. People would say, "There they are." But if there's ever anything I hope to be, it would be to be as much of a man as my father—to have the guts and the courage that my dad did.

Lee and his son corresponded in the actor's absence, and there appeared to be a strong bond.

From 1927–33, Canada Lee was a professional fighter who moved to welterweight. In the ring, Lee participated in 200-odd fights, losing only 25. Irving Rudd posited in *Negro Digest:*

> Many people have forgotten the fact that Canada Lee was an outstanding boxer when he campaigned professionally from 1927–1933. As a simon-pure, Canada Lee was Metropolitan A.A.U. and New York State welterweight title holder, and when he gave up medal chasing in 1927, he was besieged by managers to join their stables. Lee was the Ray Robinson of his day. . . .
>
> Clever, strong, a hard puncher, Lee fought such great scrappers as Vince Dundee, Tommy Freeman, Andy Divodi, Izzy Grove, Jack Britton, Johnny Indrisano, Al Mello, Pal Silvers, Georgie Levine, Ignacio Ara and Lou Brouillard.
>
> Lee never was knocked out and declares he was floored only three times. (47)

Reports vary that Lee earned anywhere from $75,000 to $100,000 in the ring, virtually all of which he promptly spent in a lavish lifestyle. Harassment and blacklisting at the end of his life eclipsed his excesses.

It was Andy Divodi who, in 1929, ended Lee's career as a pugilist when he, using unethical tactics, according to Lee's widow, Frances, rubbed rosin in his eye. As a result of this bout which caused blindness in one eye, Lee quit the ring and obtained a glass eye.

Visually impaired and searching for something to do, Lee returned to music, establishing his own jazz band. Briefly, he worked in vaudeville. But, one day in 1934, he walked into the Harlem YMCA where Frank Wilson, the actor best known for the title role in the 1927 play *Porgy*, was casting his own vehicle. A spectator recognized Lee, and the prizefighter became a performer in Frank Wilson's *Meek Mose*.

The acerbic critic Percy Hammond of the Republican *New York Herald Tribune* wrote that the 1928 *Meek Mose*, in which Lee was not cast, was "a mess of oversweet theatrical marmalade produced last evening at the Princess. The effort was pathetic" (16). Fannin Belcher, a black scholar, also said that the play had a "minstrel aroma in dialogue and characters" (230). Ten thousand people came to the open-air presentation of the 1934 *Meek Mose* in which Lee participated, its embarrassment and ineptness notwithstanding.

Meanwhile, America tottered on the brink of economic collapse. While hundreds stood in soup lines in the midst of the Great Depression, 75 percent of those without work were African Americans. Theatre mirrored the times.

Lee's next activity foreshadowed the fighter he was to become. He was Blacksnake Johnson in a volatile 1934 production of Paul Peters and George Sklar's *Stevedore*, a play that dramatically portrayed the agony of troubled dock workers. It was Lee's first known controversy of many more to come. He was best at roles closer to his assertive and sometimes aggressive personality.

The play caused such alarm by 1935 that the headline of a column in *The Afro-American* ran, "Congress Alarmed Over 'Stevedore' Lynch Drama." The article read:

> *Stevedore*, played by a mixed cast, deals with the attempt of a Southern white girl to pin a charge of rape on a stevedore to save her white lover from prosecution after he has beaten her. The charge precipitated a lynch attempt and a mob of whites invaded the colored colony on the banks of the New Orleans wharves but were resisted by armed white and colored laborers who repulsed them with bullets (Clipping file, Moorland-Spingarn Collection, Howard University Library, n.p., n.d.).

The New York Times Theatre Review, on 2 Oct. 1934, noted: " . . . the final scene on the barricade, in which . . . struggle is visualized in gunfire, gathering mobs and flying bricks, remains a climactic triumph" (18:2). Lee chose roles of heroes, and amazingly, power brokers of Hollywood, Broadway, and other venues often permitted him.

The theatre and the government were unusually liberal in the 1930s. Out of the needs of the Great Depression and under the aegis of Franklin Delano Roosevelt's Works Progress Administration, Congress created the Federal Theatre Project of 1935–39. With a grant of $46 million Harry Hopkins, Relief Administrator, gave National Director Hallie Flanagan money to put 13,000 unemployed people to work. Eight hundred and fifty-one were black. They earned $23.86 a week, regardless of the size of the role.

They performed, according to sources that vary, in either 16 or 22 different Negro units in New York City, Peoria, Raleigh/Durham, Birmingham, San Francisco, Hartford, and Los Angeles, among other cites. They played in classics, contemporary drama, vaudeville, circus acts, children's theatre, and the legendary Living Newspaper, the provocative and in-depth stage equivalent of the movie newsreel or documentary. Churches, tents, high schools, and regular theatres housed these groups.

Kevin O'Morrison also wrote me:

> As for the Federal Theatre—particularly the Federal Theatre at the old Lafayette Theatre at 131st Street and Seventh Avenue, in Harlem—I saw only a few pieces there. What I saw were memorable—for their vigor and exuberance . . . the sheer joy of the actors in being able to be on a stage practicing their craft before their community. . . . Uptown in Harlem, there was no such thing as a wall. Hot emotion—whether of grief of joy—flowed from stage to audience and back, in a never-interrupted connection. . . . When I arrived in [New York City] in May, 1937, [*Macbeth*] was still among the "hottest" subjects of discussion among theatre folk . . . (25 Feb. 1980).

Jack Carter, a handsome, extremely tall actor of color, starred as the royal thane, and the beautiful Edna Thomas played Lady Macbeth. A 21-year-old Orson Welles directed and John Houseman headed the New York City Negro Unit.

Canada Lee played a cigar-smoking Banquo in the voodoo inspired *Macbeth,* which had genuine witch doctors and voodoo drummers, a choir, and a cast of 100. The spectacle opened on 14 April 1936 at Harlem's Lafayette Theatre. On opening night, police had to quell the overflow crowd that spilled onto the sidewalk. Newspapers reported that a festival spirit and glaring Hollywood floodlights as well as a brass band of 80 pieces came to Harlem on 14 April 1936 to celebrate the opening of the most ambitious venture of the Negro division of the Federal Theatre Project—a different version of Shakespeare's *Macbeth* with an all-Negro cast.

Junior League matrons sat next to black domestics in the racially mixed audience. Audiences loved the play. Some people were seeing one for the first time in their lives. On Relief Night, the night set aside for welfare and poor patrons, spectators could come for as little as five cents. It was a theatre for the community.

The critics, however, were not all kind. Brooks Atkinson of *The New York Times,* in a review of 15 April 1936, believed *Macbeth* "missed the sweep and scope of a poetic tragedy (25)." In an undated newspaper clipping, Sylvia Taylor wrote of Lee, "Banquo he played with a fervor that would have appalled Shakespeareans from Macready to Greet" (n.p.).

Percy Hammond, of *The New York Herald Tribune* exclaimed:

> The Negro Theatre, an offshoot of the Federal Government, gives an example of deluxe boondoggling at the Lafayette in Harlem, presenting *Macbeth* with considerable pomp and circumstance.... The actors sounded the notes with a muffled timidity that was often unintelligible. They seemed to be afraid of the Bard though they were playing him on their own home grounds. Mr. Jack Carter, as Macbeth, burst out in oratory . . . and so did Mr. Canada Lee. . . . Miss Edna Thomas impersonated Lady Macbeth with a dainty elegance that defied all traditions except the WPA (16 Apr. 1936).

So incensed were the voodoo drummers and the witch doctor that legend has it that they first sought the advice of John Houseman about whether or not Hammond was a bad man. Houseman assured them that he was. They promptly descended into the basement of Harlem's Lafayette and began weird chanting and drumming. In three days, Percy Hammond was dead. The newspapers credited pneumonia.

Roi Ottley of the *New York Amsterdam News* was glowing in his accolades for the entire cast. Thomas Anderson, an actor and close friend of Lee's, in a personal interview with me on 25 November 1977, stated that Canada Lee was "a dynamic actor who could create a mood without ever having to 'get into it.'"

Lee's foray into the government-sponsored Federal Theatre Project continued with the role of Yank in Eugene O'Neill's *S. S. Glencairn or One-Act Plays of the Sea (1937)*. White critics were bewildered by black actors attempting Eugene O'Neill, although Paul Robeson and Charles Gilpin had played the role of the Emperor Jones earlier. That role, however, was seen as one for a black actor. On 30 October 1937, Brooks Atkinson wrote of the WPA production of the O'Neill tetralogy:

> Although the Harlem mummers put on a bizarre *Macbeth* two seasons ago, and have every logical right to play any dramas that interest them, they cannot light the proper fire under the melting pot of Mr. O'Neill's British tramp steamer (23:2).

Atkinson asserted that the Harlem Players were not able to speak impeccable British English: "The fine plays of O'Neill deserved a much more sensitive performance than the Negro actors could provide" (23:2). The critic pronounced the casting irrational.

Conversely, St. Clair Bourne, a black critic for *The New York Amsterdam News*, was more reflective than reactionary on 6 November 1937:

> The capable players of the Negro theatre have undertaken Eugene O'Neill and under the circumstances have done it well. I say "under the circumstances" because the O'Neill characters are just about the most difficult to portray. Difficult even for players acquainted with the types, they constitute a towering obstacle to the basically different Negro actor.... Canada Lee comes through with a good job, especially in *Bound East for Cardiff* (16).

The twentieth century ended with many white critics and audiences, however well-intentioned, believing that African American actors should play only those roles designated for black actors. But it was the Federal Theatre that began the practice of black actors playing in classics, including Shakespeare.

In spite of mixed reviews of his Federal Theatre performances, Lee worked on Broadway as well. He was Henry in a 1937 rendition of *Brown Sugar*, with Butterfly McQueen as "an over genteel parlor maid in an apartment of iniquitous leanings" (*New York Times Theatre Review* 3 Dec. 1937, 29:2). Lee's branching out and networking remained important, showing that he was preparing for a full-fledged career in the theatre.

As contacts and Lee's talent continued to pay off, William DuBois's *Haiti*, a drama about the revolution that won freedom for the Haitian slaves in 1802, appeared on the Federal Theatre stages in 1938. Rex Ingram was first cast in the starring role of Henri Christophe. Initially, Canada Lee was Bertram; then he moved to the starring role.

Lee had exposure to a number of people, including powerful whites able to open doors for him, especially Orson Welles and John Houseman. Lee also had exposure to major critics. Such visibility led to work in Hollywood and on Broadway. However, the Federal Theatre left a mixed blessing on many of its actors, including Canada Lee. In addition to the benefits, there was the beginning of the House Un-American Activities Committee in 1938. That year, Martin Dies, a Congressman from Beaumont, Texas, began investigating the theatre in search of Communists under every theatrical flat. By 1939, after a series of hearings consisting of truths, half-truths, hearsay and untruths, Congress closed the Federal Theatre and ordered the records destroyed. Congressman J. Parnell Thomas, a Republican from New Jersey, cited *Haiti* as a play with "Communist leanings."

Abram Hill, an African American playwright who wrote *Liberty Deferred* for the Federal Theatre Project, mentioned at a luncheon at Tuskegee University on 14 November 1982, that he and a trainload of others, under subpoena, took a train ride from New York City to Washington, D.C. to testify before the Dies Committee in 1939 on Canada Lee's behalf. Lee's name appears 16 times in the HUAC hearings. It was a frightening time, long before Joseph McCarthy of Appleton, Wisconsin, began his investigations in the late 1940s and early 1950s.

Dick Campbell, singer, actor and director, wrote to me on 5 January 1978, of the Federal Theatre:

> The artistic impact of the Federal Theatre Project (FTP) was without precedence in the annals of the American Theatre. I subscribe to all of the fantastic glory heaped upon it by all the writers of the past who chose to chronicle its history. It was the beginning and finally the end of the National American Theatre. The killing of the FTP by an act of Congress was a collective murder by bigots and bums aided by a Broadway crowd of producers who feared that the FTP might lead the ticket buyers away from Broadway shows to the free theatre of the neighborhoods.... People who never saw a stage play in their lives were frequenting the workshops of the FTP and enjoying art that they always felt was only for the Broadway crowd who could pay for it, not for recipients of "welfare." And what a pity! The stupid Broadway producers never had the intelligence to realize that the FTP was developing an audience for the commercial theatre that would one day pay off.

Campbell was an associate of Lee and the last director of the New York City Negro Unit.

Meanwhile, with the closing of the only government-sponsored theatre America has known, Lee again went to Broadway in a cameo appearance as Drayton, opposite Ethel Waters as Hagar in DuBose and Dorothy Heyward's *Mamba's Daughters* in 1939. Georgette Harvey was Mamba; Fredi Washington played Lissa; and Willie Bryant, Gilly Bluton.

Drayton, old and feeble, is about to be laid off, amidst taunts from the younger men who resented him in the days of his Samsonian strength. The final insult comes when Drayton is assigned to work with a woman in the fields. Hagar is his partner. She is more of a blessing than a curse. Many critics, including Carl Van Vechten, praised *Mamba's Daughters*. Brooks Atkinson was not so enthralled and wrote a scathing review, which he retracted under pressure. With the closing of this Broadway production, America found itself moving toward war.

World War II brought many changes for the theatre. John Houseman, in the Foreword to John O'Connor and Lorraine Brown's *Free, Adult, Uncensored: A Living History of the Federal Theatre,* posited:

> As the Great Depression lifted and the economy began to pick up under the stimulus of an approaching war, the Federal Arts Projects became superflu-

ous and politically embarrassing. The Federal Theatre was liquidated, buried and largely forgotten in the new excitement of World War II (x).

Money now went into defense instead of art. Canada Lee found himself without the opportunity afforded by government funds, but with other excellent opportunities, as a direct result of the Federal Theatre Project. Langston Hughes wrote in *The New York Age* of Uncle Sam as a producer:

> For both the musical and dramatic actor of color, the Federal Theatre of the depression period was more than a gift from Roosevelt. It seemed like a gift from God. Not only did it bring forth food in a lean period, but it brought forth such real contributions to the art of the stage. . . .
> Top authorities in the Federal Theatre, Hallie Flanagan and Elmer Rice, believed in no color line. For the first time in America, in a sustained manner, Negroes were able to create their own plays and musicals, act in them, and also gain experience in directing, scene designing, and the other technical aspects of theatre which had hitherto been closed to them. With few previous exceptions, it was the Federal Theatre that dared to cast Negro actors in non-Negro roles, not only on Broadway, but in its units elsewhere as well. The Federal Theatre broke down not only the old taboos against colored Americans as backstage technicians, but the bars against colored actors playing other than racial roles (10).

While Canada Lee suffered greatly in his short life, he truly benefited from the FTP in terms of range of roles.

Lloyd Richards strongly stated from his Yale office in 1985: "The Federal Theatre was one of the benefits of a very bad time. It gave dignity to the profession by acknowledging the actors as an important part of the fabric of this country. It is as significant as the creation of the endowments" (28 Jun. 1985). With the closing of the Federal Theatre Project, African Americans sought other funding.

Mainly with ticket sales made more possible by celebrity attractions, the Negro Playwrights Company came into being. In 1940 this group, a black community theatre, presented Theodore Ward's *Big White Fog.* Canada Lee had the leading role of Victor Mason who, disillusioned and in despair, gives his life's savings of $1,500 to the *Black Star Line,* a fleet of three ships, all used and in poor condition, that would take African Americans back to Africa. Such was Marcus Garvey's quixotic vision.

Marcus Garvey, a native of Jamaica, and a revolutionary in America, laid the groundwork for the Universal Negro Improvement Association (UNIA) of the 1920s and early 1930s, a utopian concept for those blacks who had given up on America and felt that returning to Africa was their only hope.

Big White Fog was highly controversial when first presented by the Federal Theatre Project in 1938. Theodore Ward, the playwright, was bitter with every right to be. On 15 June 1977, Ward announced in a lecture at the University of Iowa that, as a young man, he had seen Marcus Garvey with his plumes, part of Garvey's flamboyant regalia, and had been affected. He also stated, "My father threw my first play in the fire, saying it was the work of the devil." Bitterness pervades Ward's drama.

Many white Americans considered *Big White Fog* too radical and leftwing. Many black people were embarrassed by it, as well, since it espoused Communism, Garveyism, and materialism. According to Rena Fraden, "middle-class race leaders resisted mightily being lumped into what they considered a 'typical' portrait of the African American citizen, especially one that depicted them as losers and second-class citizens" (125).

Ralph Warner describes *Big White Fog:*

> The play begins on Dearborn Street in the Black belt of Chicago in August of 1922, when prosperity was sweeping the land and crumbs are falling from the masters' tables into hungry Negro mouths. Victor Mason, father of a family of four, and his wife are the protagonists of the play.... Victor Mason ... resolves to struggle for what he considers the only path toward security and freedom ... the Garvey movement (n.d., n.p.).

The play ends in violence, with the Mason family being evicted from their home and Victor Mason being killed. Black audiences, in particular, boycotted the play. Whites were made uncomfortable.

Doris Abramson reports:

> According to the *Daily Worker*, 24,000 white New Yorkers and only 1,500 Negroes saw *Big White Fog*. ... *Big White Fog* remains a good example of a bold play in the politically conscious genre by a Negro who made no concessions to the white man's theatre tastes, but whose revolutionary solution was either too strong or too dated for many members of the audience, white or black (116–117).

The same may well be said of Canada Lee.

Equally daring were Orson Welles and John Houseman who catapulted Canada Lee to fame by casting him in the role for which he is arguably best known, Bigger Thomas, the black urban archetype, in Richard Wright and Paul Green's *Native Son*. This is a dramatization in ten scenes of Wright's watershed novel. The play examines Bigger's tormented life. He is a young man living in bleak poverty in Chicago who accidentally murders his employer's daughter, and then, out of fear that his black girlfriend may tell, he performs a second murder. Bigger is not a Machiavellian personality, but one who lacks education, self-esteem, racial pride, and judgment. Ultimately, he goes to the electric chair, after a white lawyer's heroic attempt to save his life.

Native Son had a long run and toured many cities, including Long Beach, Cleveland, Baltimore, Philadelphia, Detroit, Chicago, and Boston. Everywhere, it met with critical acclaim. Of Lee's performance, critic Rosamond Gilder posited in *Theatre Arts Monthly* in May 1941:

> No small measure of the play's powerful effect must be credited to Canada Lee's interpretation of the leading role. Much of what is important in the novel but is lost in the play—the profound subjective exposure of the Negro's unconscious motivations—is restored by the actor's performance. Bigger's smouldering resentment against the world as he has always known it; his unreflecting violence breaking out even more easily against the things he loves—his mother, his friends, his girl—than against the things he hates; his profound frustration stemming from the denial of his right to live; these and the varied tensions and releases provided by the succession of events through which he moves are admirably expressed by the actor in every attitude and movement of his powerful body, in his speech, his gestures, his silences (331–332).

While the critical reception was extraordinary, and audiences wept at the poignant drama, tension reigned backstage.

The director of *Native Son* and Canada Lee were involved in a salary dispute. At 9:48 P.M., 13 June 1941, the director telegraphed Lee from Los Angeles at the St. James Theatre in New York, that he was unable to give him $150 more per week. Others, the director noted, had taken cuts. The director's professional jealousy surfaced when he observed that Lee was getting more out of the gamble than he ever would. Uneasiness pervaded many other aspects of the play.

By 17 February 1942, the long-running hit met with difficulty in regard to Jim Crow. On that date, Max Johnson in *The Baltimore Afro-American* wrote about rigidly segregated seating (83 cents for some) for the audience in Baltimore:

> Despite all manner of pleas and inducements by several interested white patrons, the management of Ford's Theatre flatly refused Monday to even momentarily lower the jim-crow against colored persons, as the stage production *Native Son* opened here for a week's run.
>
> John Little, Manager of the Theatre, not only refused to allow any seats to be sold to colored in the first balcony, but reprimanded [Mrs. Wilma Ludlow] for being a white person wanting to "entertain colored" (n. p.).

The police chief of Baltimore ordered all pictures of the racially integrated cast removed simply because they showed Negroes and whites together.

Dick Campbell remarked that *Native Son* was a play that "rocked the hell out of Broadway" (5 Jan. 1978). The drama played twice on Broadway, first in March of 1941 for 97 performances. It then toured major cities, and reopened on Broadway in October of 1942 for 84 performances. *Life* magazine devoted an issue almost entirely to the play and hundreds of newspapers wrote about it. Canada Lee's widow, Frances, had a clipping service that obtained them. In spite of an avalanche of publicity, Lee endured many indignities.

The crew and management treated Lee indifferently, at best. In Long Beach, property people failed to bring his knife and gun. His dressing room there contained a cot, a chair, and no door. In spite of all, Lee was a star. The liberation of Bigger Thomas, the character, and Canada Lee, the man, came in suffering.

Slightly more than a year after *Native Son* closed, Lee appeared in the role of Sam Johnson in *South Pacific* in 1943. Mounted at the Cort Theatre by Lee Strasberg, this was not the Rodgers and Hammerstein musical, but a play about "a cynical, individualistic Negro sailor who refuses to help in the war against the Japanese until he sees that no man can stand alone" (*Current Biography 1944,* 395–396). Lewis Nichols believed: "David Lowe has acquired for the leading role one of the best Negro actors, Canada Lee.... He does not play it as well as he did the tortured figure of *Native Son,* but the part is more loosely put together" (ll:2). Lee was not a quitter, in spite of mixed reviews of much of his work.

His next vehicle, put on by the famous American Negro Theatre, was Philip Yordan's *Anna Lucasta* (1944). Lee had a cameo role of Danny, a sailor; Hilda Simms starred in the title role, and Earle Hyman, as the juvenile lead, Rudolph. Alice Childress played "a tough waterfront whore" (Gilder, Nov. 1944), and Frederick O'Neal, Frank, the bullying brother-in-law. While the play began in the basement of the Schomburg Library in Harlem, Harry Wagstaff Gribble carried it to Broadway. The reviews were extraordinary.

Rosamond Gilder assessed the play in *Theatre Arts Monthly* in November 1944:

> *Anna Lucasta* was the first play [of the 1944 season] to attract any serious consideration.... It presented an all Negro cast in a play that had nothing to do with Negro problems as such, but was concerned with the sins and wickednesses, the hopes and fears of a group of ordinary human beings (632–633).

The play made $9,500 in its first five showings on Broadway.

Burton Rascoe of *The New York World Telegram* hailed the drama with rare superlatives:

> In my opinion, *Anna Lucasta* is the most important event in our native American drama in 20 years. It is not only top notch theatre, with some of the finest acting, both comedic and dramatic, that has ever been seen on Broadway, but is the first American play, designed for an all-Negro cast, to treat Negro life without a certain amused condescension ... (31 Aug. 1944, n.p.).

So pleased were many directors at America's historically black colleges that *Anna Lucasta* became a staple of their productions. Lee was truly in the vanguard of the theatre, in spite of the pervasive Jezebel stereotypes of the black woman.

In the same year of this triumph, Alfred Hitchcock called Lee to Hollywood to play one of the survivors, Joe, the steward, in the classic film *Lifeboat*. Loften Mitchell, distinguished African American theatre historian, said to me in a personal interview:

> Canada Lee was magnificent in *Lifeboat*. He was a creature of hope when the survivors ran out of food. They were in the lifeboat, and he did the twenty-third psalm with eloquence. I don't know any other words. Beautiful scene (28 Jun. 1980).

Many praised the character Lee played, one who was not "like a pack of dogs," but one with "simple religious faith" (Spoto 147).

Donald Bogle argued:

> All the passengers symbolize specific elements in a full democratic society. A black steward, pensive and inarticulate, represents America's vast second-class citizenry. "Hey, Charcoal," the steward is greeted by Tallulah Bankhead. But when it is revealed that "Charcoal" has saved the life of a drowning white woman and her child, he becomes "Joe" and takes on heroic dimensions. The role was played with somber dignity by Canada Lee (139).

Lee continued to struggle in real life for dignity, as well.

By 1944, he had also begun to be very politically active. Narrating the radio series "New World A-Comin," Lee stressed the achievements of the Negro. This was the first radio series to devote itself to the issue of the Negro as a human being. Roi Ottley wrote the script. Every Sunday afternoon, the show aired over Manhattan's WMCA.

But Lee began to spread himself too thin. By March of 1944, he went to Washington with other entertainment moguls seeking to persuade Congress to help black soldiers, all of whom in 1944 were in racially segregated units. In June, the actor/activist participated in a rally at Madison Square Garden. This mammoth event included such prominent personages as Moran Weston of the Episcopal Church, Walter White of the NAACP, Adam Clayton Powell, Jr., of Abyssinian Baptist Church, and Dick Campbell, actor and leader of entertainment for the black United Service Organization units.

By September, Canada Lee became a member of the National Citizens Political Action Committee urging people to register and vote (*Current Biography 1944*). He was also active in Actors Equity.

At this critical juncture, Lee accepted Margaret Webster's invitation to play Caliban in her production of Shakespeare's *The Tempest* (1945). Believing that Caliban should be seen as the animal emerging as a man, Lee saw the character not simply as a monster to be played by an actor with a darkened face.

Hermine Rich Isaacs reviewed the Webster production, about which Webster had collaborated with the famous Eva LeGallienne:

> Many New York theatre-goers, conditioned perhaps by the King-Coit children's performances—the only *Tempest* of note in these parts since John Corbin and Leo Calvert's neo-Elizabethan venture in 1916—have fancied the play as a thing of shimmering surface loveliness, illuminated by flights of poetic imagination but no very profound philosophical content.
>
> ...Yet for Margaret Webster "It is not the surface pageantry but the spiritual and abstract values that have kept the play alive and make it worth doing today." It is essentially, she insists, "a play about the search for freedom, and about power and the misuse of power—major preoccupations of the current day" (89–90).

Of Lee's casting, Rich wrote:

> In picking the Negro actor for the role [of Caliban], Miss Webster made it clear that she meant to exploit his particular intensity, his power to come to grips with character, and not the pigmentation of his skin. "I do not intend," she insists, "to make Caliban a parable of the current state of the American Negro." Yet her willing eyes discover a ready parallel. "Prospero has taught Caliban the words of civilization but kept him a slave" (91).

Lee played the "animal emerging as a man" in an elaborate and powerful fish-scale costume.

Arnold Moss, who played Prospero, said to me of Lee:

He was terribly hard to work with. He and I were good friends, but he was hard to budge if he thought he was right. He did another naughty thing on the tour besides going to sleep on opening night—Canada wanted me to come in via stage left instead of stage right. We rehearsed for twenty minutes and were twenty minutes late opening.
    The Motleys had designed the set and costumes. On opening night, Canada had a friend of his make a whole new costume for him. This was a strange creature no one had seen before . . . 11 Jan. 1981).

Newsweek argued in an article titled, "Tempest on a Turntable": "Lee's Caliban is both articulate and monstrous, which is probably all that one could demand of the grotesque role" (83). (It was rumored that the actor made over $1500 a week in *The Tempest*). Lee was a politically aware man who had used the theatre as a vehicle of political vision. The role of Caliban brought him considerable critical acclaim as well as pressure to become more involved in civil rights.
    On 31 January 1946, according to *The New York Times,* Lee demanded the ouster of Mississippi senator Theodore G. Bilbo.

[Senator Mead] dashed into the corridor and received a petition from Canada Lee, Negro actor, and returned for his speech.
    The petition, bearing the signatures of some 25,000 New Yorkers obtained by the Citizens' Committee of the Upper West Side, demanded the expulsion of Senator Bilbo from the Senate for "conduct unbecoming a member of Congress" (1 Feb. 1946, 19:1).

Senator Bilbo, author of *Take Your Choice: Separation or Mongrelization,* arrogantly declared: "We have already determined that the Negro race is physically, mentally and morally inferior to the white race" (98). Warning that intermarriage was deadly, because the mixing of the races would defile white purity, he admonished talented blacks such as W. E. B. DuBois that they should thank God for the drop of white blood that made it possible.
    Bilbo was twice voted Governor of Mississippi and served three terms as U.S. Senator. He voted against the anti-lynching bill, the anti-poll tax bill, and the Fair Employment Practices Committee in 1945, all three of which were defeated at the time of his vote. He introduced a bill in the Senate for the voluntary resettlement of American Negroes in West Africa. Such a courageous step as delivering the petition against Bilbo was the beginning of Canada Lee's death knell.
    On the heels of this political boldness, Lee was among the first African Americans to produce a play on Broadway. (Miller-Lyles-Sissle-Blake produced *Shuffle Along, Runnin' Wild,* and *Chocolate Dandies;* Ethel Waters and

Earl Dancer produced *Africana*.) Lee and Mark Marvin produced Maxine Wood's *On Whitman Avenue* (1946). Wood wrote me:

> I knew Canada only very casually until I gave him a copy of the play to read. He was moved by it and since no Broadway producer had snapped it up, and feeling strongly that the play *must* be produced on Broadway, he decided to produce it with his friend Mark Marvin. He also liked the role of David Bennett, which he played (20 Aug. 1979).

The hurdle of finding enough money was considerable.

Fredi Washington wrote:

> Lee and his partner were unable to interest one single solitary Negro in New York in helping to back this play. Out of the $50,000 which is what *Whitman's* budget called for, the producers were able to get but $1,000 from a Negro, and that investor is a Chicagoan, far removed from the heart of the theatre world. The other $49,000 came from white investors.
>
> ... Of course there are not too many of us who have money to invest in any venture, but when you see new bars being opened daily in Harlem where there are far too many already, you wonder why some of these people would not invest in projects which have the ability to make the lot of the Negro better (newspaper clipping on *On Whitman Avenue*, n.d., n.p.).

Financial struggle was only part of the difficulty.

Opening in May of 1946, the play, directed by the well-known Margo Jones, depicted David Bennett, a black returning war veteran, unable to find housing in his own country. A liberal white college student rents her parents' second floor flat to Bennett while the parents are on vacation. The neighbors refuse to let their children play with the Bennett children. The parents of the liberal daughter, upon their return, are shocked to see the black couple, expecting a child, in the apartment. A committee is formed to protect the neighborhood. After considerable pressure, the black couple surrender the apartment key in a gripping moment.

Reviews were mixed. Lewis Nichols insisted that Lee overacted. Fredi Washington argued that Lee underplayed the part. Langston Hughes ranked the play with *Uncle Tom's Cabin, In Abraham's Bosom, Stevedore, Big White Fog,* and *Deep Are the Roots*. He stated in a signed, typed review for *The Chicago Defender:*

> *On Whitman Avenue* ... is the most effective play I have ever seen dealing with the problems of Negro-white relationships in America....
>
> *On Whitman Avenue* has just about everything in it. For most of the New York drama critics, it has too much. The critics did not like the play. But the

audiences do. The night I saw it, people laughed, cried and applauded all the way through. Negroes are particularly moved by it. To us it is almost too real. We forget that it is just a play. . . . Canada Lee heads a splendid cast . . . (22 Jun. 1946).

Hughes gave credit to other actors including Will Geer, Hilda Vaughn, both white, and Abbie Mitchell, the well-known and respected African American actress, who played the mother.

The black press and other more liberal newspapers came to the defense of the play. Many in the white press devoted considerable space to a barrage of hostile, negative criticism. *People's Voice* argued in the play's defense on 18 May 1946,

> Another excellent play of Negro life is in the process of being lynched by the "kept" dramatic critics on Broadway. But *On Whitman Avenue* must not be allowed to fold; the message it gives with truly superb dramatic power must still be heard by hundreds of thousands of white and Negro theatergoers in our city (n.p.).

The community wrapped its arms around the play; there was a public forum at the New York Public Library at 104 W 136 Street on Friday, 31 May 1946.

A rabbi, a high school student, Assemblyman Leo Isaacson, and several famous people wrote statements of support. Eslanda Goode Robeson, Paul Robeson's wife, gave kudos to the work: "I called in at 887 Whitman Avenue Friday night at the Cort Theatre and was deeply gratified to see the script I had liked so much successfully translated from the page to the stage" (clipping file on *On Whitman Avenue,* Tuskegee University Archives, n.d., n.p.).

Eleanor Roosevelt's comments in *The New York World Telegram* admonished:

> We the people are today in a period of retrogression. We do not want to be reminded of our unpleasant shortcomings. We do not want to face up to the big problems that we have to meet as a great people if we are to accept our place of leadership in the world. It is much easier and pleasanter to be a little people—and involves so much less responsibility (n.d., n.p.).

Mrs. Roosevelt attended the drama, and took a photo with Canada Lee. Maxine Wood also stated in a letter to me on 20 August 1979:

> *On Whitman Avenue* was tried out in Buffalo and Detroit before coming to New York City. The Detroit run was extended to three weeks and we could

have played there many more to sold out houses. It was there a year after severe race riots occurred in Detroit. In fact its police commissioner had come to Buffalo because of "race riot weather" in Detroit; he hoped to stop the play from coming here.

Canada [Lee], aware of racial tensions in Detroit, on his own initiative, chose while the play was in the city to live in the black neighborhood. He had not done this in Buffalo nor had any other members of the cast.... On *Whitman Avenue* received rave reviews in Detroit. We thought we were coming to New York City with a hit, but the play had very mixed reviews on opening night.

... In 1946, the play was called "controversial," and "too angry" by some critics.... Reviews and articles in the black press were excellent.... The play was in repertoire in the Soviet Union for at least eight years, and was translated into Portuguese and Spanish.

The play that Lee produced and performed in had an impact on Lorraine Hansberry who in 1959 saw her similar work on housing discrimination, *A Raisin in the Sun,* go to Broadway. Unlike Hansberry's work, *On Whitman Avenue* did not do as well financially, or in critical reception. Ralph Matthews offered a salient observation in the Baltimore *Afro-American:*

> According to the paid reviewers, the play was either the most dismal flop or the season's outstanding hit, dependent upon their respective points of view. I found it reached neither extreme but was a powerful revelation of an acute problem which faces colored people in general, regardless of whether they are war veterans or not . . . (clipping file, Tuskegee University Archives, n.p., n.d.).

Matthews' review was incisive.

With *On Whitman Avenue,* Lee's work became more and more controversial. The House Un-American Activities Committee in 1947 suggested that "one might consult Canada Lee's account of the promotion efforts for . . . *On Whitman Avenue . . .* in *The New York Times* August 11, 1946, . . . it is a brilliant account of how left-wing groups work" (U. S. Congress House Committee Hearings). This suggests HUAC's tragic and pathetic incapacity to distinguish between seekers of justice and subversives.

From this powerful slice of pathos, Lee, in 1946, continuing to show that the black actor had a wider range than virtually any critic or audience member would have believed possible, moved on to play the complex Bosola in John Webster's *Duchess of Malfi.* Brooks Atkinson liked the play: "People who are familiar with Canada Lee's recent performances are no doubt prepared for the marked development in his acting . . . a good elemental actor has acquired mastery of the stage. Here he is playing in white face" (16 Oct. 1946, 35:2). A special white paste and wig helped to create the illusion that Lee was white. Bosola was central to the play.

Lee's next role—equally controversial and equally central—was that of the fighter Ben Chaplin in the film *Body and Soul* (1947). Bosley Crowther remarked on 10 November 1947:

> It is Canada Lee who brings to focus the horrible pathos of the cruelly exploited prizefighter. As a Negro ex-champ who is meanly shoved aside, until one night he finally goes berserk, and dies slugging in a deserted ring, he shows through great dignity and reticence the full measure of his inarticulate scorn for the greed of the shrewder men who have enslaved him, sapped his strength and then tossed him out to die. The inclusion of this portrait is one of the finer things about this film (21:2).

Ben Chaplin was a reflexive role; Lee played himself. *Ebony* indicates that Lee was 40 years old when he returned to the ring via celluloid, with actor John Garfield beating him in a fixed fight.

Shortly after the release of *Body and Soul*, Lee found his contracts canceled. Unwilling to play the Hollywood game of stereotypes so very prevalent at the time, Lee could no longer get regular work and virtually none in mainstream films or theatre. In a rare article, Lee stated in *Opportunity* in the winter issue, 1948:

> My *Body and Soul* experience was in contrast to the time I worked in *Lifeboat*. Though I had been assured the role of the Negro sailor would do much to advance the cause of colored people, production wasn't very far along when I noticed that the script called for the Negro to be in a corner by himself, while the Nazi mingled freely—and, in fact, dominantly among the group. I didn't like it, but couldn't do anything about it (20–21).

Canada Lee also mentioned in this article that a prominent Caucasian actor repeatedly spoke of "niggers" and how he wished they were slaves.

That Caucasian actor had his wish. Lee's next role was just that, George Wilson, the troubled head slave in the Theatre Guild's stirring production of Dorothy Heyward's *Set My People Free* (1948). The play was written in dialect, with little historical balance. Frederick Douglass did not speak dialect, for example. But lack of an authentic whole was only one problem.

Initially, the Theatre Guild had cast Rex Ingram in one of the major male roles. However, during the rehearsals, according to Thomas Anderson who was Jesse Blackwood in the production, police arrested Rex Ingram on criminal charges and took him to prison. (25 Nov. 1977). Letters in the Theatre Guild Collection at Yale University's Beinicke Library express the dismay of several key members in the organization that Ingram had put them in a difficult position, especially financially. But Lee rescued the Guild.

Newsweek reported on 15 November 1948:

> the Theater Guild offers *Set My People Free* . . . an almost-forgotten page in American history—the abortive slave uprising of 1822 that was to have freed the Negroes of Charleston and avenged them of their white owners. A program note affirms that "the plan of procedure given in the play is the actual stratagem" of Denmark Vesey's rebellion.
>
> . . . But it is in the realization of the foredoomed Vesey and of George Wilson, the loyal house servant who betrayed him, that the play is most successful. Here the concurrence of good writing and the admirable acting of Juano Hernandez as Vesey and Canada Lee as the self-tortured Wilson makes for absorbing and emotionally disturbing theater (82).

The New York Star observed: "Mr. Lee suggests with eloquence the timeless, tragic frustrations of his role in life. More often he seems conventionally smug, and a little uncomfortable, too, in the bulldog livery the Guild has given him" (17). Thomas Anderson, eventually stage manager for *Set My People Free,* informed his friend Canada Lee that the opening night was sold out (25 Nov. 1977).

On the doorstep of fame, in 1949, Lee, beset by mounting racial pressures, appeared in the film *Lost Boundaries,* an important one in a series Hollywood made on the theme of "passing." (A good many fair-complexioned African Americans "passed" for white in order to get into public accommodations denied Negroes who could be identified as such.) Lee was cast in a small, but impressive role as Lieutenant Joe Thompson.

Based on a true story in a short novel by William L. White, which appeared in *Reader's Digest,* the film shows a light-skinned black physician played by Mel Ferrer, who poses as white in a New England town for 25 years. The doctor marries a fair-complexioned woman and his children are also fair-skinned. He becomes successful and accepted by his community. Crisis grips the family, whose members have been perceived as white for years, when the Navy, in World War II, discovers their black identity and refuses the doctor a commission. Lee, as the police officer (a role not in White's novel), comforts the doctor's son, who had not been told that he is black.

According to Samuel William Bloom in his doctoral thesis on audience behavior and the Negro image in film, Atlanta banned *Lost Boundaries:*

> As Gunnar Myrdal [author of *An American Dilemma*] saw so well, all of the United States was uneasy about its behavior toward racial minorities, the Negroes in particular, and preferred to avoid facing the fact of its discrep-

ancy with the national credo of egalitarianism. It might be expected, therefore, that this would be the area in which the freedom of the film would be challenged, and so it was.

In Atlanta, Georgia, *Lost Boundaries* was banned. The Board of Censors of that city invoked an ordinance which claimed that the film's exhibition " . . . will adversely affect the peace, morals and good order of said city" (33).

Many in the press gave more favorable opinions.

Newsweek, in an article called "Superior Documentary," argued in its 4 July 1949 issue:

> As the Negro doctor, forced to renounce his race to follow his career, Mel Ferrer makes a compelling tragic figure.
>
> As directed by Alfred L. Werker and bolstered by a uniformly excellent supporting cast that includes Canada Lee, this restrained and courageous treatment of a delicate theme stands up as one of the best movies made since the war.

Historically, African Americans could attend only two medical schools in the United States in 1949, Howard University in Washington, D.C., and Meharry in Nashville, Tennessee. Canada Lee and Mel Ferrer, in their characterizations, mirrored life for America in 1949. Many in the audience were uncomfortable.

The political climate was becoming increasingly threatening in 1949. As a result, Lee and others organized a peace conference. Forces were already in motion which would bring Lee's career to an end. Maxine Wood recalls:

> 1949 was a time of terror, due to the activities of the [House] Un-American [Activities] Committee and people like Walter Winchell and Sidney Hook who were hysterically against the Conference [Cultural and Scientific Conference for World Peace at the Waldorf Astoria Hotel in New York, March 25, 1949] and put pressure on the sponsors to resign. Some did. Canada Lee was, unfortunately, one of them, stating publicly that he never agreed to sponsor the conference though the letter of acceptance was on file. His resignation was a great disappointment to me. I reasoned that perhaps because of the reign of terror in 1949 against liberals . . . and their difficulty in finding work in their profession, Canada felt obliged to "cleanse himself" of any so-called left leanings.
>
> Canada . . . was a very warm-hearted human being who acted and took action from the dictates of his "gut feelings"(20 Aug. 1979).

In spite of Lee's resignation and disassociation from the liberal left, which lost him the support of many previous friends, HUAC continued to hound him. Rarely employed now, he was $18,000 in debt.

Lee was damaged, not only by HUAC, but by the Judith Coplon trial when his name was "flushed from FBI files on hearsay evidence" (Kanfer 179). Coplon, accused of espionage, was convicted in 1949 of having conspired to pass government secrets to her paramour, a Russian spy. An informant reported that Lee, Fredric March, and other entertainment figures were her traveling companions. This accusation destroyed Canada Lee.

At some point, perhaps even before *On Whitman Avenue*, according to Maxine Wood who knew nothing of Lee's first wife, Lee and Juanita Canegata apparently divorced. He married Frances, a Caucasian, in 1950. She said to me in a personal interview at her home in Huntington, New York, on 26 June 1980:

> The whole era of McCarthyism literally killed the individual economically and with social pressures. Canada was included via insinuation. . . . This period was representative of unbelievable fear! In Canada's case, they (FBI) were anxious to get him to condemn Paul Robeson. They offered Canada complete clearance, so that he would be able to work again.
>
> They wanted Canada to split the people—"Divide and conquer." Canada was controlled, but he told them where to go. Canada admired Paul Robeson. He did disagree with him.
>
> When they (FBI) tried to force him . . . these two men came to our apartment in New York without an appointment and asked to see Canada privately. Canada's being blacklisted continued very strongly. Had *Cry, the Beloved Country* been an American production, I doubt that he would have gotten the part.

Lee's son, Carl, also shared with me how the FBI followed the family (30 Mar. 1982).

Canada Lee was to make one more film, and that, probably his greatest, Alan Paton's *Cry, the Beloved Country* (1952). In spite of political persecution and blacklisting at home, Lee had developed a considerable reputation abroad. This extended the influence of his work and led to continuing acting opportunities. Though his career in the United States was at an end, his esteem abroad led to his last role. *Ebony* believed *Cry, the Beloved Country* to be the best movie ever made dealing with a black theme (Jul. 1951).

The actor played the Zulu pastor, Stephen Kumalo, the black father whose son, Absalom, kills the white son of Jarvis. Stefan Kanfer in *Journal of the Plague Years* observed: "This was his most controlled and moving performance" (180). The film was Sidney Poitier's first, and Canada Lee's last.

The Natal Daily News, on 3 August 1950, gave front page coverage to the premiere: "The world premiere of *Cry, the Beloved Country* will be held in South Africa early in the new year of 1951 with a simultaneous showing in Durban, Cape Town and Johannesburg. Mr. Zoltan Korda, producer of the film, gave this information . . . today" (1).

On 28 June 1980, by Frances Lee's swimming pool, Loften Mitchell remembered:

> Canada Lee as he uttered the worst, slid his hand down his cane in the film and said, "You must tell it, umfundisi. Is it heavy? It is the heaviest thing of all my years. . . . It was my son that killed your son" (180–181 of *Cry, the Beloved Country*).

Newsweek agreed with Mitchell in its 29 January 1952 review:

> The particular power and poignancy of the drama lie in the way the two fathers come together in a relation transcending their personal losses and the traditional conflicts of the community: the white father . . . finding himself free of bitterness, and the colored father . . . preserving his faith and his love for the son about to be hanged (n.p.).

Some in America still viewed Canada Lee as being politically motivated by performing in this film.

Alan Paton, the author of *Cry, the Beloved Country*, reflected in a letter to me on 19 January 1982: "I do not think that he [Canada Lee] was a politician at all, but I am sure that he was under great pressures, especially from black people, to make a political statement. He was essentially a private person." But Walter Winchell, Sidney Hook, and J. Edgar Hoover sought to make Lee's life very public.

Kevin O'Morrison wrote me about Lee's offer of work in foreign countries:

> He said that spokesmen for the governments of Italy, Israel, and Ethiopia had offered him his own theatres in those countries—theatres in which to work as he chose; theatres with a company of actors, and supporting ensemble—technicians, regisseurs, etc. (His performance in *Cry, the Beloved Country* had obviously had a deeper effect abroad than here in the U.S.—where his major reward was a kind of overnight "Pop" notoriety: greater than he had before, to be sure, but of a kind that he *had* had before, and which had faded as quickly as it had occurred). "Kev," he said, "I don't want a theatre in Italy—or Israel—or Ethiopia. I just-want-to-work-HERE-as-a-free man. An artist.(25 Feb. 1980).

Frances Lee had photos of Lee preparing to do *Othello* in Rome. It was not to be.

Lee's many activities cost him his home, his career, his health, and his life. What forces affected Canada Lee's sudden rise and fall? When, ironically, the government, which had once funded art, decided to investigate the theatre in search of Communists, Lee's controversial career stood out. He had demanded defiant roles in American theatre and film and made one film abroad. He had attended and spoken out at American rallies, and delivered a petition asking for the ouster of a biased Mississippi senator.

In 1977 Barney Josephson of The Cookery and formerly of Café Society, the first interracial night club in America, reported to me in a telephone interview that Lee knocked out the teeth of two sailors who harassed him because they resented his white date. The actor proceeded to dance as the Shore Patrol handled the matter. Josephson, himself, was eventually blacklisted and forced out of business, possibly because of this incident (25 Nov. 1977).

Adding to complications was Lee's health. By 1949, he was severely afflicted with high blood pressure and sought medical treatment in Europe. He opted for two sympathectomies, an operation not performed in America at the time, but one that partially severed nerves as it relieved high blood pressure, a major disease for the African American.

Kevin O'Morrison wrote to me about Lee's surgery:

> He wanted to be free of the blood pressure that he was certain would kill him—or, worse, cripple him. And it was now obvious that what he had told me about the offer of theatres vs. the situation here was a necessary prelude to his "explanation" for the surgery he now told about . . . why, that is, he demanded of his surgeon (a shocked surgeon, I should imagine), that both operations be performed as close together as "humanly" possible . . . they may, indeed, have been back to back. . . . What is certain is that they were performed dangerously close to each other. So close that were it not for Canada's outsized stamina, the operations could not have been survived. AND the operations were a success—as he told me of the relief he felt after the operations, his face momentarily eased its tensions (. . . an actor doing a sense-memory exercise often alters his metabolism as a result of the power of memory. . . . Canada was totally an actor, and I had a real glimpse of what his early days of post-operative recovery must have been like). "It was wonderful—wonderful," he said, "to be rid of the tension." But the moment he resumed his narrative, his face was again tense and pained. "Forty-eight hours after I was back in the States, Kev, it was like I never had the operations." I didn't understand. "I had it back," he said. "You had *what* back?" I said. "The *nerves* are cut." "Doesn't matter," he said. "I've got it" (25 Feb. 1980).

Lee's tension was aggravated while he was on location in South Africa. While filming *Cry, the Beloved Country*, he and Sidney Poitier had to enter rehearsals as bonded servants of Zoltan Korda, and convince South African police that they were American actors who did not need passes. They lived on a farm together 26 miles outside of Johannesburg, having been forbidden by the laws of apartheid from staying in hotels.

Upon Lee's return to America, Walter White of the NAACP warned the actor not to make waves. But Lee's fiery spirit could not be contained. He continued to be politically active, and went hungry, as a result of the blacklisting.

Ted Poston revealed:

> Walter Kirschenbaum of the Jewish Labor Committee recalled today that he had been at the White Plains protest meeting as a speaker when Lee arrived. "I remember that he was very hungry and said he'd had to rush up there without dinner. He was very grateful when someone went out and got him a sandwich. I didn't learn until a few days later why he hadn't eaten (n. p., n.d.).

Thomas Anderson, Lee's closest friend, recalled in a soft, poignant voice Lee's loss of his New York home, which had an elaborate hand-painted porcelain bathroom (25 Nov. 1977). Lee's closest relatives, except for his wife, were unaware of his plight. A few weeks later, Lee was gone. Uremic poisoning claimed him. The obituaries ignored the blacklist.

On 9 May 1952 Harlem exploded when it learned of Lee's fatal attack of uremic poisoning. Anderson stated quietly, "Both kidneys were gone" (25 Nov. 1977). At the funeral at Harlem's Salem Methodist Church, actor Arnold Moss read these lines, which Lee had spoken as Caliban in *The Tempest*:

> Be not afraid: the isle is full of noises
> Sounds and sweet airs that give delight and hurt not.
> Sometimes a thousand twangling instruments
> Will hum about mine ears; and sometimes voices
> That, if then had waked after long sleep,
> Will make me sleep again; and then, in dreaming,
> The clouds methought would open and show riches
> Ready to drop upon me, that, when I waked,
> I cried to dream again. (act II, scene ii.)

Moss then commented:

> And when Canada spoke those lines, each performance, I couldn't help thinking that the "noisy isle" he was *thinking* about was the Manhattan where he spent most of his life. And where, he would "wake" and "cry to dream again" of the possibility of its riches (11 Jan. 1981).

Adam Clayton Powell, the flamboyant Congressman from Harlem, stepped to the dais, turned out the light on the podium, and said: "Canada Lee made his race a badge of military courage.... America has been cheapened by the death of Canada Lee.... What an irony that such a man—such a tremendous personality—such a vitally American person should be charged with being Un-American" (*The Afro-American*, 24 May 1952, n.p.).

Canada Lee has been judged by *Time* as "an actor of the order of Robeson" (7 Apr. 1941). He was also a selfless activist, seldom, if ever, as well known as Paul Robeson. In his all too brief 45 years, Canada Lee was an activist and actor whom fellow actors rose to applaud—in the theatre, there can be no higher tribute.

Works Cited

Abramson, Doris E. *Negro Playwrights in the American Theatre, 1925–1959.* New York: Columbia University Press, 1967.

Anderson, Thomas. Personal interview with author. 25 Nov. 1977.

Atkinson, Brooks. "From Broadway to Harlem," *The New York Times Theatre Review,* 7 May 1935, n.p. [review of *Sailor Beware*]

———. "'Macbeth' or Harlem Boy Goes Wrong, Under Auspices of Federal Theatre Project," *The New York Times,* 15 Apr. 1936, 25:4. [review of *Macbeth*]

———. *The New York Times Theatre Review,* 30 Oct. 1937, 23:2. [review of *S. S. Glencairn*]

———. *The New York Times Theatre Review.* 16 Oct. 1946, 35:2. [review of *Duchess of Malfi*]

Belcher, Fannin S. "The Place of the Negro in the Evolution of the American Theatre, 1767 to 1940," Ph.D. diss., Yale, 1945, 230.

Bilbo, Theodore. *Take Your Choice: Separation or Mongrelization.* Poplarville, Mississippi: Dream House Publishing Company, 1947.

Bloom, Samuel William. "A Social Psychological Study of Motion Picture Audience Behavior: A Case Study of the Negro Image in Mass Communication," Ph.D. diss. University of Wisconsin-Madison, 1956.

Bogle, Donald. *Toms, Coons, Mulattoes, Mammies and Bucks: An Interpretive History of Blacks in American Films.* New York: Continuum, 1996.

Bourne, St. Clair. "Lafayette Players Do O'Neill Show Well," *The New York Amsterdam News,* 6 Nov. 1937, 16. [review of *S. S. Glencairn*]

Campbell, Dick. Letter to author. 5 Jan. 1978.

"Canada Lee, 45, Actor, Boxer, Jockey, Dies," *The New York World Telegram Sun,* 10 May 1952, 22.

"Canada Lee, Actor on Stage, Screen," *The New York Times,* 10 May 1952, n.p.

"Canada Lee Back in Ring: Ex-Pug Makes Comeback in Boxing and in Films," *Ebony,* Aug. 1947, 16–17. [*Body and Soul*]

"Canada Lee, 45, Is Dead; Stage and Film Star," *New York Herald Tribune*, 10 May 1952, n.p.

"Congress Alarmed Over 'Stevedore' Lynch Drama," *Afro-American*, n.p., n.d.

"Crowds Jam Streets as 'Macbeth' Opens," *The New York Times*, 15 Apr. 1936, 25:3.

Crowther, Bosley. *New York Times Film Review.* 10 Nov. 1947, 21:2. [review of *Body and Soul*]

"Cry, the Beloved Country," *Ebony*, July 1951, 57–62.

Current Biography Yearbook 1944, New York: H. W. Wilson Company, 1944. 394–396.

"Final Tribute Paid to a Great Actor, Canada Lee," *The Afro-American*, 24 May 1952, n.p.

Fraden, Rena. *Blueprints for a Black Federal Theatre, 1935–1939*. New York: Cambridge University Press, 1994.

Freidin, Seymour. "Boxer, Jockey, Band Leader, Canada Lee Becomes Star Actor," *The New York Herald Tribune*, 30 Mar. 1941, 5.

Funeral Program of Canada Lee, 13 May 1952.

Gilder, Rosamond. *Theatre Arts Monthly*, May 1941, 331–332. [*Native Son*]

———. *Theatre Arts Monthly*, Nov. 1944, 632–633. [*Anna Lucasta*]

Gill, Glenda E. "Canada Lee: Black Actor in Non-Traditional Roles," *Journal of Popular Culture*, winter issue, 1991, 79–89.

———. "Careerist and Casualty: The Rise and Fall of Canada Lee," *Freedomways*, vol. 21, no. 1, 1981, 14–27.

———. *White Grease Paint on Black Performers: A Study of the Federal Theatre, 1935–1939*. New York: Peter Lang, 1988.

Hammond, Percy. "*Meek Mose*, A Solicitous Study of Negro Life as It is Seen by an Afro-American Actor," in *The Theaters Section, New York Herald Tribune*, n.d., 16.

———. "A W.P.A. *Macbeth*," *New York Herald Tribune*, 16 Apr. 1939, 16.

"Hitchcock Throws Eight People and the Nazi Who Torpedoed Them Together in an Open Boat," *Life*, 31 Jan. 1944, 77–81. [*Lifeboat*]

Hughes, Langston. "Federal Theatre Led the Way to Plenty of Integration on Broadway," *The New York Age*, 2 May 1953, 10.

———. Hand signed, typed review for *The Chicago Defender*, 22 June 1946. [*On Whitman Avenue*]. (courtesy of Maxine Wood)

Isaacs, Hermine Rich, "This Insubstantial Pageant," *Theatre Arts Monthly*, Feb. 1945, 89–93. [*The Tempest*]

Johnson, Max. *The Baltimore Afro-American.* 17 Feb. 1942, n.p. [review of *Native Son*]

Josephson, Barney. Telephone interview with author. 25 Nov. 1977.

Kanfer, Stefan. *A Journal of the Plague Years.* New York: Atheneum, 1973.

Lardner, John. "A Play about a Negro Revolt," *New York Star*, 5 Nov. 1948, 17. [*Set My People Free*]

Lee, Canada. Letter to Paul Green. 8 Dec. 1942. (courtesy of the Southern Historical Collection, University of North Carolina at Chapel Hill)

———. "Our Part in *Body and Soul*," *Opportunity*, winter issue, 1948, 20–21.

Lee, Carl. Personal interview with author. 30 Mar. 1982.

Lee, Frances. Personal interview with author. 26 June 1980.

"Lynching on Broadway," *People's Voice*, 18 May 1946, n.p. (courtesy of Maxine Wood)

"Making of *Lost Boundaries*, The," <http://www.seacoast.com/louis/lostfilm.html>

Matthews, Ralph. Baltimore: *Afro-American*, n.p., n.d. [review of *On Whitman Avenue*]

"Mead Takes Hand at Filibustering," *The New York Times*, 1 Feb. 1946, 19:1.

Mitchell, Loften. Personal interview with author. 28 June 1980.

Moss, Arnold. Letter to author. 30 July 1980.

———. Postcard to author. 29 Nov. 1980.

———. Telephone interview with author. 11 Jan. 1981.

Natal Daily News, The. 3 Aug. 1950, 1.

Norford, George. "On Stage . . . ," *Opportunity*, summer issue, 1947, vols. 24–26, 164–166.

"New Plays in Manhattan," *Time*, 10 Jan. 1944. [*South Pacific*]

Nichols, Lewis, "The Play," *The New York Times Theatre Review*, 30 Dec. 1943, ll:2. [*South Pacific*]

O'Connor, John and Lorraine Brown. *Free, Adult, Uncensored: The Living History of the Federal Theatre Project*. Washington, D.C.: New Republic Books, 1978.

O'Morrison, Kevin. Letter to author. 25 Feb. 1980.

On Whitman Avenue. Clippings of articles and reviews. Tuskegee University Archives.

Paton, Alan. *Cry, the Beloved Country*. New York: Charles Scribner's Sons, 1948.

———. Letters to author. 8 Sept. 1981, and 19 Jan. 1982.

"Peace: Everybody Wars Over It," *Newsweek*, 4 Apr. 1949, 21.

Peters, Paul and George Sklar. *Stevedore*. New York: Covici, Friede Publishers, 1934.

Poitier, Sidney. Letter to author. 3 Feb. 1981.

Porter, Russell, "5 Women Placed on Tentative Jury in Communist Trial," *The New York Times*, 10 Mar. 1949, 1–2.

Poston, Ted. "Plight of His Kin in U.S. Job Recalls How 'Whispers' Broke Canada Lee," [Canada Lee Went Hungry on the Doorstep of Fame.] (clipping file of the State Historical Society of Wisconsin), n.d., n.p.

Rascoe, Burton. *The New York World-Telegram*, 31 Aug. 1944, n.p. [review of *Anna Lucasta*]

Richards, Lloyd. Personal interview with author. 28 June 1985.

Roosevelt, Eleanor. "Racial Problems," *The New York World-Telegram*, n.d., n.p. (courtesy of Maxine Wood) [*On Whitman Avenue*]

Rudd, Irving. "Program for Pugilism," *Negro Digest, The* Apr. 1946, 47–50.

Spoto, Donald. *The Art of Alfred Hitchcock*. New York: Hopkinson and Blake, 1976, 147.

Stafford, Bart Lanier, III. Letters to author. 18 Sept. 1977, and 6 Apr. 1982.

"Stevedore," *The New York Times Theatre Review*, 2 Oct. 1934, 18:2.

"Superior Documentary," *Newsweek*, 4 July 1949, 72. [*Lost Boundaries*]

Taylor, Sylvia, "Canada Lee Has Many Trades—Master of Them All," (clipping found in the Moorland-Spingarn Collection of the Howard University Library), n.d., n.p.
"Tempest on a Turntable," *Newsweek*, 5 Feb. 1945, 82–83.
Time, 7 Apr. 1941. [*Native Son*]
United States Congress House Committee Hearings, 80th Congress, Senate Library, vol. 1138, 1947. (University of Iowa Government Documents)
Ward, Theodore. Lecture at the University of Iowa, 15 June 1977.
Warner, Ralph. "A Vital Drama of Negro Life," (clipping file of The Moorland-Spingarn), n.d., n.p. [*Big White Fog*]
Washington, Fredi. Newspaper clipping on *On Whitman Avenue,* n.d., n.p. (courtesy of Maxine Wood)
Webster, Margaret. *Don't Put Your Daughter on the Stage.* New York: Alfred Knopf, 1972, 119–194. [on *The Tempest*]
"When the Slaves Rose," *Newsweek,* 15 Nov. 1948, 82. [*Set My People Free*]
Wood, Maxine. Letter to author. 20 Aug. 1979.
———. *On Whitman Avenue.* New York: Dramatists Play Service 1944. (courtesy of Maxine Wood)

Pearl Bailey in *Hello Dolly*, 1975, The Minskoff Theatre. Courtesy of the Billy rose Theatre Collection, The New York Public Library for the Performing Arts. Astor, Lenox and Tilden Foundations.

Chapter VIII

Pearl Bailey:
The Black Dolly Gallagher Levi

"Will there be no more white Othellos?"

During the seminar "Past and Present Regulations of Race and Ethnicity in the Theatre: Has Anything Changed?" the only white male of fifteen seminarians present asked the question, "Will there be no more white Othellos?" He believed, strongly, that white actors were losing good roles to minority actors, and especially bemoaned the possibility that the theatre might never again have a Sir Laurence Olivier play Othello. As the only African American member of the panel, I challenged the white male who was clearly asserting that only a white male could pose as the Moor in the sterling manner the role required. The occasion was the November 1998 annual meeting of the American Society for Theatre Research in Washington, D. C. There were tense moments and a fervent discussion session.

I called on Errol Hill, eminent Shakespearean scholar, who was in the audience. While I admired Sir Laurence Olivier as one of the greatest Shakespearean actors of the twentieth century, I hoped that his "minstrel Othello," where he blackened his face, rolled his eyes in stereotypic fashion, walked in an effeminate manner and carried a red rose, would not be the image my student clientele would have of Othello. Hill responded that critics said, "He [Olivier] walks like a Negro and talks like a Negro," confirming my protest that color, alone, nor even vast experience as a Shakespearean actor can always determine how well one human being can perform a role.

A similar question surfaced when the black *Hello Dolly!* opened in October 1967, at Washington's National Theatre and moved on to Broadway at the St. James Theatre, between 1967 and 1969. David Merrick as impresario selected Pearl Bailey to play Dolly Gallagher Levi, the husband-hunting widow from Yonkers. Bailey used her influence to see that an all-black cast got the roles. For this, she received considerable criticism, from both black and white, including the President of Actors Equity, Frederick O'Neal, a fair-minded African American who pondered whether the performers "were sacrificing their principles for a few bucks" (quoted in Woll 228). O'Neal even wanted an integrated show. He was almost always a balanced man.

Musicals are the bread and butter of Broadway. Most theatergoers wish to be entertained, so *Oklahoma, Show Boat,* and *Paint Your Wagon* have been crowd pleasers and escapist in nature. Black musicals, historically, have brought in large crowds and considerable revenue. Perhaps they have the same kind of appeal for both black and white that Silas Green from New Orleans once did, when frenzied people flocked in droves to see black people sing, dance, and "cut the fool." The buffoon was a part of minstrelsy, but so were the pretty women, the music and dance.

Clorindy, A Trip to Coontown, and *Shuffle Along* were early black musicals that brought large crowds and strong audience appeal. O'Neal, who helped co-found the all-black American Negro Theatre (1940–49) was being practical and generating good will in his position as the only black President of Actors Equity in his concern about *Hello Dolly!* being integrated.

Carol Channing, who created the role of Dolly Gallagher Levi in 1964, had made *Hello Dolly!* hallowed ground for white actors. Bailey's response to her critics was simply: "A lot of talented people showed up, and what's wrong with them having a good job? What is good for the Negro? What is good for the Negro is good for every man..." (*The New York Times,* 19 Aug. 1990, 21).

Through Pearl Bailey's influence, Cab Calloway, a close friend of Bailey, and a multi-talented man, netted the leading role of Horace Vandergelder, a "mean and respectable man." Morgan Freeman, an unknown at the time, made his Broadway debut as a professional dancer in *Hello Dolly!* Thomas Anderson, a veteran actor of color since Virgil Thomson's 1934 *Four Saints in Three Acts,* was chosen as Calloway's understudy. Mabel King played Ernestine. Roger Lawson was Ambrose Kemper. Jack Crowder took on the part of Cornelius Hackl. The role of Irene Molloy, Dolly's competition for Vandergelder's heart, went to Emily Yancy. Billy Daniels was Vandergelder in a 1975 revival at the Minskoff Theatre. In the eyes of some, such audacity and temerity were a sacrilege.

Nevertheless, the title role won for Miss Bailey a special 1968 Tony award, and a standing ovation. Bouquets of flowers cascaded on the stage. The long-running Broadway musical also brought President Lyndon Johnson to the National Theatre. Bailey publicly recognized him in the audience one night, remarking in her typical style, "I didn't know this chile was going to show up." Then she brought him on stage for a sing-along chorus of the title song. It was probably the first time that a President of the United States served as a chorus boy (Wilson 21).

There had been a history of White House support for people of color in the theatre initiated by Eleanor Roosevelt during the Great Depression. "The Johnsons took up the new *Dolly* much as Eleanor Roosevelt had prominently attended *Swing Mikado* and *Mamba's Daughters*" (Woll 228). Eleanor Roosevelt had also supported *On Whitman Avenue* in 1946. Lyndon Johnson's support of Pearl Bailey and the all-black *Hello Dolly!* was a key element in the support of this historic production.

Bailey's role of the matchmaker who finally gets Horace Vandergelder to the altar by feigning interest in helping him get a wife other than herself has been a plum one in popular culture, the American theatre, and film. The musical was based on Thornton Wilder's *The Matchmaker* and, in 1969, starred the very talented Barbra Streisand in a $20 million film version, with Walter Matthau as Horace Vandergelder. Several other actors have played Dolly—Betty Grable, Ginger Rogers, and Martha Raye. When Pearl Bailey died, Carol Channing remarked, "The entertainment world has lost one of its most creative performers of our time. Her talent was unique and endearing" (Wilson 21).

Current Biography Yearbook 1969 reported: "'Dolly is the highest office to which the American woman can aspire,' a reviewer noted, and Miss Bailey has been elected to it by acclamation'" (24). Critic Clive Barnes exclaimed about Bailey's portrayal of Dolly:

> frankly my sensitive white liberal conscience was offended at the idea of a nonintegrated Negro show . . . But believe me, from the first to the last I was overwhelmed. For Miss Bailey this was a Broadway triumph for the history books . . .
>
> By the second act the audience was not merely eating out of Miss Bailey's hand, it had started to chew at her fingernails. When she came to the actual "Hello Dolly!" number with that entrance into the Harmonia Gardens down the red carpet, the curtains at the top parted just slightly, she slipped in, paused and then, while the audience roared, came down the steps like a motherly debutante . . . As she pranced, hips wagging and eyes a'joy, around on the runway in front of the orchestra . . . the audience would have elected her Governor if she'd only named the state (61:1).

Actors in the show were equally effusive.

Morgan Freeman, who played Rudolph, a dancer, in the 1967 Broadway production of *Hello Dolly!*, said to me:

> One of my biggest lessons I got, I got from Pearl Bailey in my first Broadway show, *Hello Dolly!*, Pearl Bailey was never late. She gave 100 percent every performance, eight times a week. Her love affair with the audience was genuine (8 Feb. 1997).

This sentiment is often expressed.

Cab Calloway wrote:

> There she'd stand at the top of the stairs, her sloe eyes sparkling above high cheekbones, her plumage-laden picture hat parading above a scarlet dress and high button shoes, as the second act of *Hello Dolly!* got off to its rousing start. Then down she'd strut, the girl I brought to Broadway 22 years before—now my grown-up friend Pearl Bailey. She'd greet everyone in her rumbling pipe-organ voice, and her fellow players would answer in that unforgettable refrain: "Hello, Dolly—well, hello, Dolly, it's so nice to have you back where you belong" (153).

Calloway, the "flamboyant band leader who strutted and scat-sang his way to enduring fame as the 'Hi-de-ho' man of jazz" (Wilson 20 Nov. 1994), was born in 1907. Eleven years older than Pearl Bailey, and a star since 1931, Calloway had opened doors to his protégé and close friend Pearl Bailey, whom he clearly adored.

A number of people adored her, and there were, of course, detractors. Richard Nixon appointed her "Ambassador of Love" in 1970 and Ronald Reagan awarded her the Presidential Medal of Freedom in 1988. Pearl Bailey was the darling of conservative white America. Some African Americans, as a result, believed she was an embarrassment. Except for the controversy swirling around *Hello Dolly!*, Bailey was virtually anti-political. *Current Biography Yearbook 1969* noted: "'I belong to nothing except humanity,'" she told Joan Barthel in an interview for the *New York Times* (November 20, 1967). . . . People ask me, why don't I march. . . . I march every day in my heart'" (25).

Marching is not the only way to effect change, of course. Bailey, as her life progressed, and as money became more plentiful, did become involved in several charitable causes for which she was honored. Some knowledge of her background is essential to understanding her pronouncements, with which many people of color disagreed.

According to *Current Biography Yearbook 1955*, "Pearl Mae Bailey was born in Newport News, Virginia on March 29, 1918 [to Joseph James and

Ella Mae Bailey] and started dancing and singing at the age of three" (34). She was the youngest of four children. Miss Bailey's father was a minister of the House of Prayer, a sanctified church. It was in this church that the young Pearl Bailey came to know the rhythms of call and response.

She also came to know the heartache any child experiences when one's parents bicker. She said in her autobiography, *The Raw Pearl,* for her parents "Sunday also seemed to be Argument Day. Papa and Mama regularly had a red-hot one going right after church. Then Mama's flat steamer trunk used to get pushed out in the hall. Mama would push it back in" (6).

Following the divorce, Pearl Bailey went to Washington, D.C., at age four, with her father, but much later, in 1933, joined her mother and three siblings in Philadelphia. By now, her mother had married a second time, a man named Walter Robinson. Bailey's early ambition was to be a school teacher. However, at the age of 15, she won an amateur contest in Philadelphia. Then, another award at Harlem's Apollo Theatre came, and she was bitten by the performing bug forever.

Sarah P. Morris wrote:

> Throughout the rest of the 1930s Bailey performed extensively as a singer and dancer on the Philadelphia-area entertainment circuit. One summer she toured with singer Noble Sissle's band as a specialty dancer. Another summer during her late teens she performed in the red-light districts of tough Pennsylvania mining towns like Pottsville, Wilkes-Barre, and Scranton. It was during this wild time that she married for the first time; the marriage— to a drummer—lasted only eighteen months (67).

Of the Pennsylvania mining towns, Bailey wrote in *The Raw Pearl:*

> Pottsville, Pennsylvania, at that time was wide open. All of the coal region was known for sporting houses, or what was commonly called the red-light district. (They really did have red lights in the windows.) Minersville Street was the busiest street in Pottsville; the girls even jumped on the running boards of the cars to catch "tricks" (24).

While Bailey never strayed into the world's oldest profession, she did enjoy tips from the procurers and other business men of Pottsville.

Pearl Bailey again moved to Washington, D. C. in 1940 and for the next several years played major nightclubs in New York City—the Apollo Theatre and Cafe Zanzibar—and clubs in the Baltimore and Washington, D. C. areas. She went on very lengthy tours from Texas to California with the United Service Organization (USO) riding or sleeping on the berths of trains. At the clubs, Miss Bailey claims she made $18 a week in tips. She earned $15 a week base pay in the Pennsylvania mining towns: "three for rent, three for board, nine dollars left for clothes, and don't forget Mama got at least a dollar and a half. She didn't ask; she just deserved it because she was Mama" (Bailey 27).

It was in the 1946 Broadway postwar black musical, *St. Louis Woman*, at the Martin Beck Theatre, that many feel Pearl Bailey first reached stardom. Edith Isaacs observed:

> Pearl Bailey, a talented member of the younger generation in the theatre [was] Butterfly in *St. Louis Woman*, her first good opportunity on Broadway. The musical was written by Countee Cullen and Arna Bontemps, music by Vernon Duke, and with Ruby Hill in a leading role (141).

Miss Hill was Della Green, *the* St. Louis woman. On 1 April 1946, Howard Barnes wrote in the *New York Herald Tribune:* "Pearl Bailey . . . pulls the show up by its shoestrings every time she makes an entrance" (quoted in *Current Biography Yearbook 1955* 35). Bailey won the 1946 Donaldson Award for best newcomer on Broadway.

Allen Woll stated:

> *St. Louis Woman*, [Harold] Arlen's postwar venture into black musical drama, differed strongly from the *Cabin in the Sky* and *Porgy and Bess* tradition by its reliance on black writers. Arna Bontemps adapted his 1931 novel *God Sends Sunday* with the assistance of Countee Cullen, who died shortly before the show's premiere. Rouben Mamoulian, of *Porgy and Bess* fame, was also brought in to direct the show.
>
> *St. Louis Woman* was noted for its remarkable cast (199).

According to Woll, Bailey lamented, "Once I sang a song called 'Tired,' and they began to associate it with me. I became a lazy-moving, tired, slow-dragger. Nobody ever pictured me kissing the leading man" (199). This was true of many African Americans on the stage, a fact that many have pointed out a vast number of times.

But Bailey did have the advantage of working in a play by black writers who were accomplished. Cullen held a Harvard M.A. and had been a star of the Harlem Renaissance of the 1920s and early 1930s. Bontemps was a professor at predominantly black Fisk University in Nashville, Tennessee, and a very close friend of Langston Hughes. There is a book that contains the many letters they wrote one another, *Arna Bontemps-Langston Hughes Letters, 1925–1967* (New York: Dodd Mead, 1980), collected by Bontemps. But Bailey was marginalized in her role.

She had only two numbers in *St. Louis Woman*, "Legalize My Name," and "A Woman's Prerogative." But she made the most of them and so dominated the show that she eclipsed the famous Nicholas Brothers tap-dance team. They were always a class act. Rex Ingram, who played bar owner, Bigelow Brown, and boyfriend of the St. Louis woman, was all but ignored after Bailey sang.

Following the success of this Broadway production, Bailey found herself in demand in both Hollywood and on Broadway, as well as in some of America's most prestigious night clubs in New York and Las Vegas. Her night club stints included the Latin Quarter in Boston and the Savoy Ballroom in Harlem. She was at Ciro's in Hollywood, and the Desert Inn and the Flamingo in Las Vegas. Some of her hits included the famous "Tired," "Bill Bailey, Won't You Please Come Home," "Two to Tango," and "Row, Row, Row Your Boat." Two Paramount films came her way. In 1947, she was cast in their *Variety Girl*, and in 1948, in *Isn't It Romantic?*

On 31 August 1948, Miss Bailey married a second time into a turbulent domestic union with a man whose name she refused to put in writing. Miss Bailey, in a truly magnanimous gesture, wrote in *The Raw Pearl*: "I will call him Jim. He was a good-looking, brilliant, wealthy Washington playboy. The wealth was from his family's real estate business" (50). This was a marriage in which there was constant abuse. It lasted until 20 March 1952. When Pearl Bailey decided to divorce him, she learned that all the mortgages had been put in her name, and she was $70,000 in debt. "Jim" even traded Miss Bailey's car in on another Cadillac for his girlfriend, prior to the divorce.

Pearl Bailey was a risk taker, but one who within two years mustered the courage to leave "Jim" and six months later, to marry Caucasian jazz drummer Louis Bellson in London, on 19 November 1952. In 1952, few white men were marrying black women, and far fewer interracial marriages occurred at all. Virtually 95 percent of interracial marriages in 1952, celebrity or otherwise, were black male and white female. Bellson and Bailey adopted two children, Tony, a son, and later, a daughter, Dee Dee. Bailey's marriage to Bellson lasted almost 38 years, until her death, and it was reputed to have been happy. They also performed together.

Bailey was sought for Hollywood films in the 1950s. The roles, however, were not very flattering, although she is fondly remembered for many of her performances. She was Frankie, Carmen Jones's "good-time" friend in the highly touted 1954 movie *Carmen Jones*, a film based on George Bizet's opera. Oscar Hammerstein, II, wrote the musical. Otto Preminger directed, Samuel Goldwyn produced, Dorothy Dandridge was Carmen, and Harry Belafonte, her lover, Joe. Olga James was the character, Cindy Lou, the sweet girlfriend of Joe. Brock Peters played the villainous Sergeant Brown and Joe Adams was the sexy prizefighter, Husky Miller, the black counterpart of Escamillo. Donald Bogle asserted: "Pearl Bailey was an open delight as she belted out a rousing 'Beat Out That Rhythm on the Drum'"

(169). Her earthiness, bright colored dresses of greens and blues, and her gift for ad lib made her a favorite in this film, which still frequently airs on the American Movie Channel.

Bailey had stereotypical roles, in the main. In 1954, also, she was Madame Fleur, the madam of a well-to-do West Indian house of prostitution, in the Broadway production of Truman Capote's *House of Flowers* at the Alvin Theatre. It opened 30 December 1954. The play lasted for 165 performances. Bailey wowed the audiences with her "What is a Friend for?" Walter Kerr noted in the *New York Herald Tribune:* [Pearl Bailey] was "easily raffish, demonically secure, justifiably confident" (quoted in *Current Biography Yearbook 1969* 24). Kerr's polite term, "raffish," for vulgar was not his sentiment alone. "The production cost $269,000 and included such well-known performers as Juanita Hall as Madame Tango, Diahann Carroll as Otillie, and Geoffrey Holder as the voodoo practitioner" (Jarmon 33). Then, Bailey played the maid, Gussie, in *That Certain Feeling,* a 1956 film starring Bob Hope and Eva Marie Saint.

The famous *St. Louis Blues* (1958), a fictionalized film biography of the blues composer W. C. Handy, featured Nat "King" Cole in the title role, Ruby Dee as his girlfriend who advocates "the Lord's music," Eartha Kitt, who sings "the devil's music," and Juano Hernandez as the tyrannical, excessively religious father who is so convinced that his son has taken up the devil's music that he throws the son's cornet in front of a moving horse wagon. Bailey was a warm Aunt Hagar to W. C. Handy.

While making the *St. Louis Blues,* Bailey attempted the role of superwoman. According to Cab Calloway, she did her own cooking, shopping, and cleaning (156). Calloway also mentioned that while working on the film, Bailey was also working Las Vegas. "For three weeks, she'd finish her show at 1:30 A.M., rush off to be in the California studio by 8 A.M., finish at 3:00 P.M., and catch a plane back to Vegas for shows at 8:30 and midnight" (156). It was this self-abuse that contributed to her health problems.

Miss Bailey also played Maria, the cynical cookshop woman, in the Metro Goldwyn Mayer movie version of *Porgy and Bess* with Sammy Davis, Jr. as Sportin' Life, Sidney Poitier as Porgy, and Dorothy Dandridge as Bess. Bogle thinks:

> Pearl Bailey could be counted on to be sassy, sensible and inventive. She was not taken in by sham, and never in her lifetime was anybody going to pull the wool over her eyes. Yet, independent and sure-footed as she was, Bailey was never pure cantankerous mammy. There was a streak of gentleness to her, and at times she was the cheerful aunt jemima who might rousingly speak her mind but who at heart meant no one any harm. Her distinguishing characteristic throughout her career was her astounding vivacity. Often

her energies seemed too broad and outlandish for a medium that requires subtlety and restraint. Who could forget how she lifted *Porgy and Bess* from its idealized, insulted world? As the shrewd, perceptive Maria she presented audiences with a chatty presence who could not abide idealization or falsification. If anything, her performance uncovered the shallowness and dishonesty of the stereotype figures that dominated the production. Pearl Bailey was genuine (189).

Perhaps it was this genuineness that also added to her appeal.

"Most of her audience is familiar with her endearing penchant for embellishing a song by ad-libbing and employing chit-chat and asides. The technique is frequently referred to as Pearlie May's throwaway style of delivery" (Jarmon 34). Bailey also added a feather boa, other furs, and rhinestones in creating her stage presence.

Her work in the 1960 *All the Fine Young Cannibals* is legend. In it she played Ruby Jones, a self-destructive blues singer who has drunk too much in her lifetime, and who assists a white musician, played by Robert Wagner, to fame. They live together in what Hollywood would have its viewers believe was a non-romantic relationship. Gary Null observed:

> The film tries hard to capture the period rhythm, but the plot is contrived. A varied collection of people mill around Miss Bailey as she trots from her bedroom to the club. Pearl Bailey is fine as the singer, however, and her funeral exalts the Negro race as the "force of rhythm" in the music world (167).

Her next film, *The Landlord,* with Lee Grant, was ten years later.

Meanwhile, Bailey's health, due to overwork, became a major factor in her professional image. In 1964, she was admitted to the hospital for exhaustion. She was 46. In February of 1965, she was again admitted for overwork. On 22 April 1965, in New York, she collapsed (Calloway 156). Four days later, she fell on her knees after coming off the stage.

Two years later, she opened in *Hello Dolly!* The show ran for two years on Broadway and then went on tour of major cities in the United States. Much to the dismay of her fans, Pearl Bailey quit the tour of *Hello Dolly!* when it was to have opened at the Uihlein Hall Performing Arts Center in Milwaukee in May of 1970. Even Cab Calloway, the leading man, arrived at the Pfister Hotel to register, where the desk clerk broke the news of the cancellation to him.

The *Milwaukee Journal* reported:

> Pearl Bailey Tuesday turned her back on the biggest payday in the *Hello Dolly!* national tour, put 70 performers out of work and raised the hackles

of about 18,000 Milwaukeeans who were deprived of seeing her in the much lauded musical comedy....

The scheduled eight performance engagement had been sold out with the greatest week's gross in the city's history, $140,000. The gross also topped every engagement the company had played on its tour.

Miss Bailey reportedly was to receive 10 percent of the gross in addition to a five figure salary for the week. The newspaper referred to Miss Bailey as "capricious," without knowing her reason for abruptly leaving the show. The set had been put on the stage and had to be "struck." Stagehands had to be paid and money for tickets refunded. Fatigue was a likely reason she left.

On 12 February 1972, Pearl Bailey, after a series of heart attacks, had yet another one, this one so severe that she was believed to be dead. As a result, perhaps, in the 1970s she diversified her life and career. She wrote books, having already penned her well-known autobiography, *The Raw Pearl*, in 1968. Autobiographies of women often have silences, where they leave out some details of sexual coercion and patriarchal power. Men may be even less revealing. Miss Bailey wrote cook books in addition to autobiography. It is unknown how much of her life she left out and, so, her life story may be her own perception of how things occurred.

In 1971, Miss Bailey starred in an ABC television series, *The Pearl Bailey Show*. She then considered retirement. Sarah P. Morris stated:

> Even after announcing in 1975, at the age of fifty-seven, that she was retiring from show business, Bailey remained in the public eye. She made numerous TV appearances on commercials, game shows, sitcoms, dramas and specials. In 1975, she was named a special advisor to the U.S. mission of the United Nations General Assembly. She costarred with comedian Redd Foxx in the 1976 film comedy *Norman . . . Is That You?* She received a Britannica Life Achievement Award in 1978 and was fêted with an "all-star" TV tribute in 1979. In 1981, she provided the voice for Big Mama, the owl in *The Fox and the Hound*, an animated film (68).

Diversification, too, had its rewards.

In 1977, according to Calloway, she received an honorary doctorate from Georgetown University, where she also gave the Commencement Address. In January of 1978, Bailey, at 58, enrolled as a full-time freshman at Georgetown. This took a great deal of courage. She made the Dean's List and in 1985 completed a B.A. in Theology, a degree she had abandoned in the 1930s.

Pearl Bailey's life was affected by a lack of formal education during her most productive years. Very few African Americans of her era earned college degrees. In 1918, the year she was born, through 1954, legal segregation prevailed in the public schools and in many colleges and universities. Additionally, Miss Bailey was born into the working class. There was an elite black middle class, defined by degrees and money. Bailey had only the latter, eventually, and a lot of naturally endowed talent. Her personal life, arguably, may have been very different had she had the advantage of a formal education sooner.

Ever a trooper in spite of disadvantages, on 11 July 1990, Pearl Bailey underwent knee surgery, performed by Dr. Richard H. Rothman, at the Pennsylvania Hospital in Philadelphia. Miss Bailey suffered from degenerative arthritis and had an operation common to many, especially those over the age of 65. She recovered enough to give a concert with Wynton Marsalis.

But on 17 August 1990, as she was packing her bags to go to New York, she called out "Louis!" and her heart gave out (Calloway 158). Louis Bellson rushed Miss Bailey to the Thomas Jefferson University Hospital in Philadelphia. During her brief hospital stay, her husband slept on a cot at her bedside. She did not linger in pain.

Approximately 2,000 people attended the services at the Deliverance Evangelistic Church while many more paid their respects outside. Lena Horne and Ella Fitzgerald sent flowers. Cab Calloway was a pallbearer who spoke these words: "Pearl was love, pure and simple love. I mean it from my heart and soul, that Pearl Bailey was something you'll never see again" (*The New York Times*, 24 Aug. 1990, B, 7). Rabbi Harold S. White said at her funeral: "Her life was a song" (Calloway 158). Louis Bellson was heartbroken. He said that he could never return to their home at Lake Havasu, Arizona without her (Feather 1 Sept. 1990). He agreed to attend other ceremonies and tributes many made to this theatrical legend.

Pearl Bailey broke many barriers, and according to many sources, without any visible appearance of bitterness or anger. Will there be no more white Othellos? Of course, there will be. Patrick Stewart is a recent excellent one. Will there be only white Dolly Gallagher Levis? No. Roles no longer belong to one racial group. While Pearl Bailey cannot get credit for all of the non-traditional casting that has evolved in the twentieth century, for *Hello Dolly!* she made history in the annals of the American theatre. That history, unfortunately, has not all been positive. There is still a great deal of resentment over all-black shows, and not all of it from Caucasians.

Woll discovered the following after a study done by Actors Equity revealing shocking statistics, much of this in the uproar over the all-black *Hello Dolly!*

> The New York State Commission for Human Rights investigated theatrical hiring policies the following year (1968), and its conclusions were similar to

those of Equity's study. Of the 523 actors in 22 Broadway shows in March, 1968, only 57 were black, 7 Hispanic, and 1 of Asian origin. Backstage statistics were equally dismal. Of 664 production employees on Broadway that season, only 14 were black. Although the stagehands' union had been integrated in 1955, only 2 of the 381 working on Broadway that season were black (227).

Frederick O'Neal had mixed feelings about the all-black *Hello Dolly!*, but preferred not to speak to David Merrick, a producer of considerable stature. O'Neal, a native of Mississippi who went to New York City during the Great Depression, was a man of even temperament, who had experienced the pain of the racial divide, but believed, ideally, in an integrated society and fairness. Even he admitted, though, "We gauge progress in this area by the number of Negroes engaged for roles not racially designated" (quoted in Woll 228).

In a world that fought for integration in the 1960s, there seems to be a perpetual ideological struggle regarding separation and integration in the decades that followed that era. In the more than 30 years since the all-black *Hello Dolly!* crossed the boards of The National Theatre and the St. James, one must acknowledge that different world views regarding separation and integration have not ceased. Pearl Bailey wanted a role not racially designated, and got it for herself and others.

The argument began, perhaps, with Marcus Garvey in 1921 with his Universal Negro Improvement Association and his Back to Africa movement, one clearly outside of the world of theatre as we define it in the arts. It was a major argument that consumed many in the 1960s when Martin Luther King, Jr. declared that we must integrate. Malcolm X, until the latter years of his life, argued for separation. It is an argument facing public schools and colleges at this very hour. The argument continues today with August Wilson and Robert Brustein, most visibly, but it is a deep concern affecting most in the theatre, whether it be on Broadway, in regional theatres, on college campuses, or in local community houses.

Any assessment of Bailey's total career and life would cause one to reflect that Pearl Bailey, imperfect as all humans are, embraced mankind and gave many of audiences, as well as her friends and family, a great deal of pleasure.

Works Cited

Associated Press, "Pearl Bailey's Love Is Remembered at Her Funeral," *The New York Times,* 24 Aug. 1990, B, 7:1.

Bailey, Pearl. *The Raw Pearl.* New York: Harcourt, Brace and World, 1968.

Barnes, Clive. "Pearl Bailey Captures Audience From Start," The *New York Times Theater Review,* 13 Nov. 1967, 61:1.
Bogle, Donald. *Toms, Coons, Mulattoes, Mammies and Bucks.* New York: Continuum, 1996.
Byrd, Rudolph. *Generations in Black and White.* Athens: University of Georgia Press, 1993.
Calloway, Cab. "Unforgettable Pearl Bailey," *Reader's Digest.* Aug. 1991, 153–158.
Current Biography Yearbook 1955. New York: H. W. Wilson Company, 1955, 34–36.
Current Biography Yearbook 1969. New York: H. W. Wilson Company, 1969, 23–25.
Feather, Leonard. "Drummer Bellson Brings Big Band to Disneyland; Jazz: The Musician-Composer Is Trying to Look Forward after the Funeral of His Wife, Pearl Bailey. His Daughter, Dee Dee, Will Join Him," *The Los Angeles Times,* 1 Sept. 1990, F, 1:5.
Freeman, Morgan. Personal interview with author. 8 Feb. 1997.
Isaacs, Edith. *The Negro in the American Theatre.* New York: Theatre Arts, 1947.
Jarmon, Laura C. Entry on Pearl Bailey in *Notable Black Women of America,* ed. Jessie Carney Smith. Detroit: Gale, 1992, 32–34.
Joslyn, Jay. "Pearl's Exit Irks 'Dolly' Fans Here," *Milwaukee Journal,* n.d., n.p.
Morris, Sarah P. Entry on Pearl Bailey in *Black Women in America: An Historical Encyclopedia.* Darlene Clark Hine, ed. Brooklyn: Carlson Publishing Company, 1993, 66–68.
Null, Gary. *Black Hollywood: The Black Performer in Motion Pictures.* New York: Citadel Press, 1975. (courtesy of Ed Hancock)
"Pearl Bailey Mourned as Person of Love," *The Chicago Tribune,* 24 Aug. 1990, sec. 1, 13.
Peterson, Bernard L., Jr. *A Century of Musicals in Black and White: An Encyclopedia of Musical Stage Works by, about, or Involving African Americans.* Westport, Connecticut: Greenwood Press, 1993.
Thomas, Robert E. "Chronicle," *The New York Times,* 12 July 1990, B, 4:3.
Wilson, John S. "Pearl Bailey, Musical Star and Humorist, Is Dead at 72," *The New York Times,* 19 Aug. 1990, 21.
———. "Cab Calloway Is Dead at 86; 'Hi-de-hi-de-ho' Jazz Man," *The New York Times,* 20 Nov. 1994, 22.
Woll, Allen. *Black Musical Theatre: From Coontown to Dreamgirls.* Baton Rouge: Louisiana State University Press, 1989.

Ruby Dee and Ossie Davis (photo by Anthony Barboza). Permission granted by Tony DuPuis.

Chapter IX

Ossie and Ruby are One!

"Ossie and Ruby are one!"

—Dick Campbell

These words, declared to me by the late Dick Campbell on 3 June 1992, describe one of the twentieth century's most talented artist/activist couples, Ossie Davis and Ruby Dee. They have sustained dual careers for more than 50 years and have undertaken vast professional projects in theatre, film, radio, and television as a couple and as individuals. Married 50 years on 9 December 1998, they celebrated by raising $300,000 for "twelve community theaters, $25,000 apiece, in tribute to the theaters where they began their careers" (Kinnon 49).

Their work, which has included the traditional classics, has focused more heavily on African Americans and the works of African American writers and playwrights. Ossie Davis, who foremost wishes to be remembered as a writer, wrote:

> If we can create for our people; work for our people; belong to our people; we will no longer be forced into artistic prostitution and self-portrayal in the mad scramble, imposed upon us for too long, to belong to some other people. It is time for us who call ourselves artists, scholars and thinkers to rejoin the people from which we came. We shall then, and only then, be free to tell the truth about our people and that truth shall make us free (quoted from "Purlie Told Me!" in Fletcher 67)!

This credo has informed the daily activities of Davis and Dee, their performances, and the upbringing of their children.

The charismatic Ossie Davis and Ruby Dee are the proud parents of three adults: Nora, an educator; Guy, a blues musician, and Hasna, a middle-school principal. Their children have married accomplished spouses, and there are seven grandchildren. As of this writing, 14 January 1999, Ossie Davis's mother is also alive.

Ossie Davis and Ruby Dee have lived a life of courage and risk taking. Although they were called before the House Un-American Activities Committee (HUAC), they were not destroyed. As a result of Ruby Dee's name appearing in *Red Channels* (a newspaper column of the HUAC era that listed those thought to be subversive), she and Davis have missed opportunities that might have been theirs had they opted for a safer haven. Their struggle has been perpetual.

Dee was born into a troubled family of teenage parents, Edward Nathaniel Wallace and Gladys Hightower. The marriage was doomed; after the divorce, Wallace took a second wife, one much older than he, Emma Amelia Benson. Ruby called her mother. Ruby Wallace grew up in a home with a great deal of tension, although her stepmother was exceedingly good to her, supplying money and encouraging her talent.

The intelligent, beautiful, and resourceful Ruby Wallace entered Hunter College and eventually, while employed virtually full-time, earned a B.A. degree in romance languages. On 31 August 1941, she married a 23-year-old, four-foot, 65-pound midget, Frankie Dee Brown, a promoter for Schenley Distiller's Corporation. The marriage was short-lived, although sources differ as to the date of the divorce. Brown dropped his last name because Ruby liked the name Dee, which she has retained to this day.

Ossie Davis's life, which began in financial poverty, was far more stable than Dee's early years. But it was vintage rural South of the 1920s and 1930s. Davis's father, a self-taught construction engineer who could not write his name, ran into difficulty with the Georgia Ku Klux Klan who resented his job. While they looked threatening, Davis's father appeared unafraid, and so he was never physically harmed. Georgia police, in one of their gleeful pranks, poured molasses on the head of the young Ossie Davis. To this day, Davis is haunted by the fact that he laughed, but had he not, he might not have survived.

Moreover, Davis slept on a park bench in 1939 when, as an aspiring young actor, he left Howard University without a degree, and first arrived in New York City. He found himself in jail and labeled a vagrant by a white policeman. Ossie Davis ate 25 cent meals in Father Divine's "Heavens" during the Great Depression. Father Divine was a highly controversial religious leader in Harlem who fed the poor and housed a number of women in his "Heavens."

A bubbly but serious Ruby Dee, who initially appeared more assertive than Davis, gave a speech at Carnegie Hall in support of Ethel and Julius Rosenberg, alleged spies, who were on trial for espionage in the 1950s. So visible was Miss Dee, the activist, that she appears in FBI files, with Davis tainted by association with her. He spent a great deal of his time picketing for better conditions for actors in the union, Actors Equity. Davis reflected: "Many a battle over racism, segregated theaters, McCarthyism, the Cold War and nuclear hysteria was fought on the floor of our union meetings" (*With Ossie and Ruby* 227).

In a diversified dual career, after a period of more than 50 years as performers, Dee and Davis finally began to get national recognition. In 1995, President and Mrs. Clinton honored them with the National Medal of Arts at the White House. In 1996, the Association for Theatre in Higher Education (ATHE) cited them for Lifetime Achievement at their 1996 annual conference held at the Marriott Marquis, New York City. In the *ATHE NEWS*, May 1996, the society wrote: "Ruby Dee and Ossie Davis are extraordinary theatre artists and writers whose work on stage, film and television has earned them numerous honors and awards" (1). *Ebony* observed:

> They are both members of the Theater Hall of Fame and in 1989 received NAACP Image Awards for their work in Do The Right Thing. In 1994, they were honored with the Silver Circle Award by the Academy of Television Arts and Sciences . . . (Kinnon 196).

Their major national recognition was long overdue! Their recognition in many smaller circles had occurred a long time ago.

Ruby Dee

Ruby Dee has performed consistently since 1940. A number of seasoned people in theatre circles regard her as one of the most accomplished and experienced female actors alive today. Having been on the stage since she was a teenager, much of Miss Dee's success can be attributed to an extraordinary style of underplaying.

Dick Campbell made the following statement about Ruby Dee to me on 3 June 1992:

> She's had a powerful career—both she and Ossie. She's probably the No. 1 actress in America today who has had more experience than other black actresses who are still alive. She is one of the most talented actresses in the business today, barring none, black or white. She is just the top person, in my opinion, in the theatre today [who is] female.

> She can interpret and negotiate any kind of role. She has the capacity, knowledge, and the experience to represent the American stage in any acting category. That woman is absolutely talented. She studied and prepared herself a long time ago. I don't know any actress, black or white, who can exceed or excel her work. If she were not black, she would be the No. 1 actress in America in the eyes of others—she would be recognized.

Dee's color and gender were probably the chief factors in her not being more nationally celebrated sooner.

Born in Cleveland, Ohio, 27 October 1924, Dee is a highly versatile actor who has constantly faced the racial and gender divide. For example, she played Cordelia in 1965 opposite Morris Carnovsky, a white actor. Bernard Grebanier, critic, wrote, "When Morris Carnovsky played Lear against Ruby Dee; when the Vivian Beaumont Theatre gives me a black Orsino and Maria, I *am* upset—not out of racial prejudice, but out of respect for Shakespeare's plays" (Grebanier 534). In spite of this sneering, Dee has focused on her acting and not the critics.

As a virtual unknown on the national landscape, in 1950 she played the wife of Jackie Robinson in the Hollywood film *The Jackie Robinson Story*. *Ebony* asserted in its June 1950 issue:

> With no pretense of presenting more than the bare skeleton story of the first Negro in the major leagues, *The Jackie Robinson Story* is, according to its hero, who plays himself, "just a success story on the screen—nothing more." Co-hero of the story is Brooklyn boss Branch Rickey, who is presented as sort of an Abe Lincoln of baseball (87).

Ruby Dee is barely mentioned. Two identified photos, one showing her comforting Robinson, and the other urging him to stay in school, are her only credits in the article. But she was in Hollywood.

Rearing a family and doing various work, by 1958 Dee was highly effective in the movie *The St. Louis Blues* as the soft-spoken romantic interest of blind musician W. C. Handy, played by Nat "King" Cole. Juano Hernandez played the religious zealot who believed that blues is the work of the devil and, as a result, throws his son's cornet in front of a moving horse carriage. Pearl Bailey played the proud aunt. A final tableau of Dee, Hernandez, and Bailey standing in the wings, as Cole and Eartha Kitt sang Handy's signature piece at Carnegie Hall was a "tear-jerker."

Other movies kept beckoning and Ruby Dee accumulated experience and training. Konstantin Stanislavski (1863–1938),

> Russian actor, director and teacher . . . created the most influential "system" of acting in the Western world. . . . Stanislavski advocated a balance between

the actor's inner experiencing of the role and its precisely attuned physical and vocal expression (Stanton and Banham 353).

Dee does this and more, having been trained in "The Method" by actors from Russia, through the American Negro Theater. As Christine in Louis Peterson's drama turned film, *Take A Giant Step*, in 1960, she comforts an adolescent black male with a shattering performance. When the young man, Spence, says that he hates being "colored" in a white neighborhood, Dee declares in the softest imaginable voice, with profound subtlety of movement, "If you hadn't been colored, you'd have never met your grandma," whom Spence adores.

Dee's silences, body movements, and grimaces are equally unforgettable as Ruth, Sidney Poitier's wife in the highly touted film *Buck and the Preacher* (1972). As Poitier's wife, also named Ruth, in Lorraine Hansberry's play adapted to film, *A Raisin in the Sun* (1959), it is Dee's quiet anger, shifting moods, and non flamboyant rage that helped this play, with its all-star cast and director, become a staple of the American theatre.

African American film critic Donald Bogle was not as laudatory as many critics about *A Raisin in the Sun*.

> As the wife who agonizes over cleaning someone else's home . . . , Ruby Dee proved successful with a difficult character. . . . Before *A Raisin in the Sun*, Ruby Dee had run through the perfect wife-girl-friend bit to the point where she was—as one newspaper called her—"the Negro June Allyson." . . . Although she occasionally rose above her material—her breakdown after Poitier's death in *Edge of the City* was extremely powerful—even in her good work, Ruby Dee . . . appeared to be the typical woman born to be hurt. Everything about her suggested frustration and pain. Her voice trembled and broke. . . . She looked . . . terribly underfed and unloved (*Toms, Coons* 198–199).

This style seemed intentional.

However, her low-key demeanor, Dee says, is unintentional (1 Sept. 1992). I submit that it is this very style, deliberate or not, that has been a major factor in propelling her into a career that has spanned more than 50 years.

Ruby Dee began her career with the American Negro Theatre (ANT) in 1940. The group had workshops for sharpening their skills. The ANT worked in the basement of the old Schomburg Library in New York City's Harlem. The late Frederick O'Neal and Abram Hill co-founded the group, setting up rigid rules of discipline. "Actors were fined if they were late for rehearsal" (O'Neal 24 June 1980).

On 25 August 1946, *The Daily Worker* reported: "The overall purpose of the American Negro Theatre is to revolutionize Negro participation in the theatre—to project men and women on the stage as men and women rather than exotic distortions" (n.p.). With this group, which included many now famous actors of color, Dee played the title role in the road production of Philip Yordan's *Anna Lucasta*. Hilda Simms created the role in 1944. The play went on to Broadway in 1946, under the influence of Harry Wagstaff Gribble.

Of her work with the ANT, Ruby Dee reflects:

> It was one of the most significant times in my life. Relationships were very special. It was a theatrical family. I've never had that experience since then. My time in Harlem was the most exciting time of my life. The ANT was my first training and schooling—the first time I had thought of technique. It was the most comprehensive involvement I have had. People came from the Soviet Union. They loved the group. Abe [Hill] and Fred O'Neal respected them (1 Sept. 1992).

The ANT boasted Sidney Poitier, Alvin and Alice Childress, Isabel Sanford, and Earle Hyman, in addition to Hilda Simms.

Dee's first role, in 1940, was that of Cobina, a young debutante in love with a poor man, in Abram Hill's biting satire about the black bourgeoisie, *On Striver's Row*. The play showed black strivers imitating wealthy white society with its maids and debutante balls. E. Franklin Frazier, a sociologist, later wrote a treatise on America's black bourgeoisie, a small group obsessed with color, academic credits, and cash.

Dee's neighbor and professional associate, professor and playwright William B. Branch, wrote:

> Ruby Dee, in my book, has long established herself as one of the most accomplished, as well as important, actors in the U.S. Her brilliance of talent, seemingly boundless, has spanned the decades from the American Negro Theater's *Anna Lucasta* on Broadway in the 1940s to Spike Lee's *Jungle Fever* in films in the 1990s, with major contributions all along the way. I particularly relish memories of her arresting performance as Lena in Athol Fugard's *Boesman and Lena* opposite James Earl Jones, and her luminous rendering of Julia in Alice Childress's *Wedding Band*—both Off-Broadway, and both among the finest characterizations I have ever seen. Along with her artistry, however, is Miss Dee's well-known reputation as a fighter—both in and out of the industry—for human rights and dignity, especially for African-Americans. This has undoubtedly cost her dearly, in terms of career opportunities unoffered or withheld. But she has nevertheless managed to survive, even to triumph, with her integrity unchallenged and her accomplishments undenied (29 June 1992).

Fellow actor the late Thomas Anderson, who played the stableman in *Wedding Band*, spoke on how in that play she changed from being the ingénue she had cultivated as Lutiebelle Gussiemae Jenkins in Ossie Davis's 1960 play, *Purlie Victorious:*

> Ruby Dee is a fine actress and a kind person. In *Wedding Band*, she gave up being an ingénue and putting her hands on her hips. She accepted becoming the older actress (28 Mar. 1992).

Miss Dee says of her ability to handle roles requiring different ages: "I've had this capacity to go through ages doing what was required. This is not a challenge. It is something I've been able to do since I was 18" (1 Sept. 1992). It is no challenge for her to capture hearts, either. It's part of her theatrical magic.

At the Ethel Barrymore Theatre, between 11 March 1959, and 25 June 1960, Ruby Dee caught the eyes of major New York critics. Walter Kerr of *The New York Herald Tribune*, wrote on 12 Mar. 1959:

> Miss Dee is the pregnant wife who must act as peacemaker [in *A Raisin in the Sun*] between generations. Wan, winsome, holding back the tartness that is always ready at the edge of her tongue, this wraithlike figure slowly comes into focus as the bond between embattled souls.... With a light shift of her voice, she commands a rebellious child to kiss her goodbye; with an unobtrusive gesture, she flicks an ironing board from a sofa so that a lounging and slightly fatuous college boy can relax in a tenement (n.p.).

Of her performance in *A Raisin in the Sun*, Richard Watts also stated in *The New York Post* "There are ... excellent performances ... by Ruby Dee as the wife" (12 Mar. 1959).

John Chapman of *The Daily News* believed: "Ruby Dee is touching as [Sidney] Poitier's wife" (12 Mar. 1959). Brooks Atkinson of *The New York Times* asserted: "Ruby Dee's young wife burdened with problems ... bring[s] variety and excitement to a first-rate performance" (12 Mar. 1959). John McLain of *The New York Journal American* observed, "Ruby Dee is consistently first class in this highly demanding assignment" (12 Mar. 1959). Edith Oliver of *The New Yorker* asked, after the film version of the play, "Is there a better young actress in America?" (8 Apr. 1961). The answer was, arguably, no, even though Claudia McNeil and Diana Sands as Mama Younger and Beneatha may have, at moments, eclipsed Dee's quiet power.

The quiet Dee diversified early in her career as did Ossie Davis. As a young woman, she managed not just theatre and film, but major spots on television, as well. Bob Lamm wrote: "Ruby Dee, Claudia McNeil, and Carl Lee [Canada Lee's son] all won Emmy Awards nominations for their performances at a time when it was rare for blacks even to appear in dramatic roles in television" (74). Lamm continued:

> "Express Stop to Lenox Avenue," which aired on 9 May, 1963, offers a penetrating look at the impact of a racist society on the black middle class. Written by Adrian Spies, the episode stars Ruby Dee as Jenny Bishop, a nurse who has "made it" in white society partly by hating her blackness and renouncing her roots "uptown" on Harlem's Lenox Avenue. Jenny is shaken when the aunt (Claudia McNeil) who raised her brings Jenny's cousin Lonnie Hill (Carl Lee) to Alden General so that he can apply for a job as an orderly. The nurse does not want her colleagues to associate her with Lonnie (who has a troubled history on Harlem's streets) or with the hospital's black orderlies (whom she bitterly insists have "no self-respect, no pride, no shame") (75).

Lamm reminds his readers that this show aired during the days of Eugene "Bull" Connor, the Birmingham, Alabama, Police Commissioner who turned dogs and fire hoses on civil rights demonstrators in 1963. It was also the year that Medgar Evers, a prominent NAACP leader, was murdered in Mississippi. It was an era mired in controversy.

Another major moment came for Dee in her controversial performance of Julia in Alice Childress's *Wedding Band* in 1966. Miss Childress said of Dee's performance:

> She was just wonderful. She did it for the first time at the University of Michigan and then she did it at the Ivanhoe Theater in Chicago. And then she did the New York City production at Joe Papp's New York Shakespeare Festival at the Public Theater in New York. Joe Papp and I co-directed. He was the producer. I did the teleplay and it was done on ABC and Ruby played in that. She was just marvelous. She was nominated for an Obie Award for best lead role for her New York performance (6 Aug. 1992).

Wedding Band: A Love/Hate Story in Black and White is an interracial love story in an era when miscegenation laws forbade marriage between the races in many states, not just the South. The play lacked spectacle, physical violence, and true sensationalism.

The content focused on the love affair between Julia Augustine, a black seamstress, and Herman, a white baker, in Charleston, South Carolina, set against a backdrop of World War I in 1918. Herman and Julia have been involved for ten years when the play opens.

Black and white neighbors and family oppose the relationship. Blacks find it especially difficult to understand how Julia can love a white man. The couple prefer to marry, but the law of South Carolina forbids it. Herman brings Julia a wedding band to celebrate their tenth year together, but she must wear it on a chain around her neck. Herman also brings a cake from his bakery, but no friends join in the celebration.

While there is no physical violence in the play, the emotional violence is hard to bear. As Herman becomes ill with the "war-time influenza," his mother and sister come to try to take him away. The mother expected her son to be somebody. Instead, in her opinion, he has become a "poor bakerson layin' up with a nigger woman." She further complicates matters when Herman has hopes of leaving for the North where he and Julia might marry by demanding that Herman pay her back for the loan she has given him to establish his bakery. Julia is no model of propriety, either, using considerable profanity to Herman's mother.

The play ends with Herman's death. Julia holds him in her arms where he dies in their dwelling. The couple would have been happy had not strongly opposing forces, including laws, been too formidable. Trudier Harris writes: "Inhuman laws combine with inhumanity to make life much more of a struggle than it needs to be" (70).

Of the 7-11 December 1966 performances of *Wedding Band* at the Mendelssohn Theatre of the University of Michigan, Ann Arbor, an unidentified critic wrote: "Ruby Dee gives a moving portrayal of the leading feminine role . . ." (Source unknown, possibly *The Detroit Free Press*, 17 Dec. 1966). Ann L. Marchio of *The Michigan Daily News* observed:

> Not only a vibrant personality off stage, Miss Dee forces the character of Julia into the viewer and does not relent until the climactic conflict at the end of the first scene (8 Dec. 1966).

Clive Barnes noted: "Ruby Dee, loving and defiant by turn, defensive and tortured, was flamboyantly credible" (27 Oct. 1972). Few, if any, other critics have used "flamboyant" to describe Dee.

Mical Whitaker, who served as producer/director of "The Ossie Davis/Ruby Dee Story Hour," a weekly radio show heard "from 1974–1976 on 65 radio stations nationwide on the National Black Network" (biographical statement on Miss Dee provided by Emmalyn II Enterprises 26 May 1992), and sponsored by Kraft Inc., declared: "The thing I loved so much was Ruby Dee's closing statement, 'Swing gently in a just right breeze.'" Whitaker went on,

> She has strength and quiet power. She was aware that our radio show reached and had a lot of appeal to prisoners, most of whom are black male. She and I would choose material that would be inspiring to them (27 Mar. 1993).

Dee's ethos is subdued.

Another of her many performances that was highly touted was that of Lena in the 1970 work of Athol Fugard, *Boesman and Lena*. Stanley Kauffman wrote of her performance in that play at Circle in the Square:

> the glory of the production is Ruby Dee's performance of Lena.
>
> Four summers ago, in the middle of a converted baseball field in Ypsilanti, Michigan, I saw Miss Dee as Cassandra in a production of The Oresteia, her tiny form filling that huge space, prophesying death in the king's house and a future for herself. Lena fulfills that prophecy. When Miss Dee enters, her eyes have taken command of her being, have taken it somewhere else. Her body can do anything she asks of it, and she asks a great deal, but it is her voice that she has now developed to heroic range, from simper to demonic fury. With an imagination that conceives largely, with completely reliable techniques, with fire and pity and powerful spirit, this little woman becomes a giant, making this mud-creature into a protean figure. It is the best performance I have seen in the American theatre since Judith Anderson's Medea (Kauffmann 25).

To this, Clive Barnes adds even more accolades about *Boesman and Lena*:

> Never for a moment do you think she is acting—even, and this is the trick, when she is at her most stagey.... Her frail sparrow-figure, her bright, unsubdued eyes, her voice ..., her manner, her entire being, have a quality of wholeness that is rarely encountered in the theatre (Current Biography 1970 109).

Dee, herself, regrets that she has had far more restricted than classical roles.

She has played Cassandra in Aeschylus's *The Oresteia*, Kate in Shakespeare's *The Taming of the Shrew,* and Cordelia in *King Lear.* In 1982, on television, Dee was Mary Tyrone, the "lace-curtain" Irish wife and mother, in an all-black production of Eugene O'Neill's *Long Day's Journey into Night* opposite Earle Hyman as the male lead. She has also been in Molière's *The Imaginary Invalid*.

Moreover, Dee took on the challenging role of the aging white southern belle, Amanda Wingfield, who pursues her sad illusions that she had 17 gentlemen callers in her youth, in Tennessee Williams's *The Glass Menagerie* at Arena Stage, Washington, D. C. in 1989. Amanda also hopes for at least one gentleman caller for her emotionally crippled daughter, Laura. Chris Gilmer published the following from an interview he conducted with Dee about the role:

> DEE: I didn't realize the depth of our prejudices and how much in place they are. There were comments in reviews about a Black woman having gentlemen callers, men who were bankers and so forth, incredible for a Black family. Well, when Tennessee Williams was writing, I had an uncle

who lived in Washington. He was a bail bondsman. He did not have an education, but he was very wealthy (243).

Amanda is a universal figure. Predominantly white universities do not hesitate to produce *The Glass Menagerie*. Black casts on historically black college campuses put on *The Glass Menagerie* throughout the twentieth century, as well. Few, if any, audience members raised their eyebrows, since white plays were the regular fare for black actors on historically black college campuses for much of the twentieth century. Only when black actors in white plays have come to regional theatres and Broadway have there been questions about credibility.

In spite of these challenges that a female actor of color faces, more kudos have come from the critics for Dee's performances in works by and for African-Americans. In 1988, she starred in Ron Milner's touted play, *Checkmates*, on Broadway. Invited by Ricardo Khan of Crossroads Theatre, in 1994 Ruby Dee was in African American playwright Pearl Cleage's *Flyin' West*, a provocative melodrama. The play also was mounted at the Kennedy Center. Four black women strike out for the West, Nicodemus, Kansas, in the 1890s as a better option than living in the Deep South. Blizzards, droughts, and locusts were more manageable enemies than racism. Wil Parrish further enlivens the play.

Black and white critics have given non-legitimate negative evaluation of Dee's classical portrayals. Ruby Dee declared, "Whites are not pigeonholed. I've played very few leads" (1 Sept. 1992). She hopes: "There will be a new set of classics in another twenty years—those writers among us who are never heard—[Toni] Morrison, [Alice] Walker, and [Zora Neale] Hurston." (1 Sept. 1992). Since those words were uttered, Morrison won the Nobel Prize for Literature in 1993, and Walker and Hurston are more and more widely read and put on stage. Dee goes on, "As valuable as Shakespeare and O'Casey were, we've got to get the newer writers on the map" (l Sept. 1992).

With her normally subtle portrayals, Dee has revolutionized the theatre and films about urban America, much as have Wesley Snipes, Morgan Freeman, Denzel Washington, Angela Bassett, James Earl Jones, and Al Freeman. In 1989, Dee played the romantic interest opposite Ossie Davis in Spike Lee's unsettling *Do the Right Thing,* a film that dramatized urban violence. Donald Bogle wrote: "Ruby Dee has rarely been able to unleash her gift for idiosyncratic comedy" (*Toms, Coons* 323). This she did, however, in Lee's film.

In the 1991 *tour de force* of Spike Lee, *Jungle Fever*, Dee says little, but immobilized audiences with her facial expressions, raised arms, and other stage business. As the mother of two sons, one (played by Wesley Snipes) involved in an adulterous relationship with a white woman, and the other consumed by drugs (played by Samuel L. Jackson), Dee's performance was overwhelming. As Mahalia Jackson sings a moving gospel song in the background, actor Dee tries, in vain, to prevent the character played by her actor-husband, Ossie Davis, from killing their dope-infested son with a flaming pistol as he quotes scripture.

Of Spike Lee, Dee says, "Spike hires people who can flesh out his notion, and he lets you do it. He's very generous in that respect. He's open-minded and tough-minded. In working for Spike, you feel you must do more than your best" (1 Sept. 1992). Dee also said of Lee, "He trusts the artist." Producers trust Dee's quiet power to mesmerize—those who have been fortunate enough to witness her art.

However marginalized Dee and her sister artists may have been, this has not deterred her from playing to exquisite perfection those roles she has claimed. She still continues to quietly triumph on stage, film, television, radio, and in her marriage and motherhood.

Ossie Davis

I first met Ossie Davis in an elevator at the Sheraton Hotel in Philadelphia during the Thanksgiving season of 1973. He was the keynote speaker for the National Council of Teachers of English (NCTE) and I was in attendance. As I recall, we were the only ones in the elevator. I immediately recognized him and said, "You're Ossie Davis," to which he replied, in jest, "No, I would not be Ossie Davis for the world." While still in the elevator, as my memory recalls, he gave me his home office address and telephone number, since as a member of the Lyceum Committee at the University of Texas at El Paso, I wished to recommend him and Ruby Dee for our Lyceum Series.

His NCTE keynote speech was one of the most extraordinary I have heard. He had wisdom, a rich plethora of material, and a compelling bass voice. He spoke on language, society, and the impact language has on mankind. It was one of many moving speeches he has given.

The actual fulfillment of bringing him to El Paso was delayed almost two years while he and Ruby Dee took off to Africa to film *Countdown at Kusini*. But on 10 February 1975, they came to the University of Texas at El Paso where I was their host. The *El Paso Herald Post* wrote on 25 January 1975: "Their appearance in El Paso is one of many tour stops for concert readings of literature written mostly by black authors" (5).

They read with great feeling at the Plaza Theater downtown to a packed house. They dressed in evening wear and, occasionally, sat on high stools. A minister of one of the black churches was there on complimentary tickets I sent him after he had admonished his clerk who read my promotional announcement in a Sunday service prior to the Davis/Dee reading, "Sister, any more of those theatre announcements, see me first." I assured him, prior to the reading, that this was not a finger-popping, get-in-the-alley-with-Sally event, but one of dignity and refinement. He was most laudatory after having heard the actors. This is one of many instances where black performers and members of lyceum committees must overcome negative misconceptions in the black community.

I most remember Ossie Davis reading Paul Laurence Dunbar's "Ante Bellum Sermon" with a skill of verisimilitude that I have seldom seen. Ruby Dee read from Langston Hughes's piece by the persona Jesse B. Semple, "Dear Dr. Butts," and she and Davis read many pieces together, seldom in unison, but clearly in tandem. The evening was a rich, enjoyable learning experience.

There was a lavish dinner at the top of a downtown El Paso bank before the reading. The El Paso Alumnae Chapter of Delta Sigma Theta Sorority held a reception at the home of one of the members after the performance. They placed a bowl of fruit in their hotel room and gave Miss Dee a large bouquet of long-stem, American Beauty red roses as the reading ended. Both Dee and Davis came to the first class in Black Literature that I ever taught for coffee and conversation; we included as many others as possible in the Conquistador Lounge at the University of Texas at El Paso. Faculty, students, and townspeople came to that, including John West, Chair of the University of Texas at El Paso's Department of English at the time.

I last recall a face-to-face meeting with Mr. Davis when he and Miss Dee came to Tuskegee Institute the fall of 1982, when I was Department Head of English and Foreign Languages there. He and his wife were filming *A Walk through the Twentieth Century with Bill Moyers,* with one scene shot at the famous monument of Tuskegee Institute's founder, Booker T. Washington, where Washington lifts the veil of ignorance from the face of a student. I met with Dee and Davis, accompanied them to Booker T. Washington's home, The Oaks, and attended a cocktail party where they were honored at the home of President and Mrs. Benjamin F. Payton.

At the time of our last visit, Ossie Davis was 65. He was born on 18 December 1917, in Cogdell, Georgia, to Kince Charles and Laura Davis. He grew up in Waycross. "His father was a railroad construction engineer, then an unusual occupation for a Negro in the Deep South" (*Current Biography 1969* 114). Davis's father could not write his name. Whites treated his father badly, providing the first motivation for Davis to become an activist. His father was also a great storyteller and read the Bible often, clearly one reason Ossie Davis is so gifted as a playwright and actor, himself.

Upon graduation from high school, Ossie Davis hitchhiked to Washington, D. C., and enrolled in the historically black Howard University. There he came under the profound influence of Sterling Brown, an African American drama critic, poet, and professor. Davis also came under the influence of Alain Locke, a giant among black intellectuals of the twentieth century who was a philosopher and drama critic. He asked Davis about his career path.

With the impatience of youth, Davis left Howard University without a degree at the end of his junior year, New York City bound, but "tarried" an extra week beyond his planned departure in order to hear Marian Anderson's 1939 Easter Sunday concert at the Lincoln Memorial. Davis wrote about the famous event in his and Dee's autobiography, "It married in my mind forever the performing arts as a weapon in the struggle for freedom" (86). Davis's first stay in New York City was an exercise in surviving poverty, as he sought an acting career. And so, he enlisted in the army.

After a stint in the army between 1942–45, where even the soldiers' visits to prostitutes were segregated, Davis returned to Valdosta, Georgia, when Dick Campbell, director of the Rose McClendon Players, recommended him for a part in Robert Ardrey's *Jeb*. Davis left immediately for New York City once more.

He played the title role of Jeb Turner in the play, which opened at the Martin Beck on 21 February 1946. Ruby Dee was Libby George. The romantic attraction was instant. In 1947, they both toured with Philip Yordan's *Anna Lucasta,* with Davis playing the romantic lead, Rudolph. Earle Hyman created the role in 1944. Davis and Ruby Dee were so busy that they had to marry on their day off on 9 December 1948. Their marriage and child-rearing have always been interwoven with participation in the theatre, film, television, and radio.

In 1950, on Broadway, Davis played Jacques in *Wisteria Trees* and, in 1951, the angel Gabriel in Marc Connelly's *Green Pastures,* a role created by Oscar Polk, in a play made famous by Richard B. Harrison in the plum role of "de Lawd." Davis's contributions are massive both as playwright and actor. His *Curtain Call, Mr. Aldridge, Sir,* a readers' theatre production about the 19th century African American Shakespearean tragedian, Ira Aldridge, has not gotten its due. It was published by Thomas D. Pawley and William Reardon in *The Black Teacher and the Dramatic Arts.*

One work that seems to have been of particular significance to Dee and Davis was their involvement in *The World of Sholom Aleichem* where members of The Group Theatre performed in 1953 in the basement of the Barbizon-Plaza Hotel in New York City. Howard DaSilva and Morris Carnovsky offered Ruby Dee the role of the Defending Angel. Davis was stage manager (*With Ossie and Ruby* 241). This work meant a great deal because it showed both Davis and Dee that they could make their own job opportunities and it showed them the positive ties between African Americans and Jews.

While Davis, several times in his life, read at synagogues and Jewish centers, in 1957 he moved to Broadway where Lena Horne, for the first time, starred on Broadway in *Jamaica,* a new musical with Ricardo Montalban, Josephine Premice, and Joe Adams. The book was by E. Y. Harburg and

Fred Saidy; the music, by Harold Arlen, with lyrics by E.Y. Harburg. Ossie Davis was Cicero. The venue was the Imperial Theatre, with David Merrick as producer. *"Jamaica* ran for 555 performances at the Imperial Theatre in 1957–58" (*Current Biography Yearbook 1985,* 196). But sadness loomed as well.

Davis's father died January 1958, with Ossie Davis visiting both during the illness and for the funeral. It was a bitter irony that Kince Charles Davis did not get to see his son's major breakthrough. Davis replaced Sidney Poitier as Walter Lee Younger, a black man seeking dignity in a dignity-stripping world, in Lorraine Hansberry's *A Raisin in the Sun,* but it was Davis's own work, *Purlie Victorious,* that brought him, literally, to the door of fame when it opened on Broadway at the Cort Theatre on 28 September 1961.

Davis took five years to write the comedy *Purlie Victorious.* Alexander Allison *et al.* wrote in 1974 in *Masterpieces of the Drama:* "In his sunny and exuberant *Purlie Victorious,* the black playwright and actor Ossie Davis celebrates the demise of Southern white supremacy" (889). *Masterpieces of the Drama* anthologized *Purlie Victorious,* along with mainly white classics. Allison *et al.* continue:

> This [white supremacy] he lays to rest in the person of Stonewall Jackson Cotchipee, the "Ol Cap'n," owner of a peon plantation in Southern Georgia. Outwitted by Purlie Judson and his followers, the Cap'n departs this life in an apoplectic rage and is turned into a piece of statuary before our eyes (889).

As in Jonsonian comedy (889), there are the stereotypes of the obeisant Gitlow; the ingénue, Lutiebelle Gussiemae Jenkins [one of Dee's favorite roles] and the Mammy, Idella. Davis, himself, played the preacher, Purlie. This was an act of courage, since Davis faced criticism for writing and portraying a stereotype.

His courage was most exemplified when, in a revolutionary decade, he delivered the eulogy of Malcolm X in 1965. Malcolm X, in his time, was vilified. In 1999, he has been honored by the United States Post Office with his image on a stamp in the Black Heritage Series. While he is now considered one of the most influential African Americans of the twentieth century, Malcolm X was a pariah in much of America when Ossie Davis eulogized him.

Not just Caucasians disliked Malcolm X, who had spent time dancing in zoot suits, womanizing, and being in prison for burglary and drugs. Many in the African American community were cautious about being remotely identified with Malcolm's leadership, as well. He was a follower of Elijah Muhammad, and as a leader of the Black Muslims had once called white Americans "devils." Although Malcolm X changed late in his life and believed all men must be brothers, it was the change that may have cost him his life.

Malcolm X was assassinated in the Audubon Ballroom in Harlem in 1965, with his wife and children present. Anyone connected with Malcolm was in danger. But Davis was undaunted. These were the words he spoke at Malcolm's funeral:

> Here—at this final hour, in this quiet place, Harlem has come to bid farewell to one of its brightest hopes—extinguished now, and gone from us forever. . . .
>
> Many will ask what Harlem finds to honor in this stormy, controversial and bold young captain—and we will smile.
>
> They will say that he is of hate—a fanatic, a racist—who can only bring evil to the cause for which you struggle!
>
> And we will answer and say unto them: Did you ever talk to Brother Malcolm? Did you ever touch him, or have him smile at you? Did you ever really listen to him. . . . Malcolm was our manhood, our living black manhood! . . . And we will know him then for what he was and is—a Prince—our own black shining Prince! (*Autobiography of Malcolm X* 454)

These are bold words for a man giving tribute to a brilliant urban leader, who only late in his 39 years converted to Islam and made the pilgrimage to Mecca.

Although Davis did not eulogize Martin Luther King, Jr., who was assassinated on 4 April 1968, he did attend the funeral, a dark day in America where thousands of stunned people of all colors lined the streets of Atlanta. Mahalia Jackson sang and Andrew Young and Jesse Jackson were major presences. King's youngest daughter was five years old. These images are forever emblazoned in history through the photography of Moneta Sleet, Jr. Following the several assassinations of the 1960s—Medgar Evers, Martin Luther King, Jr., John F. Kennedy, and Robert Kennedy—Davis went to Nigeria as director to film *Kongi's Harvest*.

Meanwhile, the highly successful *Purlie*, "the first black musical to reach Broadway during the 1970s" (Woll 256) blazed on the stage. Based on Ossie Davis's *Purlie Victorious,* the musical had a highly favorable reception from audiences and critics.

> The inspiration for the Purlie tales was, strangely, The World of Sholom Aleichem (1953). . . . Davis . . . hoped that Purlie Victorious would be the counterpart to Aleichem's Jewish characterizations (Woll 256).

Davis has frequently seen positive parallels between Jewish and African American people. Cleavon Little and Melba Moore as leads won Tony and Drama Desk awards. Sherman Hemsley of CBS's *The Jeffersons* added to the strong cast.

The late 1970s through the 1990s saw Dee and Davis continuing to expand their rich work in television documentaries and special programs, including a 15 February 1999 appearance on *Cosby*, the second television series to star Bill Cosby.

By 1986, Davis appeared on Broadway for 13 months as Midge, an unconfrontational, almost blind octogenarian building superintendent opposite Hal Linden as Nat Moyer, the Jewish radical octogenarian protagonist, in the Tony–award winning play, Herb Gardner's *I'm Not Rappaport*. In 1984, Judd Hirsch created the role of Nat, with Cleavon Little as Midge. The venue is two worn benches under a rustic bridge in Central Park. The cast included seven actors. Walter Matthau and Davis, in 1997, played in the film version. *The Boston Globe* wrote: "As Midge, Davis is a man to whom urban guerilla warfare and invisibility have become second nature" (24 Jan. 1997 C8). The play is about what it means to become old and how to cope with aging in a world often indifferent or hostile to the aging.

In spite of a damaging house fire in 1987, Davis continued to work in the play, *Rappaport*, going to Jupiter, Florida to become Midge at Burt Reynolds's Dinner Theatre in 1988. Davis also worked on the famous civil rights documentary, *Eyes on the Prize*, in 1989. As a result of both performances, Ossie Davis became a well-known figure on television, Ponder Blue, between 1990–94 in CBS's *Evening Shade* with Burt Reynolds.

The year 1989 brought Davis and Dee considerable visibility in Spike Lee's film, *Do The Right Thing*, where Dee was "Mother Sister" and Davis, "Da Mayor." Danny Aiello starred as Sal, with Bill Nunn as Radio Raheem, Samuel L. Jackson as DJ Mister Love Daddy, and Spike Lee as Mookie. Donald Bogle wrote:

> No other black film drew as much attention or had as great a cultural impact as this drama, which examined a day in the life of black residents in Brooklyn's Bedford Stuyvesant section and culminated in a violent racial uprising (*Toms, Coons* 318–319).

Reviews ran from praise of Lee's talent to outright fear that he had told a story celebrating violence. Bogle continued:

> Lee wisely cast unusual and interesting performers. It is hard to recall when Ossie Davis, here using his personal warmth and generosity of spirit to turn Da Mayor into the film's true moral center, has been as much fun or as interesting (*Toms, Coons* 323).

There is an on-screen romance for Davis and Dee that made the film charming at moments in spite of the violence that is a real part of urban America. Davis's portrayal of the father who is a religious fanatic in Spike Lee's 1991 *Jungle Fever* with Wesley Snipes, Lonette McKee and Samuel L. Jackson was extremely powerful.

In 1995, Minister Louis Farrakhan of the Nation of Islam led what was called a Million Man March on Washington where black men were to atone for their sins and how they had treated their wives and girlfriends. They were to pledge to be better and they were to come together for inspiration and community. The march, however, did not limit itself to the Nation of Islam, although Farrakhan was the main leader. Black men, including many who brought their sons, came from all religious backgrounds and from across class lines. Black women were not encouraged to make the journey, although a very few showed up. It was on the buses that many black men felt the strongest sense of communion.

In 1996, filmmaker Spike Lee took on the formidable task of adapting the day to film in a movie called *Get on the Bus*. Fifteen African-American men contributed the entire $2.5 million dollar budget. The movie included Ossie Davis as an old-timer who is the spiritual conscience of the group. The men leave on a chartered bus from south central Los Angeles bound for Washington, D.C. Lee featured the purposes that led these men to understanding of themselves and others. The significance of the journey was also highlighted. Charles S. Dutton and Andre Braugher were among the other better known actors of color in the film.

Ossie Davis, since 1950, has appeared in a large number of historical ventures in films, plays, and television specials. He has several times narrated the nationally televised Memorial Day Celebration at the Capitol in Washington, D. C. One of his most controversial films was *Miss Evers' Boys* in 1997.

Miss Evers' Boys was adapted from Dr. David Feldshuh's play about a real-life Tuskegee, Alabama, syphilis experiment on black men. The United States government demanded that health workers in Tuskegee use black men as human guinea pigs. While these men believed they were being treated for syphilis, the government actually wanted to know the effects of a lack of treatment. The men were, therefore, given only a placebo, aided by the character Nurse Eunice Evers, based on a real-life nurse. She assisted the government in seeing how untreated syphilis develops. Ossie Davis, Alfre Woodard, and Laurence Fishburne starred in this HBO film. It captured 12 nominations for Emmy Awards, including Best Supporting Actor for Ossie Davis.

In 1998, President Clinton invited the survivors of the experiment, many in their 90s, to the White House for an apology. It was during the response session that a very articulate, well-dressed black man in his 90s, a survivor of the syphilis experiment, said how much he objected to being called a boy by the play/movie title. "We were *men!*" he affirmed, to a round of applause. The experiment started in 1932 and ended in 1972. Some victims received a cash settlement of $375,000 each, aided in a protracted struggle by the famous Tuskegee Attorney, Fred Gray.

Davis, in his 80s, continues to get work on college campuses, at special commemoratives, and in film. One of his "treasured experiences includes working with both Ms. Dee and their son, Guy Davis, in the storytelling, folklore and music revue *Two Hah Hahs and a Homeboy*, mounted at Crossroads Theatre" (Profile: Ossie Davis), which Ms. Dee compiled.

"Ossie and Ruby are One"

The marriage of Dee and Davis has survived more than 50 years because they determined, early on, to pray together daily and be together as much as possible. They have built trust and respect for themselves and one another. Their children have been a high priority. Their careers have survived because they have diversified their artistic portfolio and because they have a strong sense of identity. They work very hard and very long hours. They are, in a world of crass materialism, not materialists. Their reported joint fee of $15,000 per campus appearance is far below that of many celebrities. In 1961, *Ebony*, on its cover, called them "Mr. and Mrs. Broadway." While they have appeared several times on The Great White Way, they have hired black people in many capacities and nourished black friends, among them Moran and Miriam Drake Weston, also distinguished and caring people. They have not ignored white allies. They have also embraced other ethnic and religious groups, particularly those of the Jewish faith. They have consistently refused to be relegated to "artistic prostitution," (quoted in Fletcher 68) and this credo has nourished their spirit, their marriage, and their art.

Works Cited

"Actors to Appear at Plaza Theater in Lyceum Series," *El Paso Herald Post*, 25 Jan. 1975, 5.

Allison, Alexander W., Arthur J. Carr, and Arthur M. Eastman. *Masterpieces of the Drama*, third edition. New York: Macmillan, 1974. [full text of *Purlie Victorious*]

Anderson, Thomas. Telephone interview with author. 28 Mar. 1992.

Anderson, W. Calvin, "One Miracle At A Time," *American Visions*, Apr./May 1992, 21–24.

Atkinson, Brooks. *The New York Times*, 12 Mar. 1959, n.p. [*A Raisin in the Sun*]

Barnes, Clive. "Childress Play Opens at Public Theater," *The New York Times*, 27 Oct. 1972, 30:1.

Bogle, Donald. *Blacks in American Film and Television*. New York: Garland Publishing, 1988, 40–41, and 381–382.

———. *Brown Sugar: Eighty Years of America's Black Female Superstars*. New York: Harmony Books, 1980.

———. *Toms, Coons, Mulattoes, Mammies and Bucks.* New York: Continuum, 1996.
Branch, William B. Statement, 29 June 1992; Letter, 12 Aug. 1992.
Campbell, Dick. Telephone interview with author. 3 June 1992.
Carlin, Peter Ames and Sue Miller. "Two Become One," *People,* 9 Nov. 1998, 153–156. (courtesy of Jane Nordberg)
Carr, Jay. "'Rappaport' Leans Lovingly To the Left," *The Boston Globe,* 24 Jan. 1997, C8.
"Celebrating a New Decade," *ATHE News,* May 1996, vol. 10, no. 2, 1.
Chapman, John. *The Daily News,* 12 Mar. 1959, n.p. [*A Raisin in the Sun*]
Childress, Alice. Telephone interview with author. 6 Aug. 1992.
Current Biography Yearbook 1969. New York: H. W. Wilson Company, 1969, 114–117.
Current Biography Yearbook 1970. New York: H. W. Wilson Company, 1970, 107-110.
Current Biography Yearbook 1985. New York: H. W. Wilson Company, 1985, 194–198. [entry on Lena Horne]
Davis, Ossie. "Purlie Told Me!" *Freedomways,* spring 1962, 155–159.
Davis, Ossie and Ruby Dee. *With Ossie and Ruby: In This Life Together.* New York: William Morrow, 1998.
Dee, Ruby. Letter to author. 27 Feb. 1995.
———. Telephone interview with author. 1 Sept. 1992.
———. Biographical statement about Miss Dee provided by Emmalyn II Enterprises on 26 May 1992.
Fletcher, Winona L. "Ossie Davis: The Transformation of Stage Presence into Nitty-Gritty Eloquence," *Blacks in the Media,* ed. Herman C. Hudson, Occasional Papers, no. 2, Indiana University at Bloomington, 1992, 67–85. (courtesy of Winona L. Fletcher)
Gary, Beverly. "For a Negro Actress, the Curtain Rarely Rises All the Way," *The New York Post,* 13 Apr. 1956.
Gill, Glenda E. "Her Voice Was Ever Soft, Gentle and Low, an Excellent Thing in Ruby Dee," *Journal of Popular Culture,* summer 1994, vol. 28, no. 1, 61–71.
Gilmer, Chris. "An Interview with Ruby Dee," *Studies in American Drama, 1945-Present,* vol. 7, no. 2, 1992, 241–251.
Goldman, Connie. "MM Interview: Hume Cronyn & Jessica Tandy and Ossie Davis & Ruby Dee," *Modern Maturity,* vol. 37, no. 4, Jul-Aug. 1994, 64–83. (courtesy of Winona L. Fletcher)
Grebanier, Bernard. *Then Came Each Actor.* New York: McKay, 1975.
Greene, Michael E. "Entry on Ossie Davis." in *Dictionary of Literary Biography: Afro-American Writers after 1955,* 38. Ann Arbor: Gale Research, 1985, 80–86.
Haley, Alex and Malcolm X. *The Autobiography of Malcolm X.* New York: Random House, 1965.
Harris, Trudier. "Entry on Alice Childress," in *The Dictionary of Literary Biography: Afro-American Writers after 1955,* 78. Ann Arbor: Gale Research, 1985, 70.
Hill, Errol. *Shakespeare in Sable: A History of Black Shakespearean Actors.* Amherst: University of Massachusetts Press, 1984, 159–161.

"The Jackie Robinson Story," *Ebony,* June 1950, 87–91.

Kauffmann, Stanley. "Boesman and Lena," *New Republic.* 25 July 1970, 16–25.

Kerr, Walter. *The New York Herald Tribune,* 12 Mar. 1959, n. p. [*A Raisin in the Sun*]

Kinnon, Joy Bennett. "Ossie & Ruby: Is This the Love Affair of the Century?" *Ebony,* Feb. 1999, 48–196.

Lahmon, Jo Ann. "Ruby Dee," in *Notable Black American Women.* ed. Jessie Carney Smith. Detroit: Gale Research 1992.

Lamm, Bob. "*The Nurses:* Television's Forgotten Gems," *Journal of Popular Film & Television,* vol. 23, no. 2, summer 1995, 73– 79. (courtesy of Bob Lamm)

Lanker, Brian. *I Dream a World: Portraits of Black Women Who Changed America.* New York: Tabori and Chang, 1989.

McLain, John. *The New York Journal American,* 12 Mar. 1959, n.p. [*A Raisin in the Sun*]

Marchio, Ann L. "'Wedding Band' Debut Defiant, Infused with Honesty, Humor," *The Michigan Daily News.* LXXVII, no. 80, 8 Dec. 1966, 2.

"Midget Salesman," *Ebony,* Feb. 1947, 22–35. (on Frankie Dee)

"Mr. and Mrs. Broadway," *Ebony,* Feb. 1961, 110–114.

Mitchell, Loften. *Voices of the Black Theatre.* Clifton, New Jersey: James T. White and Company, 1975.

Norment, Lynn. " 'Raisin' Celebrates Its 25th Anniversary," *Ebony,* Mar. 1984, 57–60.

Oliver, Edith. *The New Yorker,* 8 Apr. 1961, n.p.

O'Neal, Frederick. Personal interview with author. 24 June 1980.

Pagan, Margaret D. "Ruby Dee," in *Black Women in America: An Historical Encyclopedia,* ed. Darlene Clark Hine. Brooklyn: Carlson Publishing Company, 1993, 313–315.

Pawley, Thomas D. and William Reardon. *The Black Teacher and the Dramatic Arts.* Westport, CT: Negro Universities Press, 1970.

Profile: Ossie Davis (one page biographical statement provided by Dee & Davis, 14 May 1996).

Stanton, Sarah and Martin Banham. *Cambridge Paperback Guide to Theatre.* Cambridge, England: Cambridge University Press, 1996. (gift of Sarah Hruska)

Watts, Richard. *The New York Post,* 12 Mar. 1959, n.p. [A Raisin in the Sun] *Wedding Band* program, University of Michigan, Ann Arbor, 7–11 Dec. 1966. (courtesy of Thomas Anderson)

Wedding Band review, source unknown, possibly *The Detroit Free Press* 17 Dec. 1966. (courtesy of Thomas Anderson)

Whitaker, Mical. Telephone conversation with author. 27 Mar. 1993.

Woll, Allen. *Black Musical Theatre: From Coontown to Dreamgirls.* Baton Rouge: Louisiana State University Press, 1989.

Reviews of *A Raisin in the Sun* were taken from *Casebook of Black Theatre Materials,* prepared by Winona L. Fletcher, for the American Dance Festival Summer Humanities Institute, Duke University, 16 June–19 July 1991.

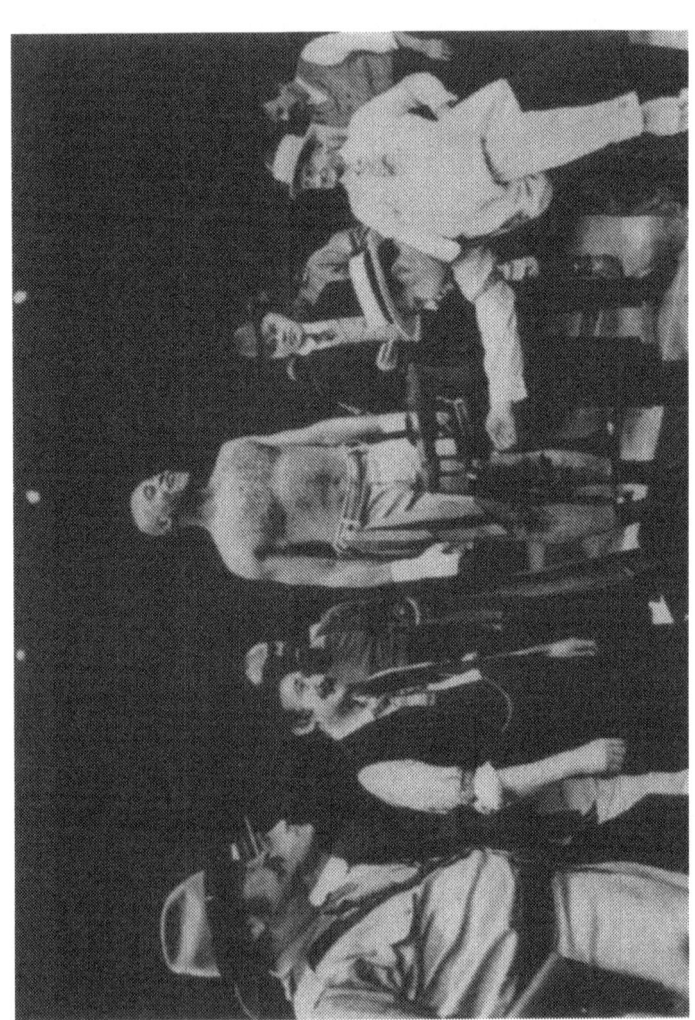

The Great White Hope, original New York theatrical production. James Earl Jones as Jack Johnson in the Herman Levin production. Wisconsin Center for Film and Theater Research.

Chapter X

James Earl Jones: "My Soul Looks Back and Wonders How I Got Over"

> *How I got over!*
> *How I got over!*
> *You know my soul*
> *Looks back and wonders, Lord,*
> *How I got over!*

These words, popularized first by Mahalia Jackson and then by Aretha Franklin, express the miracle, the awe, the virtual impossibility of James Earl Jones's staggering achievements. Most importantly of all, he has triumphed over adversity without becoming embittered. A man of dignity, class, humility, and prodigious talent, he has won two Tony Awards, for best actor in Howard Sackler's *The Great White Hope* in 1969 and in August Wilson's *Fences* in 1987, two Obies, the Vernon Rice Award, an honorary doctorate from Princeton, several Emmy Awards, a Golden Globe, the National Medal of Arts, and several NAACP honors. He has performed in more than 150 stage and screen productions.

The actor has been in at least 84 plays, almost 60 movies, and credits so massive in television, public ceremonies, and radio that it is an effort in futility to count. He is in a sustained and happy marriage, an ecstatic fatherhood, and has an understanding of his relationship with his actor father, Robert Earl Jones. Asked what was the most pleasant moment with his wife, Cecelia, he stated, "They keep happening," (15 Sept. 1998), and of the most pleasant moment with his son, Flynn Earl, James Earl Jones beams,

"They keep happening. They started from the day he was born and they keep happening" (15 Sept. 1998).

No history of the American theatre can ignore James Earl Jones. No one tome can give credit to the quality of his work. No book chapter need try. The odds he has faced would have forced many to give up long ago. This actor, who learned the classics by doing them, faced the trauma of being abandoned at an early age, seven rejections by Lee Strasberg's famous Actors Studio, a protracted hand-to-mouth existence, a fire of questionable origin that destroyed his home, resentment of his interracial dating and marriages, and a highly visible protest by 55 well-known celebrities surrounding his portrayal of Paul Robeson.

It cannot be gainsaid that there is some downright jealousy of his many splendored talents. He has worked steadily since 1951, while many actors starved. Even when he lived in a $19 a month cold-water flat on Manhattan's Lower East Side, earning less than $4,000 a year doing menial labor, he continued to work in the theatre at night. Few can match his voice. Fewer can manage the emotional investment he gives to his characters. His movements are dazzling. His humility, startling. His political savvy is enviable.

Arguably the actor who has done the greatest work in the American theatre of the twentieth century, James Earl Jones is made of high moral fibre. Having lived with his maternal grandparents in Arkabutla Township, Mississippi until the age of five, one day the grandparents drove him to Memphis, where the actor's paternal grandparents lived. It was suddenly announced that this was his new home. Jones recalls in *James Earl Jones: Voices and Silences:* "I did the only thing I could think to do. Silently, stubbornly, I hung onto the mattress [in the car], physically protesting this separation with all my strength" (31). But the trauma caused permanent stuttering, and for years he spoke only when he had to.

The near-abandonment was not carried out, and the young Jones moved with his maternal grandparents to Dublin, Michigan. Born 17 January 1931, in Arkabutla Township, Mississippi, the only child of Robert Earl and Ruth Connolly Jones who married in 1930 but separated before James Earl's birth, James Earl Jones had as parents a very young, marginally educated couple still grappling with their own maturity. His mother was a teacher with a sixth grade education, but she eventually became a maid.

His father, initially a chauffeur and butler, desperately dreamed of becoming a prizefighter and actor. Robert Earl Jones took off to New York City as a very young man in search of this dream. He worked with the Harlem Suitcase Theatre during the Great Depression, and on Broadway in Lillian Smith's *Strange Fruit* in 1945 as the lynch victim, Henry. Robert Earl Jones is a gifted actor whose timing for his dream was unfortunate. He was born too soon.

In spite of Robert Earl's efforts to see his son prior to then, the two never began to get to know one another at all until James Earl was 21 years old. In an interview with me of 28 June 1980, Robert Earl Jones said, "I invited him to come live with me in New York [in the fall of 1955]," which James Earl Jones did. They worked together as custodians, and the older Jones taught James Earl pointers about how to portray the protagonist, Othello.

Robert Earl Jones, clad in a gray and maroon jogging suit, perhaps readying for one of three New York marathons that he has run, sat in an all-afternoon session by the swimming pool of Canada Lee's widow, Frances, in Huntington, New York, on that hot summer day of 28 June 1980. Theatre historian Loften Mitchell, Robert Earl Jones, and I were guests. As the afternoon and evening moved into the next morning, Robert Earl Jones recited Paul Laurence Dunbar's "The Party" from memory. It was a moving rendition. Robert Earl Jones has been a performer, not an activist.

James Earl Jones states that his art is his politics. His favorite stage role is that of the slow-witted Lennie, a migrant worker of 1937 in John Steinbeck's *Of Mice and Men*. Lennie was not conceived of as black. On television, Jones has also played Gabriel Bird, "a Chicago policeman imprisoned for twenty years for killing his partner" (Jones and Niven 288) in *Gabriel's Fire,* and Few Clothes, a miner unionist struggling for dignity in the West Virginia coal mines in the film *Matewan*. DeFoy Glenn, an African American director in Charlotte, North Carolina, upon returning from seeing the Broadway stage production of *Fences,* said, "My hat, my shoes, my everything off to Mr. Jones," for his stirring portrayal on stage of the ex-convict and garbageman with a dream, Troy Maxon (Conversation with author circa 1987).

It is no gentle irony that James Earl Jones has won his only two Emmy Awards for Best Actor for roles designated for black men: Jack Jefferson in Howard Sackler's *The Great White Hope* in 1969, and Troy Maxon in August Wilson's *Fences* in 1987. Jack Jefferson is flamboyant, brash, and foolhardy. Troy Maxon, the protagonist in *Fences,* is a father in conflict with his son, Cory; an adulterer who brings his out-of-wedlock child home to his wife, Rose; and an illiterate garbage man, although his all-too-human dreams of becoming a major league baseball player make him universal. Daniel Larner believes Jack and Troy to be "both unique and strong and flawed" (3). Jones has excelled, here, in his portrayal of traditional roles.

The actor has played more nontraditional parts, however, than most African American actors on the stage: Deodatus Village in Jean Genet's *The Blacks* (1961), Oberon in Shakespeare's *A Midsummer Night's Dream* (1961), Caliban in Shakespeare's *The Tempest* (1962), Camillo in Shakespeare's *The*

Winter's Tale (1963), the title role in O'Neill's *The Emperor Jones* (1964), Macduff and later, the title role in Shakespeare's *Macbeth* (1966), and the retarded Lennie in John Steinbeck's *Of Mice and Men* in 1967 and 1974.

He has been the aging and unwise Lear in Shakespeare's *King Lear* (1973), the Hoosier hardware salesman Hickey, who infects his wife with a venereal disease and then kills her, in O'Neill's *The Iceman Cometh* (1973), the shrewd serf, Lopakhin, in Chekhov's *The Cherry Orchard* (1973), Judge Brack in Ibsen's *Hedda Gabler* (1980), and Othello seven times, including a Broadway production in 1982. This is the short list.

In regard to representation, James Earl Jones has a philosophy different from Paul Robeson, even though Jones has benefited from being born at a more opportune time than Robeson. In a telephone interview, Jones shared with me his thoughts on playing nontraditional roles:

> I don't think it really matters once you get into the play. It's nice to have a consistent ethnic—it's good for the audience's sake, makes it easier for them—but I've also played Claudius to an all-white cast, Gertrude and Hamlet included, and it doesn't matter. Somehow, [with] the great dramas there's enough distance either way—historic or cultural distance—so that we don't need to be pampered by so much attention to ethnic detail. I think it's wise to do so; it makes sense to do so, but I've not made it my practice.

While both Jones and Robeson have wanted authentic representation of the black man on stage, Jones, in his own words of 15 September 1998, "does not like to make too much of race when it comes to acting."

Jones has not spoken out, outside of his roles, on controversial issues. He does not want a curtain of silence to fall on his career. Direct confrontation can be deadly as it was with Canada Lee and Paul Robeson. Only through theatrical resistance can an actor of color hope to survive. In his book *James Earl Jones: Voices and Silences* (1993), Jones wrote: "I have never been an activist. . . . The stage is your podium" (227). One can *play* the flamboyant and defiant Jack Jefferson in Sackler's *The Great White Hope;* one dare not *be* him. One cannot even play Paul Robeson as Jones did in 1977 without ruckus.

When did this actor begin his long body of work? The young James Earl Jones graduated from high school in 1949, and went to the University of Michigan-Ann Arbor, determined to be a physician. High school had not prepared him for the rigor of his college science courses. He left in 1953, without a degree, believing that there was no point in taking final exams since, as a member of the Reserve Officer Training Corps, with the Korean War intensifying, he would be dead "by fall." He served his country briefly in Fort Benning, Georgia, upon his leaving college after four years.

During his last two years at Michigan, however, he began appearing in plays, including the controversial drama on miscegenation, James Gow and Arnaud d'Usseau's *Deep Are the Roots,* about a returning black war veteran in love with the white governor's daughter. James Earl Jones played Lieutenant Brett Charles, a role created by Gordon Heath in 1945 on Broadway. At Michigan, one student rose in protest, but the play went on. It was at Michigan, also, that Jones was introduced to the classics and performed the role of Epops in Aristophanes's *The Birds* and Verges, the language-challenged Constable who helps bring the villain, Borachio, to justice in Shakespeare's delightful comedy, *Much Ado about Nothing.*

His life in transition, Jones worked summer stock in Manistee, Michigan, from 1953 to 1959. It was there that he first played the title role in Shakespeare's *Othello.* He was clearly preparing for a career on stage. In 1955, Jones moved to New York and lived with his father. They began to bridge a wide chasm, although Jones admits as late as 15 September 1998, "I don't know my father, really." But Robert Earl Jones was a master teacher to his son, especially on techniques about playing Othello. The elder Jones also said to James Earl Jones: "I've not been able to make a living at this [the theatre], so if you do it, you must do it because you love it" (quoted by James Earl Jones in telephone interview with author 15 Sept. 1998).

James Earl Jones, knowing by now that he had this love, studied at the American Theatre Wing in New York City, from which he received a diploma in 1957. By October, Jones became the understudy for Lloyd Richards in the role of Perry Hall in *The Egghead* on Broadway. Jones did not get on Broadway then, but by January of 1958 made his Broadway debut as Edward, the valet, in Dore Schary's *Sunrise at Campobello,* a play about Franklin and Eleanor Roosevelt.

Joe Papp had seen James Earl Jones by now and offered him a minor role in Shakespeare's *Henry V* in 1960 at Shakespeare in Central Park where tickets sold for $9.90 each. This was the beginning of James Earl Jones's move to stardom.

Success breeds success, and Geraldine Lust, producer-director, invited Jones, at the age of 30, to play the savage yet charming Deodatus Village in Jean Genet's absurdist drama, *The Blacks,* a play about race relations with an all-black cast, which opened at the Saint Marks Playhouse off-Broadway on 4 May 1961. Some actors wore masks. It ran for three years, and the pay, for Jones, was $45 a week. He was not with the play the entire three years. Jones stated in *Voices and Silences:*

> Because black actors were involved in the theatre, the play got all kinds of militant political attention. Maya Angelou had arrived at an extreme position and was vocal about it. Abbey Lincoln was even more vocal . . . (118).

Jones recalled in his interview with me:

> It was the first time that a large number of black actors were asked to render a complex play, and it brought out of the woodwork, you might say, all of the actors who had any sort of capability of handling dialogue, handling language. The first question we were asked—the producer was not sure she could find enough black actors who had been, say, had any Shakespeare or any sort of training in poetic drama, and she did manage to get the group, the cast that you now know of (15 Sept. 1998).

Cicely Tyson, Roscoe Lee Browne, Lou Gossett, Raymond St. Jacques, and Godfrey Cambridge, among others, were in the cast.

Politically savvy at an early age, or growing in racial awareness, Jones also told Bernadette Carey of *The Washington Post* on 24 December 1967 that he felt relatively free of racial frustrations while living in New York until he took the role of Village. "In some ways that role in a powerful drama, that night after night forced me through all the hatred, disaffections and distrusts between white and black, was more real than the life I was leading" (quoted in *Current Biography Yearbook 1969* 226). Jones continued:

> Through that role, I came to realize that the black man in America is the tragic hero, the Oedipus, the Hamlet, the Macbeth . . . even the working-class Willie [sic] Loman, the Uncle Tom and Uncle Vanya of contemporary American life (226).

Upon leaving the cast of *The Blacks*, he joined the New York Shakespeare Festival once more and played Oberon in *A Midsummer Night's Dream* and the Lord Marshall in *Richard II*. He was also cast in Errol John's *Moon On a Rainbow Shawl*; it was in this play that James Earl Jones made his first stage appearance with his father.

By 1962, Jones, in a traditional role, was Henry Simpson, the Negro "chauffeur" to Albertine Prine in Lillian Hellman's *Toys in the Attic*. The characters, in middle age, still play with "toys in the attic." Julian, the brother and newly married husband of the play, showers his sisters with lavish gifts—two tickets to Europe, a piano, a refrigerator, and letters of resignations at their jobs. Wealth does not bring them happiness.

Hellman, as a playwright, wrote about greed and a relentless pursuit of truth at any price. She also treats as a pattern the notion that one must accept responsibility for one's own happiness, something that only Henry and Albertine do in *Toys in the Attic* by their having a quiet, intimate relationship in the Deep South, their color difference notwithstanding. This play was one of a number on miscegenation that crossed the boards of American stages between Edward Sheldon's *The Nigger* in 1909, and Howard Sackler's *The Great White Hope* in 1968.

Following this highly controversial play, Jones also took on the role of the animal Caliban in Shakespeare's *The Tempest,* and according to Alice Griffin, cited by Errol Hill, Jones was "a complete original . . . a savage, green-faced lizard darting his red tongue in and out, lunging clumsily at what he wanted and yelping when he was denied it" (quoted in Hill 173, from Alice Griffin, "The New York Season 1961–62," *Shakespeare Quarterly* 13, 1962, 553–57). Canada Lee had played the role of Caliban on Broadway in 1945, so this was not a first, but a significant step in Jones's upwardly mobile career.

Another first for Jones, however, and his favorite role, was that of the retarded Lennie in John Steinbeck's *Of Mice and Men,* played, initially, at Purdue University in 1967 [Robert Earl Jones was Crooks in the Purdue production], and in 1974 at the Bob Hope Theater at Southern Methodist University in Dallas. Jones said to me: "I was one of, I was probably the first black actor to play Lennie" (15 Sept. 1998). The black actor Leigh Whipper had done Crooks in the 1940 film, with Lon Chaney and Burgess Meredith.

Of Mice and Men focuses on the relationship between two migrant farm workers in California during the Great Depression. It was first published in February of 1937, but came out of Steinbeck's experiences as a farm laborer in 1922. George Kaufman helped Steinbeck adapt the novel to the stage. The play first opened at the Music Box Theatre in November of 1937, winning the Drama Critics Circle Award. Broderick Crawford played Lennie. The action takes place over three days and describes the experiences of Lennie Small and George Milton. Lennie, while slow-witted, has great physical strength and is highly destructive when upset, especially toward animals, which he kills. George guides him, mercifully, away from the saloons and whorehouses.

The two men wish to save their money so that they might buy property in the not-too-distant future. They secure work on a farm and try to execute their plan. Before this occurs, however, Lennie unintentionally kills the blonde wife of the boss's son when she reacts to him with fear. He only wants to stroke her hair. She screams. Scared, Lennie's reaction is to shake her, but he breaks her neck, because of excessive, unintentional force. George locates Lennie, hiding, and shoots him, knowing that a mob will do so in a more cruel fashion.

According to Jones and Niven:

> Critic Didier Delaunoy reflected on the implications of a black Lennie, writing in the *Black American* that "The casting of Jones in the part brings in a whole new set of thoughts and motives. His relationship with George takes on a totally different meaning. The whole idea itself would have been an explosive one in 1937, when the play was written. Today, it still has an intriguing concept, one that draws on more than the mere relationship and friendship between Lennie and George" (219).

In preparation for this role, James Earl Jones created a Lennie with drooping shoulders and a sad demeanor. He wore an old hat and carried it as a cradle for his dead animals. At Southern Methodist University, Jones visited an institute for retardates in Dallas in order to authentically depict the tragic and violent Lennie. Critical reviews were highly laudatory, and Al Hirschfeld drew a caricature of Jones in the part.

As stardom neared, James Earl Jones determined that he could afford to marry. He chose Julienne Marie, an actress whom he met while playing Othello, and she, Desdemona. The ceremony occurred in January of 1967, but the marriage was not to last. By Jones's own admission, he and she permitted his career to eclipse hers.

With many credits along the way, Jones reached stardom, knowing his life had changed during the Broadway production of Howard Sackler's *The Great White Hope* in 1967. Errol Hill called Jones's portrayal of Jack Jefferson, the character name for Jack Johnson, the first black heavyweight champion of the world, "an uncanny evocation" (172). Awards poured in. Clive Barnes wrote that the play came into the Alvin Theatre on 3 October 1968, "like a whirlwind" (40).

Jane Alexander, former well-known head of the National Endowment for the Arts, then 29, played the white Eleanor Bachman or Ellie, the black prizefighter's mistress. This was "a part in which she had to kiss a Negro and get into bed with him" (Funke 54). Alexander reported being followed as she left the theatre, and receiving obscene letters. Some called her "a traitor to her race" (54). Newspapers reported boycotts, particularly of the movie that followed the stage play.

Jack Johnson (1878–1946), the first black heavyweight champion of the world, was a colorful figure. Gerald Early declares: "Born in Galveston, Texas on 31 Mar. 1878, Johnson was the most charismatic figure and the most notorious African American figure in the American popular culture of his day" (404).

Johnson "won the crown from Tommy Burns in Sydney, Australia, on 26 Dec. 1908" (Ploski and Marr 700). On 4 July 1910, Johnson, in the 14th round, knocked out Jim Jeffries in Reno, Nevada. Early observes:

> Johnson's fight against great white hope Jim Jeffries, in July 1910, was the most discussed sporting event in American history at the time. Johnson easily won the fight but race riots broke out all over the country afterwards.... Indeed his impact has been such that his name comes up whenever a famous black male is mentioned or connected to scandal or conspicuously displays a sexual preference for white women (404).

James Weldon Johnson wrote in *Black Manhattan* that thousands of spectators at the Jim Jeffries fight howled and prayed for Jim Jeffries to "kill the nigger" (66). The taunts probably stemmed from two sets of motivation. Jack Johnson was unbeatable in the ring, and there was strong white male hostility from some camps toward alleged black male sexual prowess, which Johnson flaunted at every opportunity. He paraded his white wives and mistresses with an audacity few would dare. It was this audacity that James Earl Jones conveyed so well on the stage.

In the interview with me, James Earl Jones modestly differed with me when I called him the greatest American actor of the twentieth century: "I know that there are no great actors anywhere in the world. There are actors who sometimes do great work" (15 Sept. 1998). Few would argue that he did this in *The Great White Hope*. Jones continued,

> I think I was cast in the first place because Ed Sherin had seen me do Shakespeare, and he had three choices, myself and Yaphet Kotto and Brock Peters. I think he made sure that all of us had climbed some, what I call some poetic drama mountains, like Shakespeare, because one needed that kind of stamina to climb the mountain that was going to be presented in *The Great White Hope* (15 Sept. 1998).

A trainer worked with Jones in a regimen Jones believes was even worse than that most real prizefighters endure.

The history of Jack Johnson is important to understanding the charisma Jones had to exude in the part. In 1913 Johnson left the United States due to legal entanglements connected with white women. In 1915, in the 26th round, Johnson lost to Jess Willard in Havana, Cuba, in what Johnson and others report was a "fixed fight." Johnson drove fast, defiantly; drank hard, deliberately; and spent his money lavishly. His shoes were handmade. Reputedly, he owned five $100 suits at a time when few earned that a week.

William Wiggins, Jr. wrote:

> Jack Johnson made big money and he spent it on big cars, expensive clothes and other expensive items. In addition to the huge purse he made in the Jim Jeffries fight, Jack Johnson commanded, and quickly spent, large entertainment fees (61).

Wiggins also reported:

> Jack Johnson got married four times and had many mistresses. He always seemed to be in trouble either because or over some woman. Early in his life, he had been tricked out of all his belongings by one. He was shot in the foot by one jealous woman. He fought numerous brawls over the honor of his wife, Etta Terry Duryea, as they toured Europe in 1911. And finally, his downfall and conviction under the Mann Act was the result of sensational testimony given by one of his former lovers, Belle Schreiber (57).

(The Mann Act forbade taking underage women across state lines for sexual purposes.) The playwright reduced the four wives to one mistress and one black wife, who is stereotyped as a violent and revengeful hussy. Some felt that the play whitewashed the character of the real Jack Johnson.

Critics, as a whole, raved over James Earl Jones's portrayal. Jones shaved his head for the role and lost considerable weight, remarking that he has never been in such good physical shape before or since. Peter Hellman in *New York* described the 200-pound, six feet one and a half, 37-year-old Jones as having "butterscotch skin and eyes the color of jade" (quoted in *Current Biography Yearbook 1969* 227). Jack Kroll of *Newsweek* wrote:

> The play is Jones—in him all the juggling and overdeliberation of the work become fused and ignited in a figure at once larger than life and densely human. Jones has a great big technique without the slightest trace of emptiness or inflation. He can expand before your eyes from a flare point of inarticulate feeling to a storm system of emotion. . . . His mischievous put-on darkie [sic] humor, the complex balance of dignities and demeanings that he must constantly negotiate, his supreme physicality which is the triumphant paradox of his personal power and social impotence—all this Jones creates with a style so clear and confident that it transcends style and becomes that blend of form and energy that is acting (quoted in *Current Biography Yearbook 1969* 227).

The role was so demanding that Richard F. Shepard stated in The *New York Times:*

> Mr. Jones puts in a resoundingly energetic evening depicting the progressively embittered heavyweight champ and drinks as much as three quarts of grapefruit juice a night to keep his formidable vocal assets liquid" (n.p., n.d.).

Jones, himself, announced to Leo Seligsohn in a 2 October 1968 issue of *Newsday:* "No other play has drawn as much out of me; no other play has demanded as much. It's like a birthing" (quoted in *Current Biography Yearbook 1969*).

Jack spurns Ellie, eventually saying he will "cut it off first." Unable to take the rejection, she drowns herself. The play ends with Ellie's tragic suicide, accomplished through her jumping into a well. Barnes reported:

> Her mud-spattered body is brought in. It is laid on Jack's massage table, and Jack, tortured with a grief too much for a race to bear, let alone a man, sobs out: "What Ah done to ya . . . what you done honey . . . honey, what dey done to us?" This is a tremendous moment in the theatre—one of those moments when the heart rushes up not just to the play, not just to the players, but to that almost mystic note of communication and understanding that is perhaps the theater's most potent miracle (40).

Alexander remarked in an interview that the suicide was not the hardest part to enact. It was the scene in the first act when she submits to an inquisition by the District Attorney, who is clearly trying to find a law Jack has broken, especially sexual.

Jones continued work in the theatre in the title role of *Othello* and as Zachariah Pieterson in Athol Fugard's *Blood Knot* in 1968. By 1970, he was finally working very regularly. He was cast opposite Ruby Dee as Lena and he as Boesman in Athol Fugard's *Boesman and Lena*, and as Tchembe Matoshe, the African protagonist struggling for independence in Lorraine Hansberry's *Les Blancs*. Of his role in *Boesman and Lena*, Jones recalls: "I joined John Berry again . . . off Broadway, with Ruby Dee and Zakes Mokae. I played the brutish Boesman, who brought me back to the elemental man. I hoped I could find the elemental man within myself" (Jones and Niven 211). In this search, however, Jones found himself catapulted into a major Shakespearean supporting role.

The commercial theatre has seldom, if ever, cast a black actor in the title role of *Hamlet*. In 1945, Gordon Heath and Marion Douglass played Hamlet and Ophelia at Hampton Institute in Virginia, a historically black college. Owen Dodson directed. In 1951, Dodson, having moved to Howard University in Washington, D.C., another historically black college, cast Earle Hyman in the role of the Prince of Denmark, a part Shakespeare clearly marked for a Dane. Perhaps many feel as a white male student at Michigan Technological University said in 1995: "Black actors can't play Hamlet. It's not in the script." James Earl Jones has not played the Prince of Denmark.

But, Jones did play the evil and scheming Claudius, the brother who murders his own kin to get the throne and the King's wife in *Hamlet* in June of 1972. The venue was the open-air Delacorte Theatre in New York's Central Park, with a white Gertrude, played by Colleen Dewhurst, and Stacy Keach as Hamlet. Hamlet is a young prince; it is conceivable that by the time Jones reached stardom, he may have been perceived of as too old. Mel Gibson played Hamlet in film in 1990, certainly past his youth. It is, nevertheless, the dream of any actor who does the classics to play the indecisive, intellectual Prince in one of the theatre's best known Shakespearean tragedies.

Jones also tried his hand at directing. The vehicle was Chekhov's *The Cherry Orchard*. This play has a slow tempo as Chekhov shows the bumbling and ineffectual humans who occupy its intellectual and physical space. Jones had not had the same experience with directing as he had had with acting. Madame Ranevskaya, of the upper class Russian society of 1904, cannot change. She is hopelessly in debt, but Lopakhin, her servant, is unable to help her. Lost in an exploitative and unrequited love affair with a Parisian lover, Madame Ranevskaya zealously gives an expensive ball and lives lavishly, far beyond her means. James Earl Jones saw his grandfather in the character of Lopakhin, who buys the cherry orchard at auction, and cuts it into parcels of land for rent. He thought that he could direct it. Joe Papp had asked.

Jones revealed to me about his work in *The Cherry Orchard:*

> I started out, I conceived that show, and I started out directing it and had to relinquish the direction to someone else and take over the role of Lopakhin, so I did not see myself as Lopakhin for that cast.
> The young man I cast, I had problems with him. I had director-actor problems with him. I couldn't get across to him what I thought the direction we wanted to go with the character [was]. We had some problems. We had some difficulties, and when I had to let him go, I had to let myself go as a director, as well, and take over the role. So, it's a complicated experience for me (15 Sept. 1998).

So it was that Jones played the shrewd, practical serf who buys the cherry orchard in a triumphant coup of servant over master in Chekhov's masterpiece at the New York Shakespeare Festival.

More and more plum roles came Jones's way. According to Errol Hill, in August of 1973

> Jones gave one of his finest performances as King Lear, energetic and exciting, with Ellen Holly and Rosalind Cash appearing as his two ungrateful but singularly attractive daughters Regan and Goneril, while Lee Chamberlain played Cordelia with great tenderness. In this 1973 production Jones was directed by Edwin Sherin, who had directed him in *The Great White Hope,* and it was clear that "once again the actor and director were able to merge their talents in a highly rewarding collaboration" (174).

Critics found Jones unusually able in his portrayal. It was a triumph of an actor who never gave up.

It was at Circle in the Square in December of 1973 that Jones portrayed Hickey, the hardware salesman who comes into Harry Hope's Saloon in Eugene O'Neill's *The Iceman Cometh.* It was a role many thought belonged only to Jason Robards, Jr. But Jones acquitted himself well, if not entirely to his own satisfaction. Jones said to me:

> O'Neill wrote about the common man, I think that's first [in importance about the playwright]. And most black people in this society have common man roots, you know, none of us, most of us are not wealthy or aristocratic in any way. Although we might have been descendants from kings, the slavery period sort of equalized us to the lowest rung of life, and I think we all inherit a common man, a "commonness," and I think that's what O'Neill wrote about. My biggest problem with Hickey was that I thought I didn't have the temperament, nothing to do with race or other cultural factors. Hickey had the temperament of a fast-talking Hoosier and I didn't. That is

not my temperament, and I had a problem with it. I worked at it, but I had a serious problem with it (15 Sept. 1998).

On 9 December 1973, Louis Sheaffer wrote in *The New York Times* about Hickey's impassioned speech where he explains why he killed his wife:

> "God," Hickey cries out, "can you picture all I made her suffer, and all the guilt she made me feel, and how I hated myself! I even caught myself hating her for making me hate myself so much. There's a limit to the guilt you can feel!" (D5)

This towering performance led to Jones being Diahann Carroll's film beau in the movie *Claudine*.

In the November 1998 issue of *Ebony*, the editors named John Berry's 1974 film, *Claudine*, one of the top black films of all time. It got a Golden Globe and NAACP Award. James Earl Jones co-starred with Diahann Carroll who played the title role. Helen Dudar wrote: "The first garbageman collector in his repertory was Roop, the strutting, lecherous trash man in *Claudine*" (6). Jones considered the role of Claudine's boyfriend to be one of his best experiences in film.

In 1976, Jones took the title role in a showcase production of *Oedipus Rex*, directed by David Gild, at the Cathedral of St. John the Divine in New York City. On 21 February 1977, *Time* reported: "Actor James Earl Jones . . . commands about $200,000 per movie these days, but for twelve weekend performances in a workshop production at Manhattan's Cathedral of St. John the Divine, he agreed to work for nothing" (50). Also in the late 1970s, Jones read for students in the American College Theatre Festival Competition at the Kennedy Center, as a courtesy and as encouragement. Little did he know that controversy was about to loom again.

In 1977, *Paul Robeson*, a one-man show written by Phillip Hayes Dean, caused Jones considerable difficulty. Ossie Davis, James Baldwin, Maya Angelou, Gwendolyn Brooks, and a staggering number of 51 others signed petitions and took out full-page newspaper advertisements to see that Jones's portrayal of Paul Robeson in 1977 and 1978 be one that they and Robeson's son, Paul, Jr., considered an authentic representation of Robeson.

They formed the National Ad Hoc Committee to End the Crimes Against Paul Robeson. It is not clear that Jones was the one who had committed the crimes against Robeson. Nevertheless, Paul Robeson, Jr. personally picketed virtually every performance. Jones said in the interview with me:

> It was a phenomena of the year . . . of the time, and it happened to be a time when Paul Jr. was very sensitive to anyone doing anything about his father. He felt sharply. . . . He was guardian of his father's image and wanted no one

to do anything, good or bad.... But now, Avery Brooks does this same play and Paul Jr. does not bother him (15 Sept. 1998).

The controversy eventually died down, but Errol Hill believes,

> His portrayal of Paul Robeson in 1978... left those who witnessed his essentially one-man performance of over two hours in no doubt whatever that they were in the presence of an extraordinarily gifted actor (173).

Jones even attended one of the meetings of the opposing forces, but went on, with dignity, in his performance.

He continued to get nontraditional roles, playing Judge Brack in Ibsen's *Hedda Gabler* in 1980 at the Yale Repertory Theatre in New Haven, Connecticut. More than once, Jones strongly believed that he should protect the arts from the many funding cuts that seem to have occurred all of the twentieth century. At the time Jones played Judge Brack, he testified before the Connecticut Commission on the Arts, where funding was threatened, stating, "Culture is as necessary for humanity as food," an important part of his philosophy.

In 1983 Jones took the crucial role of Sam, the black servant, in Athol Fugard's *Master Harold... and the Boys*. Sam serves a white family with an adolescent and impudent son, Hally, in Fugard's native South Africa. According to Lee Jacobus,

> Hally reveals throughout the play (which is set in 1950) that he is more attached emotionally to Sam, the black waiter in his parents' restaurant who has befriended him, than he is even to his own parents (1229–1230).

Hally *is* Athol Fugard. Fugard's creation is autobiographical. One of the most powerful moments comes when Hally, a boy, disrespects Sam. Fugard admitted that he was exorcising ghosts on the stage with the setting in St. George's Park Tea Room in Port Elizabeth. Jones admirably assisted in this exorcism.

Soon, thereafter, in February 1982, Jones played Othello at the Winter Garden Theatre, his first time playing the Moor on Broadway, but his seventh time playing Othello in a period of 19 years. Christopher Plummer was Iago in what can only be called a brilliant performance, down to Plummer spitting on the stage when he uttered the lines of envy that drive him to his Machiavellian tactics:

> But he, Sir, had th' election:
> And I, of whom his eyes had seen the proof
> At Rhodes, at Cyprus, and on other grounds

>   Christian and heathen, must be leed and calmed
>   By debitor and creditor; this counter-caster,
>   He in good time must his Lieutenant be,
>   And I—God bless the mark!—his Moorship's
>   Ancient (*Othello,* Act I scene l).

Cecelia Hart, one of the Desdemonas, became James Earl Jones's wife on 15 March 1982, during the performance's run.

Of James Earl Jones's performance, Errol Hill wrote:

> As Othello, Jones possesses the three characteristics that Caldwell Titcomb believes are prerequisite for any actor undertaking the role. They are an imposing physique (six feet or over), a God-given organ-toned windpipe, and an extraordinary aura of personal magnetism (cited in Hill 174 from *Bay State Banner,* 3 Sept. 1981).

Jones showed, as Othello must, both strength and vulnerability.

Walter Kerr praised Jones for his very different and gentle portrayal of a scene where the fearful and bewildered Desdemona is on her knees (Hill 176 from Walter Kerr, "The Jones-Plummer 'Othello' is Twice Blessed," *The New York Times,* 14 Feb. 1982). Such an extraordinary performance of Othello, a slave of passion, led to another role where Jones did great work, the part of Troy Maxon in August Wilson's *Fences.*

Fences, as with many plays, did not begin on The Great White Way. It showcased, first, at the Eugene O'Neill Playwright's Conference Center in Waterford, Connecticut, opened next at the Yale Repertory Theatre, at some point played in San Francisco, and then at Arena Stage in Washington, D.C. Finally, it came to a triumphant run at the 46th Street Theatre on Broadway, all under Lloyd Richards' excellent direction. Helen Dudar wrote of Jones, "In Troy, Mr. Jones has a role shaped to his talents as lovingly as a master tailor cuts a bespoke coat" (section 2, l).

In his interview with me, Jones stated: "[*Fences*] was a hugely effective play even though it was not complete" (15 Sept. 1998). Jones respects August Wilson in many ways, but believes that Wilson is inflexible about rewriting, something Jones still believes *Fences* needs. On 10 May 1985, following a performance of *Fences* at Yale, Heather Henderson interviewed James Earl Jones and Mary Alice, the extraordinary and experienced actor who played Troy's wife, Rose.

In that interview, James Earl Jones talked about the authenticity of August Wilson's writing, comparing him with John Steinbeck:

> You don't often find this kind of play. Steinbeck used to write about this stratum of life, but among American playwrights, it is rare. Few writers can

capture dialect as dialogue in a manner as interesting and accurate as August's. My first experience with a play with the black sound was by a white writer, Howard Sackler—in *The Great White Hope*. That dialogue was not identifiable as Galveston, Texas; it was a poetic rendering of an idea of Southern dialect (67).

Those who attended the Dartmouth Drama Conference in March of 1998 which featured August Wilson, spoke of Wilson's unusual ability to listen. It was this ability to listen in barber shops and record language that has made Wilson a playwright Jones could interpret so ably.

Of the play and Jones, Edith Oliver wrote on 6 April 1987:

> The hero of "Fences," and hero he is indeed—a flawed giant—is a garbageman of fifty-six named Troy Maxon. Once a baseball player of professional ability, he was prevented by his color from playing in the major leagues: The time is the late nineteen-fifties—post-Jackie Robinson but too late for Troy. A baseball hangs on a cord in the back yard of his shabby house in a poor section of some Northern city, and he whacks away at it angrily throughout the action. There is no aspect of his life in which he does not feel constricted—fenced in—and in James Earl Jones' towering performance one can almost see him bursting at the seams (81).

Jones, himself, was distressed about parts of the play, not just the lack of completeness, but some language, which the audience, at times, misunderstood, especially the baseball metaphors. The father-son conflict was especially disturbing to Jones.

Audience reaction to *Fences* was powerful. Large numbers of black women stood and cried when Troy brought the out-of-wedlock child home to Rose when Troy's mistress, Alberta, dies in childbirth. Audiences felt that James Earl Jones sensitively portrayed a black man like men he had known.

With the end of *Fences,* James Earl Jones came to the conclusion that he no longer had the stamina to do eight shows a week as Broadway requires, so he has spent much of the time since the late 1980s doing television and film. He is best known to many as the voice of Darth Vader in the Star Wars trilogy and the voice of King Mufasa in the film, *The Lion King.* It is Jones's deeply rich and commanding voice that so many speak of. He has come to that voice through trial by fire. For many years he stuttered and still struggles to overcome it.

In 1995, Jones played Rev. Stephen Kumalo in the film based on Alan Paton's novel about apartheid in South Africa, *Cry the Beloved Country.* It was a role created for the screen by Canada Lee in 1952. The film brings together a white and black father in a moment of compassion after the black father's son kills the white father's son. This was a time when South Africa was rigidly and painfully a country torn apart.

How has Jones survived against so many odds—near-abandonment as a child, clear envy from many regarding his achievements, a theatre that has for much of the twentieth century stereotyped black actors, critics who can be harsh against anyone in the theatre, a profession in which most make very little money, the deep prejudice many still have against interracial marriages, and his being a black man in an America with a clear racial divide?

Jones's answer to all of this is many faceted. First of all, in terms of earning power, Jones said to me: "I entered the theatre as a realist. Nothing was a shock to me, and I needed no sort of special preparation to survive" (15 Sept. 1998). He went into therapy to deal with his near-abandonment. He recognizes that he is a stutterer as a result of this trauma of his childhood, and works hard at handling language exceptionally well. He has basically ignored some of the controversy surrounding his personal and professional life.

As to the critics, he says:

> I learned fairly early on not to read reviews. They can be quite devastating to the ego one way or the other, and neither way is healthy, so I learned back in 1964, I guess, not to read reviews, so I don't know what the critics have said about me. Sometimes my family or my agent will read reviews, and if there is something that I should know, they will share it with me, but otherwise if it's something that won't help me one way or the other, I prefer not to know. People coming back stage usually don't say things of a critical nature. It's always wise for them not to. When I visit someone backstage, I usually say just simply "Thank you very much," and not say "I liked it because, or I hated it because." It's a very vulnerable time for the performer, to go back stage and lay some heavy number on them (15 Sept. 1998).

James Earl Jones, an actor who has not just survived but triumphed over all adversity, has no bitterness about his hard times. Jones reflects:

> I don't like to express any resentment or sour grapes about my work because it's been a glorious time, and I'm happy to have been able to make a living as an actor and I have no misgivings about the kind of roles I have been given or because I'm black or white or the kind of money I've made or because I'm rich or poor. Those are really irrelevant things (15 Sept. 1998).

What is relevant is that he has performed a wider range of roles than most, and has been blessed with a good marriage, a good relationship with his son, and an acceptance of his relationship with his father. His very high visibility has made him a very positive black male figure in an era where black men are under siege. Arguably, he is the best known actor of color in the world. His art remains his politics, perhaps one of the strongest reasons he has thrived. With faith in God, he has also developed humility. It is an affirmation of what the human spirit can become.

Works Cited

Barksdale, Richard and Keneth Kinnamon. *Black Writers of America.* New York: Macmillan, 1972.

Barnes, Clive. "Theater: Howard Sackler's 'Great White Hope'," *The New York Times,* 4 Oct. 1968. 40:1.

Bradley, Jeff. "James Earl Jones Knows Feeling of Vulnerability," *Denver Post,* 23 July 1997, G, 1:5

"Building Fences: An Interview with Mary Alice and James Earl Jones," *Theater,* vol. 16, no. 3, 1985, 67–70.

Burg, Robert. "Young Actor on the Way Up," *Negro Digest,* Apr. 1966, 26–31.

Current Biography Yearbook 1969, Charles Moritz, ed. New York: H. W. Wilson Company, 1969.

Current Biography Yearbook 1994, Judith Graham, ed. New York: H. W. Wilson Company, 1994.

Deveaux, Dawn Della. *The Effects of Racism on the Theatrical Careers of Ira Aldridge, Paul Leroy Robeson and James Earl Jones.* M.A. Thesis, Austin Peay State University, 1987.

DeVine, Larry. "James Earl Jones, Broadway's Great Black Hope, Remembers the Berry-Picking Days in Dublin, Michigan," *The Detroit Free Press,* 27 April, 1969, 14–20.

Dudar, Helen. "James Earl Jones at Bat," *The New York Times,* 22 Mar. 1987, section 2, Arts and Leisure, 1 and 6. [*Fences*]

Early, Gerald. Entry on Jack Johnson in *The Oxford Companion to African American Literature,* ed. William Andrews, Frances Smith Foster, and Trudier Harris. New York: Oxford University Press, 1997, 404.

Funke, Lewis. "Jane Alexander Tells of 'White Hope' Challenge," *The New York Times,* 29 Oct. 1968. 54:1.

Glenn, DeFoy. Conversation with author. Circa 1987.

Green, Michelle. "The Struggle To Be James Earl Jones," *Saturday Review,* Feb. 1982. 22–27.

Hamill, Pete. "Theater: Gaudy Tragedy of a Black Champ," *Life,* 25 Oct. 1968, 66B-68.

Henderson, Heather. "Building *Fences:* An Interview with Mary Alice and James Earl Jones," *Theater,* vol 16, no. 3, summer/fall, 1985, 67–70.

Hill, Errol. *Shakespeare in Sable.* Amherst: University of Massachusetts Press, 1984.

Jacobus, Lee A. *Drama.* Boston: Bedford Books of St. Martin's Press, 1993.

James Earl Jones: A Select Bibliography. (courtesy of Debra Van Tassel)

"James Earl Jones," *Negro Digest,* Oct. 1962, 43–44.

"James Earl Jones—Actor Still Climbing," *Ebony,* Apr. 1965. 98–106.

"James Earl Jones," *Life,* 7 Nov. 1969. 71.
Johnson, James Weldon. *Black Manhattan.* New York: Atheneum, 1930.
Jones, James Earl. Letter to author. 7 May 1982.
———. Telephone interview with author. 15 Sept. 1998.
Jones, James Earl and Penelope Niven. *James Earl Jones: Voices and Silences.* New York: Charles Scribner's Sons, 1993.
Jones, James Earl. "Jack Johnson is Alive and Well . . . on Broadway," *Ebony,* June 1969, 54–61.
Jones, Robert Earl. Personal interview with author. 28 June 1980.
Kroll, Jack. "Duel to the Death," *Newsweek,* 31 Aug. 1981. 56.
Larner, Daniel M. Notes on book to author. 28 June 1999.
Louis, Errol. "Suppressing 'Un-Black' Art," *Essence,* vol. 16, Mar. 1986, 124.
Nicolette, David. "'Hamlet' Is a Hit in Central Park Despite Problems," *The Grand Rapids Press,* 25 June 1972, 7.
Oliver, Edith. "The Theatre: Mr. Wilson and Mr. Jones," *The New Yorker,* 6 Apr. 1987, 81. [*Fences*]
Ploski, Harry A. and Warren Marr. *The Afro-American.* New York: Bellwether Press, 1976.
Schechter, Joel. "James Earl Jones on Fugard," *Theater,* vol 16, no. 1, 1984, 40–42.
"Shadow of the Moor," *Wake Forest University Magazine,* Sept. 1993, vol. 42, no. 1, 10–17. [on Penelope Niven's book on Mr. Jones] (courtesy of Dr. Dolly McPherson)
Shakespeare, William. *Othello.* ed. Kenneth Muir. New York: Penguin, 1968.
Sheaffer, Louis. "Is O'Neill a Character in 'Iceman'!" *The New York Times,* 9 Dec. 1973, D-5. [James Earl Jones as Hickey]
Shepard, Richard F. "James Earl Jones Now a Champion on Broadway," *The New York Times,* n.d., n.p.
Shewey, Don. "On a Role: Stars on the Stage," *Harper's Bazaar,* Mar. 1987, 310–13.
Time, 21 Feb. 1977, 50.
"Top Black Films of All Times," *Ebony,* Nov. 1998, 154–162.
Washington, Booker T. *Up from Slavery,* excerpted in *Black Writers of America,* ed. Richard Barksdale and Kenneth Kinnamon. New York: Macmillan, 1974, 424–429.
West, Hollie I. "James Earl Jones: Expanding Horizons," *The Washington Post,* 21 Mar. 1975, Bl-B4.
Wiggins, William, Jr. "Jack Johnson as Bad Nigger: The Folklore of His Life," *Contemporary Black Thought,* ed. Robert Christman and Nathan Hare. Indianapolis: Bobbs-Merril Company, 1973, 53–70.
Zurawik, Dave. "James Earl Jones: A Commanding Presence," *Detroit Free Press,* 1 July 1979, C5.

Morgan Freeman at his Charleston, Mississippi ranch on February 8, 1997. Photo by Chris Webb, permission granted.

Chapter XI

Morgan Freeman's Resistance and Non-Traditional Roles

I wanted to be a man, nothing but a man.

(Fanon 113)

These words of Frantz Fanon represent the spirit of actor Morgan Freeman and his resistance against societal forces that would prevent his being a man. In the annals of the American theatre, the black actor has faced almost insurmountable odds since 1767, when Edwin Forrest created the character Raccoon in *The Disappointment* or *The Force of Credulity*. Since then, the stereotype has pervaded. Black men in particular, America's most feared and suspected group, have been represented on the stage and screen as denizens of the lower depths.

Conversely, actors like Morgan Freeman who seek nontraditional roles in Shakespeare or other classics are often seen as interlopers by critics and audiences, and sometimes as traitors in the black community. Such perceived abandonment of black roles is often tantamount to high treason among some people of color. Masses have often preferred black actors to play roles traditionally designated for black actors. Nontraditional roles often present an uncomfortable existence for both actor and audience.

Theatrical resistance of black actors to American racism of the late nineteenth and twentieth century, except during the revolutionary 1960s, was generally not an act of direct confrontation. Resistance for the Negro in any walk of life often appeared to be accommodation. This allowed reputedly powerful figures such as Booker T. Washington to survive.

In the theatre, actors who did confront the power structure by speaking out too often and too strongly were destroyed through economic enslavement, social disapprobation, the House Un-American Activities Committee hearings, and ill health. Morgan Freeman has been more politic.

Controversy has eluded Freeman, because he has avoided it, often being affected by severe criticism from some members of the black community. Just before the 1996 Academy Awards ceremony, news accounts revealed that Jesse Jackson stated that there was a problem with black actors not getting the Oscar. Freeman remarked that Hollywood was green, not black. Denzel Washington, who is perceived of as more black, has become the darling of many groups of color and was fêted as the Man of the Year by the NAACP at its 27 February 1997 Image Awards. Freeman, who was also in major films in 1996, was ignored that year.

In an effort to know more about this major figure, on Friday, 7 February 1997 graphic designer Bob Slater, photographer Chris Webb, and I boarded an airplane for Memphis, and on Saturday, 8 February 1997, rented a car, and drove the 70 beautiful miles to Charleston, Mississippi. Precisely at 1:30 p.m. on that Saturday, we buzzed at the gate, and Morgan Freeman answered. As we identified ourselves, Freeman opened the iron gate to his 120-acre ranch.

My first communication with the Freeman estate was through a call to Myrna Colley-Lee, Freeman's wife, in late August of 1996. She, in turn, made it possible for him to correspond with me on 30 October 1996, when I asked him what he considered the most cataclysmic changes on the theatrical landscape in the twentieth century. He responded in that letter:

> One could argue that there have been two cataclysmic changes on the theatrical landscape over the last... forty [years],... the first was Marlon Brando, and the other was the successful introduction of the idea of open casting. The effect of the latter is, I think, evident in the very existence of [me], Denzel [Washington], Danny [Glover], Spike [Lee], Wesley [Snipes], Bill Duke, John Singleton, Bob Johnson, Susanne Depasse, Will Smith, etc. Name your own.

Morgan Freeman, with a body of work beyond any of those he named, is representative of the many contemporary black actors doing nontraditional roles on stage and screen. He has done more than most to represent black men in different roles, and a chief characteristic of his work is resistance.

Resistance is exemplified in the most impressive work I have personally witnessed of Freeman's, the portrayal of Red, an Irishman, in the 1994 film adaptation of Stephen King's novel, *Rita Hayworth and the Shawshank Redemption*. The movie uses only the last three words of King's book. As Red, Freeman appears to be accommodating the system, but is not. Richard Schickel wrote in *Time:* "The movie needs the kind of authenticity that Freeman brings to it" (26 Sept. 1994 78). It is this authenticity that makes the film seem like reality.

As Red, a humane prisoner, Freeman's shaded nuances are so real, the experience so lifelike, the viewer's transportation to the prison so intense, that we believe we *are* in Shawshank. This actor, with a subtlety few achieve, convinces a warden whose suicide he eventually cheers that he respects him. Near the end, in the most poignant moment in the film, Freeman, as Red, quietly, but with sufficient genuine repentance, tells a Parole Commission that he does not give a damn. Ironically, they free him, after having repeatedly rejected his parole for years. As long as he was playing the role they wanted him to play, he could not get out. This final hearing is the only moment at any of the hearings where he stands up to them, and makes no effort to ingratiate himself with a smile he does not feel, or a promise he cannot keep. It is the quintessential moment of resistance.

Freeman is like a chameleon in that he can also pretend to be the docile, almost illiterate, naïve prisoner. "Naw suh, Warden," he pleads, when the warden is convinced that he knows what is going on with Andy (Tim Robbins) who escapes through a tunnel he has been digging for 19 years. Red did not know about the tunnel, but Andy had informed him that he was leaving.

While this role may *seem* stereotypical, the shrewdness behind the docile mask of Freeman, as Red, belies the "docile darky" image of stage and screen. Secondly, the friendship between Andy and Red is unusual and genuine for any two people, especially for two men from different races in the 1940s. Additionally, Andy is a man with formal education and an uncanny knowledge of investments. Red has probably not gone beyond high school. They transcend class and race in a spiritual fusion. In a shrewd and long-term plan, Andy outwits the warden not only with an escape, but with a vast sum of money he has helped the warden earn. He shares the money with Red, after Red is paroled; the latter joins Andy on an island outside of America.

When Freeman veers from the expected roles for black men, he has met with many good responses from audiences and critics, even when those roles are Brechtian or Shakespearean. Freeman has also faced hostile and uncomprehending critics like John Simon, as well as bewildered and uncomfortable audiences. Moreover, a large number of roles in his total body of work also stereotype him.

W. E. B. DuBois, at the early part of the twentieth century in his *The Souls of Black Folk*, wrote that the image of people of color needed to be changed symbolically. Economic advancement would fail if symbolic representation of the Negro did not change. It is remarkable that in spite of massive stereotyping of blacks and whites on the stage, film, and television, nontraditional casting does occur much more frequently than many realize.

A brief history of Freeman's 33-year career is instructive to understanding the power of his resistance. The name Morgan Freeman, to most out of the New York theatre circle, became recognizable in 1987 for his role as the psychotic procurer, Leo Smalls (Fast Black), who threatens to take out the eye of a prostitute he later kills in the film *Street Smart*. This is about the violent environment that writer/scholar bell hooks calls "outlaw culture." Freeman refers to Smalls as an "urban entrepreneur," who is flawed. The actor may have known other Fast Blacks on the rough Beale Street of his native Memphis, now home to B. B. King's Blues Club and Restaurant. While Fast Black is Freeman's favorite role, some of the viewing public did not like the despicable character of Fast Black, in spite of excellent critical reviews of Freeman's acting.

Freeman actually began his career 1 October 1967, as Creampuff in George Tabori's *The Niggerlovers*, at the Orpheum Theatre. Racially tense social conditions and some remnants of Jim Crow for actors of color were so pervasive in the 1967–87 period that Freeman was known only in some theatrical, film, and television circles for those 20 years. Nevertheless, his critical acclaim was so astonishing by 1987 that it caused Pauline Kael of *The New Yorker* to ask on 29 April of that year if Morgan Freeman was America's greatest actor. She determined that he was.

A few weeks after *The Niggerlovers*, Freeman made his Broadway debut, on 12 November 1967, at the St. James Theatre, as Rudolph, a dancer, in the all-black *Hello Dolly!*, featuring Pearl Bailey and Cab Calloway. Freeman is a trained dancer and equestrian. Such a work, in spite of its black cast, may have been Freeman's first nontraditional role, since the musical *Hello Dolly!* is an adaptation of Thornton Wilder's *The Matchmaker*.

Another nontraditional role was that of Boston Baboon in Bertolt Brecht's *In the Jungle of Cities* at the Charles Street Playhouse in Boston. Freeman recalls only that during production he sat and taught himself how to roll a cigarette, his only memory of that role.

He was, also in 1969, in a Philadelphia venue, the sergeant in George Farquhar's 1706 comedy, *The Recruiting Officer*, a perennial favorite of 18th century English drama, decidedly nontraditional. In the personal interview, Freeman mentioned that he had a hat of monkey hair so that when he put it on, it looked like long hair falling down his shoulders. He recalled how, falling down in a fight scene, he missed the stage and tumbled into the third row of empty seats in the theatre, but was not hurt. He bristled when he remembered that a critic writing for *The Philadelphia Inquirer* wrote that he learned his lines in a metronome. *The Recruiting Officer* was Freeman's second venture into repertory theatre, the first being in San Francisco.

In 1970, Freeman replaced Cleavon Little in the title role of the musical *Purlie,* a satire based on Ossie Davis's *Purlie Victorious.* The musical poked fun at black and white stereotypes. While Freeman did not transcend the stereotype here, he deliberately worked the stereotype in blatant fashion.

One of Freeman's best roles, also a stereotype, which catapulted him to fame, was that of Zeke, the wino, in Richard Wesley's 1978 *The Mighty Gents*. Al Hirschfeld caricatured Freeman in *The New York Times,* an indication of Freeman's growing stature. In the interview (8 Feb. 1997), the actor recalled,

> All the characters in this play were losers. They were social losers. *The Mighty Gents,* this little gang, had grown up as teenagers standing on the corner singing doo-wop songs; now they're in their 30s, standing on the corner singing doo-wop songs. Well, the talisman, I guess . . . what would you call this character, Zeke, was what they saw themselves headed for, and they hated him just on sight. He was the dregs, a besotted wino, almost out of control. . . . Opening night at the Manhattan Theatre Club, where we did it off-Broadway, in order to get on stage, I had to go to the lobby to get to my backstage position. And they wouldn't let me through the lobby. They wouldn't let me into the theatre [because of his appearance as a wino]. So, I just had to come out of character and say you're going to have to go get the producer right now. They went and got him and he said, "Oh, my God, it's Morgan."

This was necessity. He did what he had to do to those guarding the gates of the theatre.

Freeman's resistance in Shakespearean roles deserves attention as well. He played, among others, the title role in *Coriolanus* in 1979 at the New York Public Theater, and a cowboy Petruchio in *The Taming of the Shrew* in 1990. The latter was a highly resistant role in the battle of sexual politics.

Freeman especially liked the audience at the Anspacher Theatre of the New York Public where he played Casca to a Hispanic Marc Antony, the famous and excellent Jaime Sanchez. Julius Caesar was updated as a street hustler, an uptown numbers banker.

A number of critics praised Freeman's performance in *Coriolanus*. Freeman, himself, is convinced that the main woman in Coriolanus's life is Volumnia, his mother, in a clearly incestuous relationship. Opposite Gloria Foster as the mother, and Michele Shay as his pretty and gentle wife, Virgilia, Freeman's Coriolanus, according to Errol Hill, "was judged to be rich and heartbreaking, brilliant in the final scenes, and by itself justifying a visit to the theater" (189). Marilyn Stasio posited:

> Coriolanus is a great warrior, a responsible patrician leader, and a lousy politician. In his very fine, if not definitive, performance Morgan Freeman invests him with the soldier's bluff strength and the noble's heroic stance and proud disdain for the masses beneath his feet (30).

Edith Oliver observed in *The New Yorker* on 26 March 1979 that Freeman turned in "a fascinating study in temperament—of a complex, tortured man (n.p.)." T. E. Kalem believed "It takes an actor of liquid fire and the keenest intelligence to carry . . . [the role] off, and Morgan Freeman accomplishes it in this rousing production . . ." (67). Freeman said in the interview, "Earle Hyman paid me a real compliment about Coriolanus. He said, 'I have been all over the world in *Othello,* but I do not have what you have. You have magic.'"

But, as with many actors, and particularly black men playing Shakespeare, all the critics were not so kind. Freeman wrote me on 30 October 1996:

> I was once referred to as an interloper by a white critic—the notoriously sleazy John Simon. He tried to rain on my performance in Joe Papp's production of *Coriolanus.* . . . But, I think of him as a lone voice in the wilderness . . . a lone voice in the wilderness.

Simon's review in *New York* declared:

> To have a group of black and Hispanic actors, almost totally untrained in Shakespearean acting, . . . do *Coriolanus* ranks as advanced dementia. . . . Moreover, its theme is the undoing of its aristocratic hero by its excess of upper-class antipopulist fastidiousness. The consummate, uncompromising patrician is a figure far removed from the ken of most white Americans; to black and Hispanic Americans, actors or otherwise, he is, through historical and economic circumstance, even more remote and inconceivable. Morgan Freeman, who plays Coriolanus, cannot even approximate the part in sound, look, or demeanor. . . . I left at interval, which I thought would never come (85).

Marilyn Stasio agreed with Simon about the language, saying "The ear still recoils from hearing Shakespeare's heroic language masticated like chewing gum" (30). In Simon's opinion, Shakespeare's language is the only official language, and any variation on that is a sacrilege, since the variation is the language of a counterculture.

There is little question that a number of black and Hispanic actors would need to develop over a long period of years to have the skills of the British-born Shakespearean actors. However, for critic John Simon to believe that all blacks and Hispanics lack access to an understanding of Shakespeare shows a true lack of awareness on his part. For years, Negro professors on historically black college campuses have been teaching Shakespeare, and some with considerable skill in the language. Freeman, however, commented in his 30 October 1996 letter, "I have . . . been given to understand [from audiences, critics, directors, producers] that my participation in Shakespearean works has had the effect of making those plays more accessible."

This was certainly true for his 1990 portrayal of a cowboy Petruchio in *The Taming of the Shrew.* Frank Rich observed:

> Mr. Freeman does everything brilliantly, whether he is falling on the floor in a knockabout comic emulation of one of Ms. [Tracey] Ullman's temper tantrums or standing quietly in a soft spotlight to savor a reflective passage of verse or modeling an outlandish wedding costume that makes him look like a hybrid of Davy Crockett, Pancho Villa and Sitting Bull. He is one of those rare actors whose careful command of his art seems to inspire a higher level of performance from everyone around him. . . . His proud, intelligent shrew-tamer is genial and firm . . . , even when . . . good-naturedly countering her well-aimed volley of spit (1).

Shrew has to be acted in modern-day performance style so as to assuage the wrath of both traditional women and feminists. Freeman recalled in the interview, "The challenge was physical. There was a point where I had to rope her. Throw a rope and hit her with it every night." This was his primary challenge. A number of students that I teach do not like *Taming of the Shrew.* It seems to be unadulterated, unabashed sexism on the part of Shakespeare. So, Freeman's challenge was to obtain the right mix of roping Kate with a modicum more affection than a testosterone-filled Cave Man edict.

Benedict Nightingale in his preview of *The Taming of the Shrew,* which starred Freeman, asked: "Precisely how are we to bring the 426-year old William Shakespeare vividly to life in the world of Gorbachev and Madonna, Margaret Thatcher and Donald Trump (1)?" As more and more acting companies update the playwright, audiences can be critical. Freeman pulled off a deft high-wire act by not offending many.

He was equally adept in another non-traditional role, playing the chaplain in Ntozake Shange's 1980 adaptation of Brecht's *Mother Courage and Her Children,* also at the New York Public Theater. Buffeted by poverty and war, Mother Courage sacrifices all three of her children in the Thirty Years' War, including forcing her daughter into prostitution. The chaplain is Mother Courage's confidant. An unnamed critic in *The New Yorker* wrote on 26 March 1980, that this was "another splendid performance, by Morgan Freeman" (77). Of this role, Freeman wrote me:

> Will Lee [Wilford Leach, the director] set *Mother Courage* in the American Southwest during America's own 30 years' war against the Native Americans, which segued into the War Between the States. The premise is a powerful aid in legitimizing black presence and participation in America's history beyond the lackluster condition of slavery. My role as chaplain in that production became my role as a Baptist preacher of, as I recall, dubious ordainment, as was so often the case (30 Oct. 1996).

Resistance is obvious, reconfigured to accommodate race.

The year 1983 found Freeman being offered the leading role in Lee Breuer's *The Gospel at Colonus*, a traditional role of a black Pentecostal preacher, with an element of resistance, since he reads from the traditional Greek book of Oedipus with revivalist fervor. Freeman spoke with immense passion about this play in the interview, especially the catharsis experienced in both the traditional black church and traditional Greek drama, an often unexplored comparison. "That hollering and shouting that we do must have been to [Breuer] what the Greek chorus was really about—the Greeks were so emotional. You've just taken two traditions that were compatible and stirred them together," Freeman declared in the interview. Deacon Creon, Testifier Polyneices, and Evangelist Antigone personify this mix of two traditions.

In spite of Freeman's remarkable talent and remarkable opportunity on stage, screen, and television, he remains best known for some of his work in film, often also nontraditional: as an inmate who demands respect in *Brubaker*, a psychotic procurer in *Streetsmart*, a domestic in *Driving Miss Daisy*, the embattled principal in *Lean on Me*, a Union soldier in *Glory*, an army general in *Outbreak*, a bounty hunter opposite Clint Eastwood in *Unforgiven*, a shrewd prisoner in *Shawshank Redemption*, a clinical psychologist in the thriller *Kiss the Girls*, an abolitionist in Steven Spielberg's *Amistad*, and President of the United States in the very frightening movie *Deep Impact*.

A significant number of people most remember Morgan Freeman as Miss Daisy's driver, a traditional role he first created on stage. Freeman insisted, as he sat at the head of his table at his ranch on 8 February 1997, that the relationship between Hoke Coleburn and Daisy Werthan is romantic. Freeman stood up at the table, and with dramatic flair, shouted,

He was crazy about Daisy Werthan. She gave him stuff nobody had ever given him before. . . . She taught him how to read. He could actually sit up and read a newspaper after he got to be with her. He was driving a new car every other year. He had a job. He had purpose. He had her, and she had him. There's a moment in that big ice storm. Big. Huge ice storm. All can't go anywhere. He got up, put on his clothes, got in his car and drove to Daisy Werthan. And, she was talking to her son. She says, "I'm all right now. Hoke is here." They became inseparable.

Hoke sets up competition with Miss Daisy's son, Boolie, a white stereotype, so that Hoke can get his salary raised. He tells Miss Daisy, his cantankerous Jewish employer—another white stereotype—that he knows when his bladder is full and stops the car to relieve himself in the woods when she reprimands him for not stopping at the Standard Oil station to which black men could not go in that era. Such assertive language, in history, was taboo for black men, and would not easily fall out of his mouth. At the moment Miss Daisy almost fires Hoke for stealing a can of salmon, he walks in with the replacement and a persuasive story to go with it.

By the end of the film, he is the most important person in her life, as he feeds her Thanksgiving pie in the nursing home. When I saw the stage production on 21 May 1988, with Earle Hyman as Hoke, and Frances Sternhagen as Miss Daisy, the virtually all-white audience collectively wept unashamedly.

Joseph Hurley, who refers to Freeman as "an actor of near-volcanic on-stage power," in an unidentified newspaper clipping called "He's Daisy's Driver," wrote:

> A role that bridges the quarter century from 1948 to 1973 might seem to most actors a ripe opportunity for a display of pyrotechnics. Instead, Freeman triumphs by underplaying, working in barely perceptible gestures and details, the stage equivalent of the miniaturist's brushstroke pattern.

As a result of massive critical and audience acclaim, Freeman went to Hollywood to play Hoke in the 1989 film opposite Jessica Tandy who won the Academy Award for best female actor for *Daisy*.

In the interview, Freeman smiled about his current privilege of being able to choose roles and said: "One always has that choice." The theatre mirrors life. It causes people to feel. It makes us human. It brings understanding of experiences where all other mediums have failed. It immerses the audience in the experience. W. E. B. DuBois, a respected black drama critic, said,

> This is peculiarly the occasion to say a word of the relationship between the theatre and the American Negro. The stage still retains among us something

of freedom and the forward gaze. Behind the footlights one is permitted to examine and discuss truth under circumstances where literature is stilled, painting inarticulate, sculpture choked of convention, architecture drowned in waves of monstrosity and music fettered by death (292).

Morgan Freeman's resistance is powerful and liberating theatre.

As Webb, Slater, and I drove through parts of Memphis on Sunday, 9 February 1997, after the interview, I looked at the fairly small number of well-kept black middle-class homes versus the rows and rows of black projects that still linger, washed with age and deterioration. This in a major city with a 51 percent black population where Beale Street, its music and its whores, are still the major attractions for black and white people, Elvis Presley's mansion and private airplane notwithstanding.

The 1955 murder of Emmett Till, a 14-year-old black male, went through my mind as we drove to Freeman's home. Men murdered Till for "reckless eyeballing of a white woman," very near Freeman's home in Tallahatchie County, Mississippi. The drive my friends and I took through Memphis and Mississippi, 7–9 February 1997, would not have been possible 30 years ago; we would have been shot instantly, whatever our mission.

Morgan Freeman works to change the mind-set of an America that in 2000 still devotes considerable energy to fear and suspicion of black men. Freeman causes people, through the medium of theatre, film, and television, to see African Americans represented as human beings. His spirit refuses to be chained. Freeman, with conviction, stated near the end of the interview, "I did not set out to be a cowboy or a teacher. I was born to do this."

Morgan Freeman continues to create persona that are remarkable in range, depth, and power. In roles that are cast for black actors, his is a quintessential resistance. In nontraditional roles, he brings access and enlightenment not previously available. On this archipelago of human struggle and achievement, all Morgan Freeman and others wanted to be was a man, nothing but a man.

Works Cited

DuBois, W. E. B. "The Creative Impulse," in *W. E. B. DuBois: The Crisis Writings*, ed. Daniel Walden, Greenwich, Connecticut: Fawcett Publications, 1972, 292. (Originally published in *The Crisis*, May 1931)

Fanon, Frantz. *Black Skin, White Mask*, trans. Charles Lam Markmann. New York: Grove Weidenfeld, 1967, 113.

Feingold, Michael. *The Village Voice*, quoted in *Current Biography*, February 1991, 20.

Freeman, Morgan. Letter to author. 30 October 1996.

———. Personal interview. 8 February 1997.

Goodman, Jane. "Morgan Freeman Sails Along," *USA Today*, June, n.d. (Circa 1987). (courtesy of Dr. Winona Fletcher)

Hill, Errol. *Shakespeare in Sable*. Amherst: University of Massachusetts Press, 1984.

Hurley, Joseph. "He's Daisy's Driver," undocumented newspaper clipping. (courtesy of the Morgan Freeman Archives)

Kael, Pauline. *The New Yorker*, 7 July 1980, n.p.

Kalem, T.E. *Time*, 26 Mar. 1979, 67. (courtesy of the Morgan Freeman Archives)

New Yorker, The. 26 Mar. 1980, 77.

Nightingale, Benedict. "Wild Bill Shakespeare in Central Park," *The New York Times*, 1 July 1990, II, 5:1.

Oliver, Edith. *The New Yorker*, 26 Mar. 1979, n.p.

Rich, Frank. "Shakespeare in the Wild West, Shakespeare in the Park," *The New York Times*, 15 July, 1990, III, 3:1.

Simon, John. "From Wheel To Woe," *New York*, 2 Apr. 1979, 85.

Stasio, Marilyn. *The New York Post*, 15 Mar. 1979, 30.

Time. 26 Sept. 1994, 78. (courtesy of the Morgan Freeman Archives)

Ezra Knight as Othello (left), a noble but gullible Moor, and Allen Gilmore as the villainous Iago (right) in The Acting Company production of William Shakespeare's *Othello*, directed by Penny Metropulos. Photo by Bill Pierce. Courtesy of The Acting Company.

Chapter XII

Has Anything Changed?

> *[The 1992 Los Angeles riots] were a multiracial, transclass "display of justified social rage" that "signified a sense of powerlessness in American society . . . a lethal linkage of economic decline, cultural decay and political lethargy."*
>
> —Cornel West, *quoted by the Office of Cultural Affairs at Michigan Technological University in the* Michigan Tech Lode, *16 September 1994.*

The 1990s represented the worst of America: the 1991 Crown Heights tensions that exploded after a rabbi's motorcade accidentally killed 7-year-old Gavin Cato, a black boy, and a group of black men killed 29-year-old Yankel Rosenbaum, a Jewish student, for revenge; the 1992 acquittal of four white policemen videotaped beating Rodney King, and the resulting riots in Los Angeles; the 1995 terrorist bombing of the federal building in Oklahoma City; massive government infusions of money for prisons, but not for schools; the 1998 death by dragging of African American James Byrd in Jasper, Texas; the 1999 New York City shooting 41 times of Amadou Diallo, an unarmed young African immigrant street peddler, by four white policemen; and the 1999 shooting rampage that left 15 dead and several more injured at Columbine High School in Littleton, Colorado. These were terrible times.

Although theatre of African Americans mirrored some of these tragic events, the 1990s in the American theatre were also a time of extremely positive change. Nontraditional casting became more frequent, according to the Non-Traditional Casting Project. More and more African American theatre practitioners came under the protection of unions.

More authentic portrayals of the black middle class evolved, and more and more celebrities, especially Ossie Davis and Ruby Dee, continued to be actively involved in a hoped for resolution of the serious racial divide. More and more African Americans in the theatre secured professional training in their craft, although not enough in design and technical theatre, where the jobs are. But a good number of aspiring actors enrolled in the professional actor's training schools in the 1980s and 1990s, especially at Yale, Milwaukee, and the North Carolina School of the Arts.

In 1999, the National Portrait Gallery of the Smithsonian Institution mounted an exhibit on Paul Robeson, probably unthinkable 50 years before. It went on tour after it closed at the Washington, D. C. site. The National Portrait Gallery and other Smithsonian Institution sites have been exemplary in mounting exhibits of African Americans in the performing arts and in bringing in summer fellows from historically black colleges to assist.

Many problems, however, remain for the African American in the performing arts. Perhaps the most frequently asked question at the Dartmouth Drama Conference, "African American Theatre: The Next Stage," on 7 March 1998, was, "Where is the money?" At that conference, a young, black female lawyer announced that 97 percent of money in theatre goes to whites; 3 percent goes to blacks. One may posit that as the twentieth century ended, the African-American remained, financially at least, the stepchild of the American theatre. Admittedly a number of individuals of color have done well as have several black theatre companies.

Theatre remains The Great White Way, in many instances, on historically white college campuses, and patently black at historically black institutions. Any survey of most white colleges' websites for the theatre season will bear this out. Some selections for a season are more innovative than others. Most remain ultra traditional—Shakespeare's *Hamlet, Twelfth Night,* and *A Midsummer Night's Dream;* Miller's *Death of a Salesman,* Wilde's *The Importance of Being Earnest,* and Tennessee Williams's *The Glass Menagerie* are perennial favorites.

There are some exceptions. If there is a gospel choir of African Americans or a strong and persistent black student group, Hansberry's *A Raisin in the Sun* or the musical *Purlie* may get on the season, and then, often in the black box theatre, not on the mainstage. Brown University in Providence, Rhode Island, has had, for many years, Rites and Reason, a predominantly black group that got considerable recognition in the 1970s, especially under the late George Bass. Brown, in its main season, has also cast shows with African Americans, including George C. Wolfe's *The Colored Museum.* The North Carolina School for the Arts has staged Athol Fugard with actors of color, and the University of North Carolina at Chapel

Hill has presented Richard Wright and Paul Green's *Native Son*. These efforts remain the exception, rather than the rule.

Another exception occurred the summer of 1999 when the University of Iowa, in Iowa City, mounted an August Wilson Festival for its main summer season, including full productions of *Fences*, directed by Michael Kachingwe, *Ma Rainey's Black Bottom*, directed by Mary Beth Easley, and *Joe Turner's Come and Gone*, directed by Tisch Jones, an Iowa graduate, and a member of the Spelman College faculty. There was also a staged reading of *Jitney*. The artistic director, Eric Forsythe, brought in professional actors through the courtesy of Actors Equity. According to Gerald Roe, Associate Director of Educational Placement at Iowa, Forsythe had been wanting to put on Wilson's plays for a long time. The University of Iowa has also, for many years, had Black Action Theatre.

The tolerance of white students, however, for black theatre in literature classes is, generally, one play per term, and that should not cause them too much discomfort. In fact, when I, as a doctoral student, directed cuttings from Hansberry's *A Raisin in the Sun* at Iowa in 1976, with an almost all-white acting ensemble, one member told the professor, Lewin Goff, that she could not be both black and old, and refused the role of Lena Younger.

Parents have gone to deans when teachers at predominantly white universities have taught Baraka's *Dutchman*. At one institution, 17 out of 33 students walked out of a class called Problems and Ideas in Literature announcing they were not going to read "any of this black stuff" although all of the offerings were not of African American authors.

By the same token, historically black colleges are now making up for their having put on plays almost exclusively by white playwrights the first five decades of the twentieth century. The Dean of Arts and Sciences at Tuskegee in 1982–83 asked me, as Department Head of English and Foreign Languages, to fire the sole director/staff member of the Little Theatre because he put on only black plays—Fuller's *Zooman and the Sign* crossed the boards that year along with Langston Hughes's *Tambourines to Glory*. I did not fire the director, not because I agreed with a season of plays only by black playwrights, but because virtually every white school in America was doing the same kind of thing, and their faculty members were not being dismissed.

Some African American students, especially at white universities, have strongly criticized African American faculty who teach Shakespeare or Restoration and Eighteenth Century as being white people in black skin. That professor can also teach courses that include African American playwrights, but the razor cuts both ways. Eurocentric and Afrocentric behavior persist, and there is shared blame for a lack of diversity on college campuses. The problem spills over to newspaper critics, for it is the university that prepares the critics to either be objective or have biases in the first place.

Critics for major newspapers remain overwhelmingly white. A significant change has occurred since the legendary Woodie King, Jr., Director of the Harry de Jur Henry Street Settlement Theatre in New York City, gave me an interview at the Americana Hotel coffee shop on 25 November 1977, where he bemoaned a great deal about the dilemma of the black actor:

> Innovative black drama is not found in the lives of suburbia, London, or Westchester. These are the problems black actors face. Until Darwin Turner and Addison Gayle decide they want to work for the *New York Times*, we will be stuck with the present white critics. Broadway is a contented white cow. From 1959, when *A Raisin in the Sun* played, to 1969, you would be lucky to see eight black dramas on Broadway. New York got the Negro Ensemble, the new Federal Theatre, etc., to raise the level of consciousness. This was a direct result of what black poets and black studies departments did in the 1960s. This is the age of benign neglect. . . . When I was at Wayne State University, I discovered that determination is the only thing that can change white domination and the knowledge that you are correct and know what you are doing.

In the 23 years that have passed since King and I sat down for coffee at the Americana Hotel coffee shop, major positive changes have occurred in the American theatre.

In January 1995, Margo L. Jefferson, a Pulitzer Prize winner for journalism, was named Sunday theatre critic for *The New York Times*, having initially served on the culture desk since she joined the paper in 1993. Jefferson had previously been a lecturer in English at Columbia University from 1991 to 1993. Rohan Preston, a black male, is now theater critic for the *Star Tribune* in the twin cities of Minneapolis/St. Paul in Minnesota.

Beginning with the Federal Theatre of 1935–39, positive images of heroes began to emerge on the American stage. They continued to some extent for the remainder of the century. In recent years, the Non-Traditional Casting Project evolved in an effort to give more and more black actors and others opportunities to play roles not designated as black. However, far too many stereotypes remain, of both black male and female. There are still, basically, two images of the black woman—mammy or slut—however postmodern the version may be.

In the course of the twentieth century, there were gains in public accommodations. The slights that Paul Robeson, Ethel Waters, and Marian Anderson received have not been experienced in recent years, in all probability, by James Earl Jones, Morgan Freeman, or Ruby Dee. Most performing halls are open now. Most hotels accept guests with money to pay the bill. Actors who can afford the fee now fly across the country and across oceans first class. Of the few middle class who still ride the bus, no one sits at the back any longer, except by choice.

However, slights still occur out of fear or a lack of respect. Taxis have been reported to pass by black men, regardless of how well-dressed they may be or how much money they have, but, by and large, public accommodations are now open. One may drink water from any fountain; the signs, "White" or "Colored" are gone.

There have been gains in union protection. Far fewer African Americans are abused by working for no pay. Dressing rooms must have hot and cold running water and privacy. There is a limited time one can rehearse an actor or musician or dancer now without a break for a meal. Salaries for a few African American stars are in the millions, but often less than salaries for white stars. Actors Equity guarantees a basic salary for all its members who are employed. Employment for the black female actor is increasing, but at a far slower pace than that for the black male.

One black male who has achieved star status on stage and screen is Gregory Hines, who electrified audiences when he danced the main role of "Jelly Roll" Morton in the 1992 Broadway production of George C. Wolfe's *Jelly's Last Jam* at the Virginia Theatre. Jelly, a fair-skinned black man in New Orleans, hated his blackness, a major focus of the stage work on this jazz great. The flawless musical introduced the young Savion Glover who wowed audiences also in the 1996 Broadway production of *Bring in da Noise, Bring in da Funk*. Sammy Davis, Jr., who died in 1990, appealed to multiracial audiences as he tapped and sang his way to stardom from the time he was four years old. Hines, Glover, and Davis danced in vehicles with powerful historical messages. But the success of these men is not necessarily typical.

Black theatre, defined as that *for, by, about,* and *near* us, remained somewhat marginalized in its own theatres and on college campuses, in spite of considerable recognition since 1989 when Larry Leon Hamlin initiated the first Black Theatre Festival in Winston-Salem, North Carolina. Whites and blacks went in large numbers to see black theatre staged at every possible theatre that could be found in Winston-Salem.

Conversely, one white male faculty member at a private white college in Minnesota, at a seminar I conducted on "The Politics of African American Theatre, 1875–1996" for the American Society for Theatre Research in San Antonio in 1997, indicated that, although genuinely interested, he was afraid to go to the Penumbra Theatre in Saint Paul, Minnesota, because only he and a man at Burger King were among the whites in the area. His final advice on the first draft of his paper admonished whites interested in black theatre to just "send checks." He later admitted, first on an e-mail to me and in a later draft of the paper he actually presented, that some of his fears of actually showing up at the Penumbra Theatre were founded on his having been near race riots in Detroit in his youth.

Crossroads Theatre, founded in 1978, and based in New Brunswick, New Jersey, is among the largest and most prestigious of black theatres. It has successfully attracted white money. Their Web site states: "Crossroads presents honest portrayals of African American life and culture, thus building bridges of understanding and veracity between people of all backgrounds." They also provide a nurturing environment for artists who are African American.

Such big names as Anna Deavere Smith, Ruby Dee, and Avery Brooks have performed there. Crossroads has toured Atlanta, Washington, D. C., Los Angeles, the Bahamas, the United States Virgin Islands, London, and South Africa. Headed by Ricardo Khan, they have also been funded by the National Endowment for the Arts and were heralded by President George Bush.

Theatre that was well-funded was integrated theatre or white theatre. The Guthrie Theatre, for example, which has cast some African Americans, has a very strong group of supporters who buy season tickets. Arena Stage, which has been heroic in casting African Americans, and in attracting diverse audiences, has strong community and financial support.

For example,

> Kyle Donnelly's 1992 version of *The Way of the World* at Washington, D.C.'s Arena Stage . . . had the most racially mixed cast [of any other American production of Congreve's Restoration comedy in America since 1924] and, in places, a feminist emphasis (Kaplan 316).

Gail Grate, an African American woman, played one of the leading roles of Millamant, complete with fan and period costume.

New talent continued to erupt on the stage, including the brilliant Acting Company, created in 1972 by John Houseman and Margot Harley. According to a program distributed during the 1994–95 touring season:

> The Acting Company is the only professional theater company of its kind in America. Its mission is to provide young and highly talented, well-trained American actors of all cultural and ethnic backgrounds with an opportunity to develop their craft further by touring in a repertory of classic and contemporary plays; to develop a theater-going public by playing first-rate productions before diverse audiences nationwide; to conduct classes and educational outreach activities in schools and in underserved communities

across the country, thus increasing awareness and appreciation of the arts and the English language; to initiate and participate in international theater exchanges; and to build, through the ongoing participation of all its members, an extended Alumni Ensemble with an exceptional ability to perform together in a classical as well as a contemporary repertory.

The Acting Company has honored its mission.

In its 1994–95 American tour, it cast four African Americans in its production of Shakespeare's *Othello*. Allen Gilmore as the Machiavellian Iago was triumphant with a cherubic face, which seemed to have just emerged from the boy's choir. Gilmore's looks all the more enabled his character's diabolical machinations. Trained at Juilliard, Gilmore's diction was flawless, his movement, like that of a panther, and his fight scenes, impeccably choreographed and executed.

The anguish of Ezra Knight as the Moor, in dreadlocks, was strong. A black Emilia, played by Shona Tucker, was feisty. And Gary Lamont Allen was Solino, a Venetian soldier. While at least two other productions in the history of the American theatre have cast a black Emilia with a black Iago, such pairing is very rare.

The director was Penny Metropulos who stated in the program:

> I don't think we can view the characters in the context of simple black and white (either in race or motive). It examines the human psyche far too intimately to be tied up in any sort of tidy social package. We are confronted here with the potential in all of us to succumb to the darker forces within our natures.

It was her unusually universal vision that allowed her to cast four African Americans in a play that usually has only one African American, one recent exception being the 1998 Patrick Stewart production staged in Washington, D.C. where an almost all-black cast surrounds a white Othello.

In its 1995–96 season, The Acting Company toured with Shakespeare's *Henry V* with color-blind and cross-gender casting. Funding became a problem and the tour ended abruptly after its 31 March 1996 performance at the Calumet Theatre in Calumet, Michigan.

According to Camilo Fontecilla, Director of Marketing for The Acting Company, in letters of 22 November and 4 May 1999 their 1998 production of Ntozake Shange's *Hydraulics Phat Like Mean* "was part of a great evening of one-acts entitled *Love's Fire*. The work met with critical acclaim. The seven American playwrights included Eric Bogosian, William Finn, John Guare, Tony Kushner, Marsha Norman, and Wendy Wasserstein," in addition to Shange. Fontecilla added, "*Hydraulics Phat Like Mean* is a bit hard to pin down [in terms of] the plot, which was very flowing and poetic. . . . In a seductively choreographed meeting of male and female players, a man watches his lover perform a jazz composition."

The Old Globe in San Diego, the Oregon Shakespeare Festival, the Alabama Shakespeare Festival, the Guthrie, the Goodman Theatre, Arena Stage, and a host of other venues are including more and more African Americans in their productions. According to Christopher Olsen in a paper, "The Case of Mr. Saigon," given at the 1998 meeting of the American Society for Theatre Research in Washington, D.C., in 1987 "90 percent of all plays produced regionally [were] performed by all-Caucasian casts, and only ten percent of roles on Broadway [were] being cast with actors of color" (7). He continued:

> According to the AEA study of L.O.R.T. theatres conducted over the period of four seasons from 1987–1991, an increase in employment of actors of color almost doubled (11.2 to 20.9%). Increases were also found in actors of color performing in non-traditional roles (7.6 to 11.5%), however, the greatest gain was among African-Americans (7.45 to 15.6%), whereas, Asian and Native American representation remained fairly static (7).

The African-American actor became even more accepted in the 1990s. Morgan Freeman played a cowboy Petruchio on Broadway in *The Taming of the Shrew* in 1990 opposite Tracey Ullman as Kate, and Laurence Fishburne, in 1999, was Henry II opposite Stockard Channing as Eleanor of Aquitaine in the Roundabout Theatre Company's revival of *The Lion in Winter*.

Deborah Elliott, Publicist for the Oregon Shakespeare Festival, which is among the oldest and largest professional regional theatre companies in the United States, wrote me on 3 July 1995:

> This year [1995] 29% of the acting company is comprised of various ethnic minorities (13% African-Americans). My hope is that, eventually, the Festival will be a thoroughly diverse organization which accurately reflects the society we live in. But, one step at a time.

In perhaps at least two giant steps, the Oregon Shakespeare Festival in 1994 produced George C. Wolfe's *The Colored Museum* in its Black Swan Theatre and in 1995, Endesha Ida Mae Holland's *From the Mississippi Delta*, a true story by and about an African American woman who went from prostitute to Ph.D.

A student, Megan McLean, in my HU312 Shakespeare class for Summer Track A, 1999, wrote about the Alabama Shakespeare Festival:

Has Anything Changed?

They [the Alabama Shakespeare Festival] found Kent Thompson who had an extensive background in Shakespeare. He was born, raised and educated in the South before he left the country for further studies. Thus, Thompson is said to have a sensitivity to the South (Engle, Londré, and Watermeier 5) which is helpful since [Jim] Volz estimates that of the 170,000 annual ticket buyers, approximately 24,000 to 26,000 are African-American, giving the Alabama Shakespeare Festival probably the largest number of black people than any other Shakespeare Festival in the United States. Also, of the 30,000 children who participate in SchoolFest, where actual productions of Shakespeare plays are performed for school groups, 50% of them are black (4).

So, Shakespearean festivals are becoming highly sensitive to bringing in African American actors and audiences, many of whom are students. Students, of course, as a whole welcome Laurence Fishburne as *Othello* in the Oliver Parker film, or Denzel Washington in Kenneth Branagh's film of *Much Ado about Nothing*.

August Wilson, distinguished Pulitzer Prize–winning playwright, disagrees with color-blind casting. In an historic speech, titled "The Ground on Which I Stand," delivered in June 1996 at the 11th Biennial Theatre Communications Group Conference at Princeton University, August Wilson sparked a debate in the theatrical world with the following assertion: "To mount an all-black production of a . . . play conceived for white actors . . . is to deny us our own humanity, our own history, and the need to make our own investigations from the cultural ground on which we stand as Black Americans. . . . We do not need colorblind casting; we need those misguided financial resources to be put to better use" (quoted on the back of the Dartmouth Drama Conference flyer for the 7 Mar. 1998 gathering).

This speech sparked a debate in many corners and caused an outright rift between Caucasian Robert Brustein, drama critic for *The New Republic,* and August Wilson at Manhattan's Town Hall, with Anna Deavere Smith as moderator. Brustein charged Wilson with promoting "subsidized separatism" (Gates 46). On 3 February 1997, Harvard scholar Henry Louis Gates responded in *The New Yorker:* "Does his [Wilson's] argument do disservice to his own plays?"(44). Some theatre practitioners believe that Wilson has gotten into the mainstream theatres of Broadway and regional houses because his works are universal and not just black plays. Gates continued: "Certainly the brutal reductionism of August Wilson's polemics is in stark contrast to his richly textured dramatic *oeuvre*" (46). As a major point, Gates affirms: "So if you're looking for a theatre of black folk, by black folk, and for black folk—a genuinely sequestered cultural preserve—you'll have to cross the extraordinary dramas of August Wilson off your list" (48).

Actor Ruby Dee, not an actor known for timidity, embraces both traditional and non-traditional roles. In 1965, a critic attacked Miss Dee for her role of Cordelia in a production of *King Lear*. The critic said it made him ill to see black actors in Shakespeare, but she finally got her due in 1999. No longer can she say that she has seldom played leads and only the most idiosyncratic critic could find fault with her Bessie Delany. Ruby Dee's rise can only be called triumphant in the CBS televised production of Emily Mann's *Having Our Say*. William Tynan wrote in *Time* on 4 April 1999:

> The world first learned of the remarkable Delany sisters in a 1991 *New York Times* article. Self-described "colored maiden ladies," Sadie, then 103, and Bessie, 101, had overcome daunting obstacles to become successful professionals and lead lives of inspiring grace. Their story was turned into a best-selling book and a Broadway hit show. Now Emily Mann has spun her little two-character play into a glorious panoramic TV movie, joyous and touching. Diahann Carroll plays sweet, pragmatic Sadie with lovely simplicity. In the showier role of the flinty Bessie, Ruby Dee gives as rich and true a performance as you could hope to see, snatching you by the heart and never letting go (n.p.).

The 1995 Broadway show at the Booth Theatre starred veterans Gloria Foster and Mary Alice. Ms. Foster had played Volumnia, Coriolanus's mother, in the 1979 New York Public Theater production of Shakespeare's *Coriolanus*, with Morgan Freeman as her son in the title role. Mary Alice is best known as the long-suffering Rose, the stage wife of James Earl Jones in August Wilson's *Fences*.

Women's groups throughout America had viewing parties on the evening of 18 April 1999, to witness CBS's authentic portrayal of the black middle class. The triumph for Dee and Carroll was that there was a much wider audience than the one that witnessed the Broadway production. CBS had advertisements even on other channels in a massive promotion effort. Their *CBS News Sunday Morning* with Charles Osgood featured "The Other Cosby," an interview Randall Pinkston conducted with producer Camille Cosby.

Pinkston indicated that the story was one of persistence. Camille Cosby stated that the Delany sisters hand-picked her. "They expected me to protect their integrity," she calmly declared, and "to show how racist practices hurt people—are a painful experience." Mrs. Cosby continued, "*Having Our Say* is an effort to correct so much misinformation about African Americans and Americans. The most profound message is that their human spirit prevailed in spite of circumstances" (CBS 18 Apr. 1999).

Has Anything Changed?

Dee did not hesitate, almost on the heels of taping *Having Our Say,* to protest, along with her husband, Ossie Davis, the killing of Amadou Diallo, the 23-year-old street vendor from Africa. *People* reported Miss Dee's thinking: "I wake up at night in a panic that this kind of thing could happen to my sons or grandsons." Dee and Davis marched in Manhattan, only to have Mayor Rudolph Giuliani refer to the protesters as "silly" (*The New York Times,* 28. Mar. 1999, 31). Giuliani later admitted that he had made a mistake.

Has anything changed? Yes, in many, many positive ways, but in terms of money and the integration of theatre, the American stage has a long way to go. Some, like August Wilson, say that integration is not a good thing. Can there be Marc Connelly's *Green Pastures* with whites in it? Is Congreve's great Restoration comedy, *The Way of the World,* believable to many if an African American or Hispanic woman plays Lady Wishfort? The theatre reflects the world. Until the world changes, the theatre cannot.

Indeed as the twentieth century closed, the social rage of the 1990s "signified a sense of powerlessness in American society [and was] a lethal linkage of economic decline, cultural decay and political lethargy" (West n. p.). These dynamics were reflected, visibly, in the works of African American playwrights Pearl Cleage, Anna Deavere Smith, Ntozake Shange, August Wilson, and George C. Wolfe. Not all wrote exclusively on urban violence, but that is much of the content of their plays. Positives were interspersed with the gloom.

Nontraditional casting, a blessing in the eyes of many, became almost commonplace, including yet another *Macbeth,* with Angela Bassett following in Edna Thomas's footsteps as Lady Macbeth opposite Alec Baldwin as Macbeth in George C. Wolfe's production at the Joseph Papp Public Theater on 15 March 1998.

Earle Hyman (1926 -), a native of Rocky Mount, North Carolina, has played more Shakespeare in the twentieth century than any other African American actor including James Earl Jones. Hyman has played the title roles in *Hamlet, Macbeth, King Lear,* and *Othello.* He was knighted in Norway for his *Othello* in the Norwegian language. Unfortunately, he is best known as Russell Huxtable, Cosby's father, in the first *Cosby Show.* African American actors in the late part of the twentieth century rose above obstacles that were profoundly overwhelming the first seven decades of the twentieth century.

So did the 15 pioneers in this book. Those who have died—Rose McClendon, Ethel Waters, Marian Anderson, Todd Duncan, Canada Lee, Pearl Bailey, and Paul Robeson—refused to surrender their power to political lethargy. Those who yet live, at this writing—Maya Angelou, Anne Wiggins Brown, Leontyne Price, William Warfield, Ossie Davis, Ruby Dee,

James Earl Jones, and Morgan Freeman—are all, without reservation, those who have said, in spirit, if not in letter, "No surrender! No retreat!" Their talent and tenacity put them on the stage and kept them there. Art, for them, was a social weapon. They were not powerless. They have never given up. Those who have died paved the way for those of us yet living to now enjoy sitting in any space in a theatre where our money might place us. We enjoy public accommodations and other civil rights, in part, because of Paul Robeson. We can sing in any concert hall because of Marian Anderson's struggle to sing in Constitution Hall. Black actors, now, because of all these pioneers, have more of a chance of getting cast in a role, traditional or non-traditional. Against the formidable odds they faced, these pioneers, without exception, are an affirmation of the human spirit.

Works Cited

African American Theatre: The Next Stage. Printed flyer for the Saturday, 7 March 1998 conference at Dartmouth College.

Blumenthal, Eileen. "That Power-Mad Couple Seems So Familiar," *The New York Times*, 1 Mar. 1998, Arts and Leisure, 5. [*Macbeth*]

Barry, Dan. "Giuliani Meets With Black Leaders, Making the Routine Seem Momentous," *The New York Times*, 28 Mar. 1999, 31.

Delany, Sarah and A. Elizabeth (with Amy Hill Hearth). *Having Our Say: The Delany Sisters' First 100 Years*. New York: Kodansha International, 1993. (courtesy of Sylvia Matthews)

Elliott, Deborah. Letter to author. 3 July 1995.

Engle, Ron, Felicia Hardison Londre, and Daniel J. Watermeier. *Shakespeare Companies and Festivals: An International Guide*. Westport, Connecticut: Greenwood Press, 1995.

Fontecilla, Camilo. Letters to author. 4 May 1999 and 22 Nov. 1999.

Gates, Henry Louis. "The Chitlin Circuit," *The New Yorker*, 3 Feb. 1997, 44–50.

http://www.kolorscope.com/theater/scope/8034.htm#Mission (Crossroads Theatre).

http://www.theactingcompany.org (The Acting Company).

Horwitz, Jane. "At Studio, 'Godot's' Woes," *The Washington Post*, 10 Nov. 1998, 1 and B5. (courtesy of Maurine Kelber Kelly)

Hyman, Earle. Letter to author. 22 Nov. 1986.

———. Telephone interview with author. 19 Dec. 1986.

———. Personal interview with author. 21 May 1988.

Kaplan, Deborah. "Learning 'to Speak the English Language': *The Way of the World* on the Twentieth Century American Stage," *Theatre Journal*, 49, 1997, 301–321.

King, Woodie, Jr. Personal interview with author. 25 Nov. 1977.

McLean, Megan. A Look at the Alabama Shakespeare Festival. Paper submitted for HU312 Shakespeare, Track A, summer, 1999.

Olsen, Christopher. "The Case of Mr. Saigon," paper delivered for Seminar II.5 at the annual conference of the American Society for Theatre Research, Washington, D. C., 22 Nov. 1998.

"Other Cosby, The," *CBS Sunday Morning News,* 18 Apr. 1999.

Out of the Blues, an August Wilson Festival, Iowa Summer Rep '99, program. (courtesy of Gerald Roe)

Poggi, Jack. *Theater in America: The Impact of Economic Forces, 1870–1967.* Ithaca, New York: Cornell University Press, 1966.

Rodgers, Patrick and Julia Campbell, "Lethal Force," *People,* 19 Apr. 1999, 55–59. [on Amadou Diallo]

Tynan, William. *Time,* 4 Apr. 1999, n. p. [*Having Our Say*] (courtesy of Marcia Davis)

West, Cornel, quoted in *The Michigan Tech Lode,* 16 Sept. 1994, n.p.

Index

Abramson, Doris, 116
Acting Company, 210–11
Actors Equity, 60–61, 138, 147, 153, 207
Adams, Joe, 143, 164
Aiello, Danny, 167
Ailey, Alvin, 3, 13
Alabama Shakespeare Festival, 212–13
Albert, Donnie Ray, 94
Aldridge, Ira, 44, 45
Alexander, Jane, 180
Alice, Mary, 214
Allen, Gary Lamont, 211
Allison, Alexander, 165
Alpert, Hollis, 95, 100
Alvin Theatre, 14, 91, 144
American Dance Festival, 12
American Negro Theatre, 118, 138, 155–56
American Society for Theatre Research, 137, 209, 212
American Theatre Wing, 177
Anderson, Annie, 80
Anderson, Eddie, 45
Anderson, Garland, 25
Anderson, John, 27, 80–81
Anderson, Lisa M., 21, 31
Anderson, Louisa Tar, 60
Anderson, Marian, 2, 4, 75–85, 164, 208–9, 215, 216
Anderson, Maxwell, 96

Anderson, Thomas, 60, 100, 112, 125, 126, 131, 157
Angelou, Maya, 2, 17, 94, 95, 101–3, 185, 215
Anspacher Theater, 197
Apollo Theatre, 141
Ara, Ignacio, 109
Arena Stage, 187
Arlen, Harold, 165
Arvey, Verna, 93
Asante, Kariamu Welsh, 8, 14
Aschenbrenner, Joyce, 12
Ashcroft, Peggy, 42, 43
Association for Theatre in Higher Education, 153
Atkinson, Brooks, 15, 27, 29, 66–67, 92, 107, 111–12, 124, 157
Atkinson, Virgil, 92

Bailey, Charles P., 62–63
Bailey, Ella Mae, 141
Bailey, Joseph James, 140–41
Bailey, Pearl, 2, 5, 6, 137–48, 154, 196, 215
Baker, Josephine, 8–9, 42, 62, 63, 65
Balanchine, George, 67
Baldwin, Alec, 215
Baldwin, James, 37, 185
Bankhead, Tallulah, 67
Baraka, Amiri, 13–14

Barber, Samuel, 101
Barnes, Clive, 139, 159, 160, 182
Barrymore, Ethel, 27, 69
Barrymore, Ethel, Theater, 13, 157
Barthé, Richmond, 28
Barthel, Joan, 140
Bass, George, 206
Bassett, Angela, 161, 215
Beane, Reginald, 70
Beatty, Talley, 11–12, 60, 61, 68, 70
Beaumont, Vivian, Theatre, 154
Beck, Martin, Theatre, 28, 67, 142, 164
Belafonte, Harry, 143
Belasco Theatre, 65
Belcher, Fannin, 26, 110
Bellson, Louis, 143, 147
Bendiner, Alfred, 66
Benson, Emma Amelia, 152
Berlin, Irving, 65
Berry, John, 183, 185
Bessie, Alvah, 48, 108
Biberman, Herbert, 48
Bilbo, Theodore G., 107, 121
Bing, Rudolf, 101
Bizet, George, 143
Black, Hugo, 79
Black Action Theatre, 207
Black Swan Theatre, 212
Black Theatre Festival, 209
Blair, Mary, 39
Bledsoe, Julius, 26, 27
Bloom, Samuel William, 126–27
Bluton, Gilly, 66
Boghetti, Giuseppe, 81
Bogle, Donald, 36, 44, 45, 119, 143, 155, 161, 167
Bogosian, Eric, 211
Bonner, Marita Odette, 25
Bontemps, Arna, 142
Booth, Alan, 52
Booth Theatre, 214

Bourne, Saint Clair, 15, 113
Bowman, Laura, 25
Bradford, Henry, Jr., 76, 77
Branagh, Kenneth, 213
Branch, William B., 156
Brattle Street Theatre, 44
Braugher, Andre, 168
Brecht, Bertolt, 196
Breen, Robert, 94
Breuer, Lee, 200
Britton, Jack, 109
Broderick, Helen, 65
Brooks, Avery, 210
Brooks, Gwendolyn, 185
Brouillard, Lou, 109
Brown, Anne Wiggins, 2, 8, 17, 95, 96–98, 103, 215
Brown, Frankie Dee, 152
Brown, John Mason, 15
Brown, Lawrence, 41, 52, 53
Brown, Lorraine, 114–15
Brown, Maurice, 42
Brown, Sergeant, 143
Brown, Sterling, 163
Browne, Roscoe Lee, 178
Brownelle, John Charles, 29
Browning, Michael C., 42
Brustein, Robert, 148, 213
Bryant, Willie, 66, 67, 114
Brynner, Yul, 71
Buckley, Gail Lumet, 68
Bumbry, Grace, 94
Bunche, Ralph, 95
Burrill, Mary, 25
Bush, Anita, 7
Bush, George, 210
Byrd, James, 205

Café Society, 130
Cafe Zanzibar, 141
Calloway, Cab, 138, 140, 144, 145, 147, 196

Index

Cambridge, Godfrey, 178
Campbell, Dick, 22, 23, 26, 29, 31, 61, 93, 107, 114, 118, 120, 151, 153, 164
Campbell, Patrick, 38
Canegata, Juanita, 107, 128
Canegata, Lydia (Whaley), 108
Carey, Bernadette, 178
Carnovsky, Morris, 154, 164
Carroll, Diahann, 144, 185
Carter, Jack, 91–92, 111
Carter, Jimmy, 11
Carter, Robert A., 76
Cash, Rosalind, 184
Cass Theatre, 70
Cato, Gavin, 205
Chamberlain, Lee, 184
Chambers, Whittaker, 48
Chaney, Lon, 179
Channing, Carol, 138, 139
Channing, Stockard, 212
Chaplin, Ben, 125
Chapman, John, 157
Chapman, Oscar, 78
Charles, Kince, 163
Chevalier, Maurice, 8
Childress, Alice, 118, 156, 158
Childress, Alvin, 156
Civic Repertory Theatre, 22
Clark, Catherine King, 41
Clark, Kenneth, 52
Clark-Lewis, Elizabeth, 24
Cleage, Pearl, 161, 215
Clinton, Catherine, 24
Clinton, William Jefferson, 168
Cochran, Gifford, 43
Cochran, J. Preston, 11
Cochran, S. E., 95
Cole, Lester, 48
Cole, Nat "King," 154
Colley-Lee, Myrna, 194
Comathiere, A. B., 92

Comprone, Joseph, 61
Connelly, Marc, 99, 164, 215
Connor, Eugene "Bull," 158
Cookery, The 130
Coplon, Judith, 128
Corbin, John, 40
Cornelius, James, 108
Cort Theatre, 118, 165
Cosby, Bill, 167
Cosby, Camille, 214
Cose, Ellis, 3
Cotton Club, The 63, 65
Crain, Jeanne, 69
Crawford, Broderick, 179
Crawford, Cheryl, 93, 98
Cripps, Thomas, 40, 43, 45
Crossroads Theatre, 161, 210
Crowder, Jack, 138
Crowther, Bosley, 125
Cullen, Countee, 2, 142

Dale, Clamma, 94
Dancer, Earl, 63, 122
Dandridge, Dorothy, 94, 143, 144
Daniels, Billy, 138
DaSilva, Howard, 164
Davenport, Butler, 23
Davis, Chuck, 3
Davis, Guy, 169
Davis, Kince Charles, 165
Davis, Laura, 163
Davis, Ossie, 2, 4, 10, 14, 16, 31, 151–69, 185, 197, 206, 215
Davis, Sammy, Jr., 94, 144, 209
Dawson, William L., 41
Days, William, 11
Dazey, Frank, 42
Dean, Phillip Hayes, 16, 185
Dee, Ruby, 2, 4, 10, 13–14, 144, 151–69, 183, 206, 209, 210, 214–15
Delacorte Theatre, 183

Delany, Bessie, 214
Delaunoy, Didier, 179
DeLerma, Dominique-Rene, 100
Depasse, Susanne, 194
De Paur, Leonard, 61, 98
Dewhurst, Colleen, 183
De Wilde, Brandon, 69–70
Diallo, Amadou, 205, 215
Dies, Martin, 113
Diggs, Dudley, 43
Divodi, Andy, 109
Dmytryk, Edward, 48
Dodson, Owen, 45, 183
Donnelly, Kyle, 210
Douglass, Marion, 183
Downers, Olin, 96
Drake, Anne Q., 76
Drake, Joseph Fanning, 76
Duberman, Martin, 38, 46, 51
DuBois, W. E. B., 49, 102, 121, 196, 201–2
DuBois, William, 113
Dudar, Helen, 185, 187
Duke, Bill, 194
Duke, Vernon, 142
Dunbar, Paul Laurence, 163, 175
Dunbar-Nelson, Alice, 25
Duncan, Todd, 2, 17, 67, 95–98, 103, 215
Dundee, Vince, 109
Dunham, Katherine, 5, 12, 14, 60, 61, 67, 68
Dunning, Jennifer, 12
Duryea, Etta Terry, 181
Duse, Eleonora, 27
D'Usseau, Arnaud, 177
Dutton, Charles S., 168

Early, Gerald, 180
Easley, Mary Beth, 207
Eastwood, Clint, 200
Edmonds, Randolph, 25

Eisenhower, Dwight D., 52, 85
Eisenhower, Julie Nixon, 71
Elder, Lonnie, III, 16, 108–9
Ellington, Duke, 63
Elliott, Deborah, 212
Ellis, Evelyn, 92
Embree, Edwin, 47
Erlanger, Abraham, 7
Estes, Simon, 94
Evers, Medgar, 85, 158, 166

Fairtlough, Matt, 47
Farquhar, George, 196
Farrakhan, Louis, 36, 168
Farrar, Geraldine, 83
Faubus, Orval, 52
Faulkner, William, 71
Federal Theatre Project, 4–5, 16, 21–22, 110, 111, 112, 113–14, 115, 116, 208
Feldshuh, David, 168
Ferrer, José, 46, 50
Ferrer, Mel, 126, 127
Finn, William, 211
Fishburne, Laurence, 212, 213
Fisher, Orpheus, 83, 84
Fisk Jubilee Singers, 41
Fitzgerald, Ella, 147
Flanagan, Hallie, 5, 110–11, 115
Fletcher, Winona L., 10
Flowers, Martha, 102
Folies-Bergère, 8
Folkhart, Burt, 80
Fontecilla, Camilo, 211
Forrest, Edwin, 193
Forsythe, Eric, 207
Forsythe, Marian, 53
46th Street Theatre, 187
Foster, Gloria, 197, 214
Fraden, Rena, 116
Franklin, Aretha, 173
Franklin, John Hope, 83

Index

Frazier, E. Franklin, 156
Freeman, Al, 161
Freeman, Morgan, 10, 15, 138, 140, 161, 193–202, 209, 212, 214, 216
Freeman, Tommy, 109
Frohman, Charles, 7
Fugard, Athol, 160, 183, 206–7
Fuller, Charles, 16, 207

Gabriel, Gilbert, 27
Gaines-Shelton, Ruth, 25
Gardner, Herb, 167
Garner, John Nance, 79
Garvey, Marcus, 115, 116, 148
Gates, Henry Louis, 213
Geer, Will, 123
Gershwin, George, 42, 91, 93, 96, 97–98, 101
Gershwin, Ira, 42, 91
Gibson, Mel, 183
Gild, David, 185
Gilder, Richard Watson, 15
Gilder, Rosamond, 15, 117, 118–19
Gilmer, Chris, 160
Gilmore, Allen, 211
Gilpin, Charles S., 26, 39, 112
Giuliani, Rudolph, 215
Glenn, DeFoy, 175
Glover, Danny, 194
Goff, Lewin, 207
Goldwyn, Samuel, 94, 143
Goode, Eslanda Cardozo, 37
Gordone, Charles, 16
Gossett, Louis, Jr., 13, 178
Gow, James, 177
Grable, Betty, 139
Graham, Billy, Crusade, 59, 60, 70–71
Grant, Lee, 145
Grate, Gail, 210

Gray, Fred, 168
Grebanier, Bernard, 154
Green, Paul, 9, 22, 27, 28, 207
Green, Silas, 138
Greenberg, Marilyn, 49
Gribble, Harry Wagstaff, 118, 156
Griffin, Alice, 179
Grimke, Angelina, 25
Group Theatre, The 28
Grove, Izzy, 109
Guare, John, 211
Guines, James T., 10–11
Gussow, Mel, 15
Guthrie Theatre, 210

Hagen, Uta, 36, 44, 46
Hall, Juanita, 144
Hamlin, Larry Leon, 209
Hammerstein, Oscar, II, 107, 143
Hammond, Percy, 15, 110, 112
Handy, W. C., 62, 144
Hansberry, Lorraine, 13, 124, 155, 165, 206, 207
Harburg, E. Y., 164–65
Harlem Players, 112
Harlem Renaissance, 2, 3, 28, 142
Harlem Suitcase Theatre, 174
Harley, Margot, 16, 210
Harris, Inetta, 100
Harris, Julie, 69, 70
Harris, Patricia Roberts, 11
Harris, Sam, Theatre, 38
Harris, Trudier, 159
Harrison, Richard B., 164
Hart, Cecelia, 187
Harvey, Georgette, 66, 91, 114
Hatch, James V., 11, 24
Hayes, Roland, 41, 77, 80, 81
Heath, Gordon, 11, 45, 177, 183
Hellman, Lillian, 178
Hemsley, Sherman, 166
Henderson, Fletcher, 63

Henderson, Heather, 187
Henry Street Settlement Theatre, 208
Hernandez, Juano, 29, 144, 154
Heyward, Dorothy, 22, 66, 91, 114, 125
Heyward, DuBose, 22, 28, 42, 66, 91, 102, 114
Hightower, Gladys, 152
Hill, Abram, 15, 113–14, 155, 156
Hill, Errol, 40, 42, 137, 180, 184, 186, 187
Hill, Joe, 54
Hill, Ruby, 142
Hill, Wesley, 92
Hines, Gregory, 209
Hirsch, Judd, 167
Hirschfeld, Al, 70, 197
Hiss, Alger, 48
Hitchcock, Alfred, 119
Hoggard, J. C., 53–54
Holder, Geoffrey, 144
Holland, Endesha Ida Mae, 212
Holly, Ellen, 184
Holmes, Algretta, 64
Hood, James, 75
Hook, Sidney, 129
Hoover, J. Edgar, 46, 129
Hope, Bob, 144
Hopkins, Arthur, 27
Hopkins, Harry, 5, 110
Horne, Lena, 64, 67, 68, 147, 164
Houseman, John, 5, 16, 23, 111, 112, 113, 114, 116, 210
House Un-American Activities Committee (HUAC), 46, 47, 48, 113, 124, 127, 128, 152
House Un-American Activities Committee (HUAC) syndrome, 35–36
Howard, Floretta, 66, 70, 71
Howard Theater, 64

Huey, Richard, 92
Hughes, Langston, 3, 5, 15, 22, 30, 31, 115, 122–23, 142, 163, 207
Hurley, Joseph, 201
Hurok, Sol, 75, 77, 80, 82–83, 84, 86
Hurston, Zora Neale, 66, 161
Hyman, Al, 7
Hyman, Earle, 10, 118, 156, 164, 183, 198, 201, 215

Ibsen, Henrik, 176, 186
Ickes, Harold L., 78, 79
Imperial Theatre, 165
Indrisano, Johnny, 109
Ingram, Rex, 43, 67, 113, 125, 143
Isaac, Hermine Rich, 120
Isaacs, Edith, 45, 91, 142
Isaacson, Leo, 123
Ivanhoe Theater, 158

Jackson, Jesse, 166, 194
Jackson, Mahalia, 162, 166, 173
Jackson, Samuel L., 161, 167
Jacobus, Lee, 186
James, Flynn Earl, 173
James, Olga, 143
Jamison, Judith, 14–15
Jefferson, Helen, 92
Jefferson, Jack, 175
Jefferson, Margo L., 208
Jenkins, Lutiebelle Gussiemae, 165
John, Errol, 178
Johnson, Bob, 194
Johnson, Hall, 92–93
Johnson, J. Rosamond, 108
Johnson, Jack, 5
Johnson, James Weldon, 28, 180–81
Johnson, Lyndon Baines, 11, 85, 139
Johnson, Max, 117

Johnson, Vivian (Baxter), 102
Jolson, Al, 92
Jones, Bill T., 14
Jones, James Earl, 2, 5, 10, 14, 156, 161, 173–90, 209, 214, 215, 216
Jones, Margo, 122
Jones, Martin, 29–30
Jones, Robert Earl, 174, 175
Jones, Robert Edmond, 44
Jones, Ruth Connolly, 174
Jones, Tisch, 207
Josephson, Barney, 130

Kachingwe, Michael, 207
Kael, Pauline, 196
Kalem, T. E., 198
Kanfer, Stefan, 108, 128
Kaplan, Deborah, 16
Kauffman, Stanley, 160
Kaufman, George, 179
Keach, Stacy, 183
Kean, Edmund, 45
Keiler, Allan, 80
Kennedy, John F., 85, 166
Kennedy, Robert, 166
Kennedy Center, 86, 161, 185
Kern, Jerome, 42
Kerr, Walter, 144, 157, 187
Key, G. R. F., 64
Khan, Ricardo, 161, 210
King, B. B., 196
King, Billy, 77
King, Coretta Scott, 35
King, Martin Luther, Jr., 49, 71, 85, 148, 166
King, Stephen, 195
King, Woodie, Jr., 208
Kirschenbaum, Walter, 131
Kitt, Eartha, 144
Klaw, Marc, 7
Knight, Ezra, 211

Korda, Alexander, 43
Korda, Zoltan, 43, 129, 130–31
Krasner, David, 4
Krimsky, John, 43
Kroll, Jack, 182
Kropf, Howard, 41
Kumalo, Stephen, 96
Kushner, Tony, 211

Lafayette Players, 7–8, 25, 26
Lafayette Theatre, 15, 38, 111
Lamm, Bob, 157
Lardner, Ring, Jr., 48
Larner, Daniel, 175
Lawson, John Howard, 48
Lawson, Roger, 138
Leach, Wilford, 200
Lee, Canada, 2, 6, 15, 16, 66, 107–32, 175, 176, 179, 188, 215
Lee, Carl, 108–9, 128, 157, 158
Lee, Frances, 107, 109, 118, 128, 129, 175
Lee, Spike, 161, 162, 167, 168, 194
LeGallienne, Eva, 22, 120
Leslie, Lew, 64
Levine, Georgie, 109
Levine, James, 94–95
Lillie, Beatrice, 65
Lincoln Memorial, 164
Linden, Hal, 167
Little, Cleavon, 166, 167, 197
Livingston, Myrtle Smith, 25
Locke, Alain, 163–64
Luch, Arthurine, 69
Lundigan, William, 69
Lust, Geraldine, 177

MacPherson, Kenneth, 42
Malcolm X, 85, 148, 165–66
Mallory, Eddie, 67–68
Malone, Vivian, 75

Maltz, Albert, 48
Mamoulian, Rouben, 91, 142
Mann, Emily, 214
March, Fredric, 128
Marchio, Ann L., 159
Marie, Julienne, 180
Marsalis, Wynton, 147
Marshall, Thurgood, 52
Marvin, Lee, 122
Marvin, Mark, 122
Mason, Victor, 115, 116
Matheus, John, 25
Matthau, Walter, 139, 167
Matthews, Clyde Edward, 64, 65
Matthews, Ralph, 124
Maxon, Troy, 175
McCarthy, Joseph, 69, 114
McClendon, Henry Pruden, 23
McClendon, Rose, 2, 5, 21–31, 92, 215
McClendon, Rose, Players, 5, 31, 164
McCullers, Carson, 69
McDaniel, Hattie, 24, 68
McKee, Lonette, 167
McKinney, Nina Mae, 43
McLain, John, 157
McLean, Megan, 212–13
McLeish, Archibald, 29
McNeil, Claudia, 13, 157, 158
McQueen, Butterfly, 113
Mello, Al, 109
Meredith, Burgess, 67, 179
Merrick, David, 138, 148, 165
Metropulos, Penny, 211
Meyer, Annie Nathan, 29
Micheaux, Oscar, 40
Millen, James Knox, 29
Miller, Husky, 143
Miller, Marilyn, 65
Mills, Florence, 25, 63–64
Milner, Ron, 161

Minelli, Vincent, 68
Minskoff Theatre, 138
Mitchell, Abbie, 25, 27, 123
Mitchell, Arthur W., 79
Mitchell, Loften, 7, 39, 41, 119, 129, 175
Mokae, Zakes, 183
Moore, Melba, 166
Morgenthau, Henry, Jr., 79
Morris, Mark, 14
Morris, Sarah P., 141, 146
Morrison, Toni, 161
Morton, "Jelly Roll," 209
Moss, Arnold, 107, 120–21, 131
Mother A.M.E. Zion Church, 52, 53
Motley, John, 77
Murphy, Dudley, 43
Murray, Charlotte, 26
Murrow, Edward R., 85
Music Box Theatre, 65, 179

Nadel, Norman, 28
Nash, Elizabeth, 96
Nathan, George Jean, 39, 45
National Ad Hoc Committee to End the Crimes Against Paul Robeson, 185
National Association for the Advancement of Colored People (NAACP), 46–47, 79, 83, 131
National Endowment for the Arts, 210
National Theatre, 95, 138, 139, 148
Negro Ensemble Company, 16
Negro People's Theatre, 5, 21, 22, 29
Negro Playwrights Company, 115
Negro spirituals, 85
New York Public Theater, 197, 199–200

Index

Nichols, Lewis, 118, 122
Nightingale, Benedict, 199
Niven, Penelope, 179
Nixon, Richard, 48, 71, 140
Nixon, Sam, 7
Noble, Jeanne, 71
Non-Traditional Casting Project, 205, 208
Norman, Marsha, 211
Norris, J. Weldon, 97
Null, Gary, 44, 145
Nunn, Bill, 167

O'Connor, John, 114
O'Day, Caroline, 78
Odets, Clifford, 5, 29
Oliver, Edith, 157, 188, 198
Olivier, Laurence, 137
Olsen, Christopher, 212
O'Morrison, Kevin, 107–8, 111, 129, 130
O'Neal, Frederick, 6–7, 60–61, 107, 118, 138, 148, 155
O'Neill, Eugene, 9, 37–39, 43, 112, 176, 184, 187
Ornitz, Samuel, 48
Orpheum Theatre, 196
Osgood, Charles, 214
Ottley, Roi, 15, 112, 119

Papp, Joseph, 158, 177, 184
Papp, Joseph, Public Theater, 215
Parrish, Wil, 161
Paton, Alan, 96, 128, 129, 188
Pawley, Tom, 10, 164
Pekin Players, 8
Penumbra Theatre, 209–10
Peters, Brock, 143
Peters, Paul, 110
Peterson, Louis, 155
Petit, Jacob, 98
Petit, Paula, 98

Pieterson, Zachariah, 183
Pinkston, Randall, 214
Plantation Club, 63
Plummer, Christopher, 186
Poitier, Sidney, 13, 44, 94, 107, 128, 130, 144, 155, 156, 165
Polk, Oscar, 164
Pond, James B., 41
Pons, Lily, 83
Porgy and Bess, 91–103
Poston, Ted, 131
Powell, Adam Clayton, Jr., 120, 132
Preer, Evelyn, 7
Premice, Josephine, 164
Preminger, Otto, 94
Preston, Rohan, 208
Price, Leontyne, 2, 17, 95, 98, 99–101, 103, 215
Primus, Pearl, 1–2, 14
Provincetown Players, 38, 44
Provincetown Playhouse, 39–40
Purnsley, Merritt "Buddy," 61–62
Purple Onion, 102

Radio City Music Hall, 41
Rahn, Muriel, 31
Raikin, Bruno, 53
Rampersad, Arnold, 30
Rascoe, Burton, 119
Raye, Martha, 139
Reagan, Ronald, 140
Reardon, William, 164
Reynolds, Burt, 167
Rice, Elmer, 9, 115
Rice, Patricia, 78
Rice, Thomas "Daddy," 7
Rich, Frank, 199
Richards, Lloyd, 13, 115, 177, 187
Richardson, Ralph, 42
Richardson, Willis, 25
Rites and Reason, 206
Robards, Jason, Jr., 184, 185

Robbins, Tim, 195
Robeson, Anna Louisa, 36
Robeson, Eslanda Goode, 42, 123
Robeson, Paul, 2, 15, 16, 68, 77, 80, 92, 109, 112, 123, 128, 132, 176, 185, 206, 208–9, 215, 216
Robeson, Paul, Jr., 41, 49, 52–53, 185
Robeson, Paul Leroy Bustill, 35–54
Robeson, William Drew, 36
Robinson, Jackie, 47, 154
Robinson, Ray, 109
Robinson, Walter, 141
Roe, Gerald, 207
Rogers, Ginger, 139
Roosevelt, Eleanor, 46, 51, 78, 95, 123, 139
Roosevelt, Franklin Delano, 4–5, 46, 65, 83
Root, Lynn, 60, 67
Rose, Philip, 13
Rosenbaum, Yankel, 205
Rosenberg, Ethel, 153
Rosenberg, Julius, 153
Rothman, Richard H., 147
Roundabout Theatre Company, 212
Rudd, Irving, 109
Rule, Sheila, 6
Rupp, Franz, 76, 77

Saal, Hubert, 47, 51–52
Sackler, Howard, 5, 173, 175, 178, 180
Saidy, Fred, 164–65
Saint, Eva Marie, 144
St. Jacques, Raymond, 178
St. James Theatre, 117, 138, 148, 196
Saint Marks Playhouse, 177

Salvin, Sam, 63
Sanchez, Jaime, 197
Sands, Diana, 13, 157
Sanford, Isabel, 156
Sargent, Franklin, 23
Savage, Archie, 68–69
Savoy Theatre, 42
Schary, Dore, 177
Schickel, Richard, 195
Schkelderup, Thorlief, 98
Schkelderup, Vaar, 98
Schlosser, Anatol, 49–50
Schreiber, Belle, 181
Scott, Adrian, 48
Scottsboro Boys, 29, 65
Seldes, Gilbert, 25, 63
Seligsohn, Leo, 182
Semple, Jesse B., 163
Shange, Ntozake, 15, 199, 211, 215
Shay, MIchele, 197–98
Sheaffer, Louis, 185
Shepard, Richard F., 182
Sherin, Edwin, 184
Shine, Ted, 24
Shubert Theatre, 44
Sibelius, Jean, 82
Sidney, P. Jay, 70
Sills, Beverly, 100
Silvera, Frank, 107
Silvers, Pal, 109
Simms, Hilda, 118, 156
Simon, John, 15, 195, 198, 199
Singleton, John, 194
Sissle, Noble, 107
Sklar, George, 110
Slater, Bob, 194
Sleet, Moneta, Jr., 166
Smalls, Leo, 196
Smith, Anna Deavere, 210, 213, 215
Smith, Lillian, 174
Smith, Will, 194

Snipes, Wesley, 161, 167, 194
Sorel, Nancy Caldwell, 43
Southern, Eileen, 82, 83
Soyinka, Wole, 16
Spence, Eulalie, 25
Spielberg, Steven, 200
Stafford, Bart Lanier, III, 35, 48, 108
Stallings, Laurence, 22, 26
Stanislavski, Konstantin, 154
Starr, Milton, 62
Stasio, Marilyn, 198
Steinbeck, John, 175, 176, 179, 187
Sternhagen, Frances, 201
Stevens, Nan Bagby, 26
Stewart, Patrick, 44, 147, 211
Still, William Grant, 93
Stokes, Anson Phelps, 79–80
Strasberg, Lee, 118
Street, Charles, Playhouse, 196
Streisand, Barbra, 139

Tabori, George, 196
Tandy, Jessica, 201
Taney, Roger B., 36
Taylor, Sylvia, 112
Terry, Ellen, 66
Thatcher, Margaret, 199
Theatre Guild, 44, 91, 125–26
Theatre Owners Booking Association, 4, 23–24, 62
Thomas, Edna Lewis, 7, 25, 111, 215
Thomas, J. Parnell, 113
Thompson, Francesca, 7
Thompson, Kent, 213
Thomson, Virgil, 92, 101, 138
Thorndike, Sybil, 42
Tibbett, Lawrence, 83, 92
Till, Emmett, 12, 202
Toomer, Jean, 25
Torrence, Ridgeley, 37

Toscanini, Arturo, 75, 82
Tough on Black Actors, 24
Truman, Harry S, 49, 67
Trumbo, Dalton, 48, 108
Trump, Donald, 199
Tucker, Shona, 211
Tully, Jim, 42
Turner, Darwin T., 27
Turner, Patricia, 96
Tuskegee Institute Choir, 41
Tynan, William, 214
Tyson, Cicely, 178

Ullman, Tracey, 212
Union Baptist, 81
United Service Organization (USO), 93–94, 141
Universal Negro Improvement Association (UNIA), 115, 148

Vanderbilt Theatre, 30
Van Vechten, Carl, 9, 23, 31, 41, 51, 66, 114
Van Volkenburg, Nellie, 42
Vaughn, Hilda, 123
Vehanen, Kosti, 77
Verwayne, Percy, 92
Virginia Theatre, 209

Wagner, Robert, 145
Walker, Alice, 161
Walker, Joseph, 16
Wallace, Edgar, 96
Wallace, Edward Nathaniel, 152
Wallace, Henry A., 47
Wallace, Ruby, 152
Waller, Juanita, 108
Ward, Douglas Turner, 16
Ward, Theodore, 115, 116
Warfield, William, 2, 17, 92, 93, 94, 95, 98–99, 103, 215

Warner, Ralph, 116
Washington, Booker T., 15, 61, 163, 193
Washington, Denzel, 161, 194, 213
Washington, Fredi, 42, 43, 66, 114, 122
Wasserstein, Wendy, 211–12
Waters, Ethel, 2, 6, 12, 45, 59–71, 75, 114, 121–22, 208–9, 215
Waters, John Wesley, 60
Watkins, Perry, 107
Watts, Richard, 157
Webb, Christopher M., 13, 194
Webb, Clifton, 65
Webster, John, 124
Webster, Margaret, 44, 120
Weill, Kurt, 96
Welles, Orson, 111, 113, 116
Werker, Alfred L., 127
Wesley, Richard, 197
West, John, 163
Weston, Miriam Drake, 169
Weston, Moran, 120, 169
Whipper, Leigh, 29, 92, 179
Whitaker, Mical, 159
White, George L., 41
White, Harold S., 147
White, Jack E., 14
White, Josh, 51
White, Walter, 41, 46, 51, 79, 120, 131
White, William L., 126
Wilder, Thornton, 139, 196
Willard, Jess, 181

Williams, Bert, 7
Williams, Tennessee, 10, 160–61
Wills, J. Elder, 43
Wilson, August, 148, 173, 175, 187–88, 213, 214, 215
Wilson, Dooley, 7, 67, 70
Wilson, Frank, 23, 27, 43, 91, 109–10
Winchell, Walter, 129
Winfield, Hemsley, 1
Wingfield, Amanda, 10
Winter Garden Theatre, 186
Wolfe, George C., 206, 209, 212, 215
Woll, Allen, 142
Wood, Maxine, 122, 123–24, 127, 128
Woollcott, Alexander, 15, 26–27, 37
Works Progress Administration, 21–22, 110
Wright, Frank Lloyd, 28
Wright, Richard, 15, 37, 116, 207
Wycherly, Margaret, 38

Yale Repertory Theatre, 186, 187
Yancy, Emily, 138
Yordan, Philip, 118
Young, Andrew, 166
Younger, Lena, 207
Younger, Walter Lee, 165

Zanuck, Darryl F., 69
Zimmerman, J. Fred, 7

GPSR Compliance

The European Union's (EU) General Product Safety Regulation (GPSR) is a set of rules that requires consumer products to be safe and our obligations to ensure this.

If you have any concerns about our products, you can contact us on

ProductSafety@springernature.com

In case Publisher is established outside the EU, the EU authorized representative is:

Springer Nature Customer Service Center GmbH
Europaplatz 3
69115 Heidelberg, Germany

www.ingramcontent.com/pod-product-compliance
Lightning Source LLC
LaVergne TN
LVHW041626060526
838200LV00040B/1460